Mac
Work
Mac
Play

Mac Work Mac Play

CREATIVE IDEAS

FOR FUN AND

PROFIT ON YOUR

APPLE MACINTOSH

MICROSOFT®
PRESS

LON
POOLE

Drawings by Erfert Nielson

PUBLISHED BY
Microsoft Press
A Division of Microsoft Corporation
10700 Northup Way, Box 97200, Bellevue, Washington 98009

Library of Congress Cataloging in Publication Data
Poole, Lon.
Macwork, macplay.
Includes index.
1. Macintosh (Computer)—Programming. 2. Apple II (Computer)—
Programming. 3. Apple IIe (Computer)—Programming. I. Title.
QA76.8.M3P66 1984   001.64'2   84-16573
ISBN 0-914845-22-5

Printed and bound in the United States of America.

1 2 3 4 5 6 7 8 9 FGFG 8 9 0 9 8 7 6 5 4

Distributed to the book trade in the United States and Canada
by Simon and Schuster, Inc.

Portions of the first two chapters appeared in the premier issue of *Macworld* magazine.

The Art Deco alphabet in Part Three was adapted from Marcia Loeb, *Art Deco Designs and Motifs*
(New York: Dover Press, 1972), pages 41 to 53. Used by permission.

The summary of Multiplan functions in Part Four is from the *Microsoft Multiplan* manual
(Bellevue, Washington: Microsoft Corporation, 1984), pages 131 and 132. Used by permission.

Apple™ is a registered trademark, and Lisa™, Macintosh™, The Finder™, MacWrite™, and MacPaint™
are trademarks of Apple Computer, Inc. Microsoft® and Multiplan® are registered trademarks of
Microsoft Corporation. Macworld™ is a trademark of PC World Communications, Inc.

Contents

Part Four Reference

Acknowledgments

A number of people contributed significantly to the preparation of this book, and I wish to thank them all. Erfert Nielson not only drew all the MacPaint projects (except the Phyllis Tien Gallery letterhead), she conceived several of them as well. On top of all that, she also drafted the glossary and indexed the book. Alexis Seddun researched and developed many of the Multiplan projects. Lonna McDowell furnished some important contacts. Believe me, the book would have been truly dull and boring without their help.

Thanks to David Bunnell for introducing me to Andrew Fluegelman, Dan Farber, and the rest of the folks at *Macworld* magazine. I've had the pleasure of making many a Macintosh discovery with them.

Several people at Apple Computer graciously lent their support, particularly Mike Boich, Guy Kawasaki, and Patti Kenyon. The book simply wouldn't exist without the help they provided.

So many people at Microsoft Press did a terrific job bringing the book to life, I don't know where to begin. Thank you all, especially Tracy Smith, Joyce Cox, Barry Preppernau, Claudette Moore, Salley Oberlin, Karen-Lynne de Robinson, Nahum Stiskin, and Larry Levitsky.

My deepest thanks go to my wife Karin, for putting up with the hectic schedule, listening to my sometimes wild ideas, and keeping the lid on with her common sense. I know it hasn't been easy, and I really do appreciate her unfailing daily support.

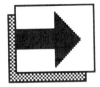

Introduction

MacWork MacPlay is for anyone who wants to have fun—and get some work done—with the Apple Macintosh computer. The book includes more than two dozen projects created using the first commercial programs available for the Mac: MacWrite, MacPaint, and Multiplan. For those who already know how to use these Mac programs, there are 27 projects to spark the imagination. For those who know how to use the Mac but not MacWrite, MacPaint, or Multiplan, three fully explained projects provide detailed, step-by-step lessons for each program. And for those who are new to the Mac, the book also illustrates basic Macintosh techniques.

Lest you think this is one of those "something for everyone" (but not much for anyone) books, relax; *MacWork MacPlay* makes no attempt to be all things to all people. For example, it is not for Mac programmers, or would-be programmers. In fact, there isn't a single line of computer programming in the whole book.

The Macintosh uses pictures as much as words, and so does this book. The illustrations that accompany the descriptions show what happens on the Macintosh. You may follow along on your own machine, but you do not have to.

What This Book Contains

MacWork MacPlay has four parts. The first part contains two chapters that introduce the Mac novice to the parts of the machine: the screen, keyboard, mouse, disks, and programs. They also explain important concepts and procedures that occur repeatedly. If you already know how to use the Mac, you can skip the first section or skim it quickly. Otherwise, you should study it carefully and practice the procedures it describes.

The second part of the book describes three projects in complete detail. One project (writing a business report) shows you how to use MacWrite. Another project (designing a letterhead) shows you how to use MacPaint. The third project (figuring your net worth) shows you how to use Multiplan. The projects in Part Two were chosen for their educational value, not because they are in any way the best use of MacWrite, MacPaint, or Multiplan. The projects and descriptions are completely independent, so you can read about all three or pick and choose among them.

The third part of the book contains 24 additional projects, presented as if they were designed and developed by 24 different people. These projects, like the ones in Part Two, are not so much recipes to follow literally as they are examples of what you can do with MacWrite, MacPaint, and Multiplan. Many of the projects in Part Three illustrate advanced features of MacWrite, MacPaint, or Multiplan not covered in Part Two. The highlights of each project are described by the fictitious person who supposedly developed it.

The fourth part of the book contains reference material. This includes a glossary, a summary of MacWrite, MacPaint, or Multiplan features, samples of type fonts, and a table of shortcuts.

Special Note to Lisa 2 Owners

A program named MacWorks makes the Apple Lisa 2 computer act like a Macintosh. This enables a Lisa 2 owner to use MacWrite, MacPaint, Multiplan, and other Macintosh programs. Thus Lisa 2 owners can also use this book. For more information on the Lisa-Mac connection, see the article "The Lisa Connection" in *Macworld*, volume 1, number 2, pages 52 to 63.

Macintosh Basics

Part One

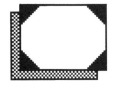

The Macintosh's Electronic Desktop

● *This chapter introduces basic Macintosh skills such as clicking, dragging, and selecting, along with objects such as icons, menus, windows, and dialog boxes.*

Imagine driving a car that has no steering wheel, accelerator, brake pedal, turn-signal lever, or gear selector. In place of all the familiar manual controls, you have only a typewriter keyboard.

Any time you want to turn a corner, change lanes, slow down, speed up, honk your horn, or back up, you have to type a different command on the keyboard. Unfortunately, the car can't understand English sentences. Instead you must hold down a special key with one finger and type in some command letters and numbers, like "S20:TL:A35," which to the car means, "Slow to 20, turn left, and accelerate to 35."

If you make a typing mistake, one of three things happens. If you type an unknown command, the car radio bleats and you have to type the command over again. If what you type happens to be wrong but nevertheless is a valid command, the car stupidly obeys. (Imagine typing A95, "Accelerate to 95," instead of A35, "Accelerate to 35.") If you type something the manufacturer didn't anticipate, the car screeches to a halt and immediately shuts itself off.

Doubtless you could learn to drive such a car if you had sufficient motivation and determination. Why bother, when so many cars use familiar controls?

Most people don't bother to use a personal computer for the same reasons they wouldn't bother with a keyboard-controlled car. Working on a computer is just not natural, and the benefits hardly seem worth the hassle of learning how to get work done in a strange and hostile environment. You have to type cryptic commands on a keyboard. Make a typing mistake and the computer may do nothing, tell you it doesn't understand, do the wrong thing, shut itself off, or destroy all the work you've done and then shut itself off. Who cares if the machine is theoretically a hundred times more efficient than pencil and paper? If using the machine rattles you so much that you can't get anything done, it is in fact less efficient and may waste more time than it saves.

What if a computer could let you work in a familiar environment, maybe like the way you work at your desk? You put the things you want to work with out on top of the desk, move them around, select one to work with for awhile, then select something else to work with, and so on. From time to time you take out other things. When your desk gets too cluttered, you put some things away, either in a file folder or in a file drawer. When a file outlives its usefulness, you toss it in the trash can. Now and then you anxiously fish around for something you didn't mean to discard, hoping the janitor hasn't yet taken it to the incinerator.

Working on a Macintosh is like working at a desk. Its screen shows a model of a *desktop,* with little graphic symbols that represent the letters, drawings, worksheets, and other objects that have been placed on it. You can move these bits of information around on the electronic desktop, select one to look at or work on, put it away, select another, and so on. You can organize these documents in folders. You can throw things away. And you can even retrieve them before the "janitor" takes them away for good.

To see the Macintosh electronic desktop, switch on the machine and insert the disk labeled System Disk.

The actual appearance of the electronic desktop depends a great deal on which disk you insert when you start up the Macintosh and on what was last done with that disk. Disks can even be set up to bypass the initial desktop configuration entirely; the next chapter explains how.

Icons: The Latest Picture Show

The little graphic symbols you see displayed on the Macintosh screen are called *icons.* Until recently, that word has referred mainly to sacred images venerated by Eastern Orthodox religions. On the Macintosh, though, an icon is a pictorial symbol for some concept or object.

System Disk

Trash

Icons on the Macintosh may all be the same small size, but they do not all look alike. For example, the icon that stands for a disk looks like a disk. The icon that represents all the things waiting to be discarded looks like a trash can. Other icons look like file folders, the front view of a Macintosh, or more abstract designs. In each case, the icon's design is meant to suggest the object represented.

Icon design alone is not always enough to absolutely identify an object on the electronic desktop. There may be two, three, or more file folder icons present at once. How can you tell which is the one you want? The name below each icon resolves this ambiguity. The next chapter explains how you can change the name of most icons.

The Pointer and the Mouse

On a real desk you can pick things up and move them around with your hands, but you can't handle the icons on the electronic desktop. You need a remote control of some sort, and the *mouse* is it. Sliding the mouse on a smooth surface moves a *pointer* on the desktop. Slide the mouse in any direction—up, down, sideways, or diagonally—and the pointer moves the same distance in the same direction.

The amount of clear space needed for mouse movement is smaller than the size of this book when closed. Should the mouse bump into some obstacle before the pointer arrives at its destination, just lift the mouse straight up, set it back down in a clear area, and start sliding again. The pointer does not move when the mouse is in midair.

Moving the mouse moves the pointer, but pressing the *mouse button* makes things happen. With the mouse button, for example, you can fasten the pointer to an icon and then move them both by sliding the mouse. This action, called *dragging,* has many uses besides rearranging icons, as later chapters reveal.

● *To drag an icon, place the pointer over it, press and hold down the mouse button, and slide the mouse.*

When you place the pointer on an icon and press the mouse button, the icon is *highlighted.* In other words, the icon changes to look like its own photographic negative; everything that was white is black and vice versa. Then, as you move the pointer (still pressing the mouse button), an outline of the icon and its label breaks away to follow the pointer. The outline shows you where the icon will appear when you let go of the button.

The mouse can also highlight an icon without moving it, an action called *selecting.* To do that, place the pointer over an icon and *click* the mouse button—press and release it quickly. Clicking on an icon does nothing in and of itself. It only selects the icon as the object to which the next command you issue will apply. This pattern of selecting an object and then specifying an action (which is exactly the opposite of the way most computers work) recurs constantly with the Macintosh; the objects and actions may change but the method never varies.

Menus: May I Take Your Order?

On most computer systems, you issue a command by typing an arcane word or two on the keyboard. Remembering such commands is hard enough from day to day. Go to Hawaii for a week and you can plan on a session with the manual when you get back.

The Mac seldom forces you to remember a command word or type any command on the keyboard. It displays all of its commands in lists, called *menus*, and lets you choose the command you want with the mouse. Don't let other computer menus you have seen or heard about prejudice you against Mac menus. People say menus are great when you're learning something but slow you down when you know the ropes. They complain that menus take over the screen, crowding out the information you're working on. They point out that, with most menus, you must still type in a code number or letter to indicate your choice. Mac menus have none of these flaws. They are unobtrusive, fast, and require no typing.

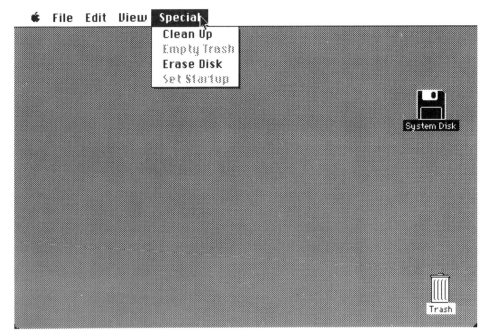

● *To see a menu, place the pointer over its title in the menu bar and press and hold the mouse button.*

The Mac hides its menus under the *menu bar*, which stretches across the top of the screen, until you ask to see one of them. When you move the pointer over one of the menu titles and press the mouse button, a menu drops down from the menu bar, temporarily overlaying a small part of the screen.

Menus act like they're spring-loaded; if you release the mouse button, the menu scrunches back up under the menu bar. But as long as you hold down the mouse button, the menu stays out where you can see it.

All of the available commands appear in black type. But it doesn't always make sense to use a command, so commands that are out of context at any particular time appear dimmed to gray. Later, when circumstances change, they appear in black type and you can choose them. For example, the Empty Trash command in the Special menu is unavailable until you throw out an icon by dragging it into the Trash (as described in the following chapter).

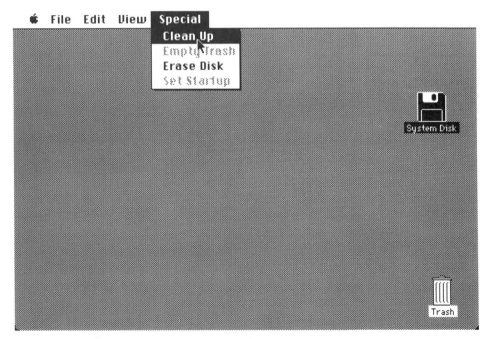

● *To choose a command from a menu displayed on the screen, hold down the mouse button while you move the pointer to the command you want. Then release the mouse button.*

Placing the pointer over an available command highlights the command, indicating it will be the one chosen if you release the mouse button then. If you move the pointer to another command instead of releasing the mouse button, the highlight moves along with the pointer. However, dimmed commands are not highlighted when you move the pointer over them because you cannot choose them.

Taking the Shortcut

While the Macintosh rarely forces you to type a command, it does provide plenty of opportunity for taking shortcuts by typing. Most keyboard shortcuts involve the use of the *Command key,* which is labeled on the keyboard with a squiggle (⌘). Much like the shift key on a typewriter, the Command key on a Macintosh modifies the effect of another key when you press them both at the same time. Of course, you do not have to strike the two keys at precisely the same instant. Holding down the Command key while you press the second key will do.

This book denotes combination keystrokes by separating the combined keys with a dash. For example, "press Command-E" tells you to concurrently press the Command and E keys. Pressing Command-E is a shortcut for choosing Eject from the File menu; either action ejects the disk that is currently inserted, like toast from a toaster (more about ejecting later in this chapter).

Not all commands have keyboard shortcuts. For ones that do, the menus list the shortcuts alongside their matching command names using a different style of notation. The Command-E shortcut, for example, is listed in the File menu next to the Eject command with the notation ⌘E. The reference section of this book contains a list of the available shortcuts.

Windows: Viewing the Contents of an Icon

The Open command, located in the File menu, lets you view and manipulate the actual information represented by an icon. The information appears in a rectangular *window,* with the icon's name written in a title bar across the top. The icon is still on the desktop but is hollow (all gray) to show it has been opened. The disk icon, for example, may already be open. If not, you can open it yourself.

● *To open an icon, first select it by pointing at it and clicking the mouse button. Then choose Open from the File menu.*

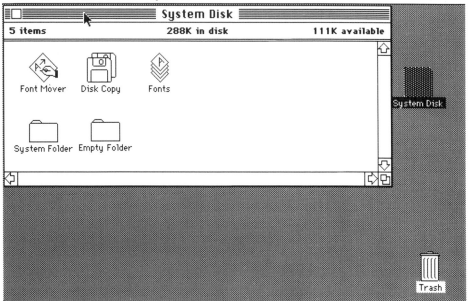

Opening a disk icon reveals more icons, each of which stands for some particular part of the information that the disk contains. Thus the disk window provides a directory of the disk contents. In fact, it is called a *directory window.*

Instead of selecting the icon and choosing the Open command, simply place the pointer on the icon and click the mouse button twice in rapid succession. This shortcut is called *double-clicking.*

Multiple Windows

Every icon has its own window. Each time you open another icon, a new window zooms into existence. The new window may fit next to the existing windows, it may partially overlap them, or it may completely hide them.

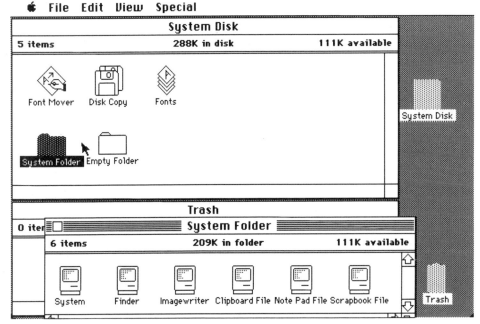

🍎 **File   Edit   View   Special**

● *To see several windows, open the*
Trash icon and then the System
Folder icon by double-clicking
on each icon in turn.

Overlapping windows have an obvious top-to-bottom ordering. It's as though you had a loose pile of papers on your desk, some on top of others and one clearly on top. On the Macintosh desktop, windows that don't overlap figure into this ordering too, though it's not as readily apparent.

The window on top, the frontmost window, has black bands in its title bar. It is called the *active window.* You can bring any window to the top and make it the active window just by placing the pointer anywhere on it (even just an edge that's sticking out behind another window) and clicking the mouse button. You can also bring an inactive window to the front by double-clicking on its open icon.

Wandering Windows

You can move a window around on the Mac desktop by dragging its title bar, just as you would drag an icon. With the pointer over the title bar, press and hold the mouse button and slide the mouse. A flickering outline of the window follows the pointer around. Let go of the mouse button, and the window jumps to the new location. Normally, moving a window makes it the active window. However, you can move a window without disturbing its top-to-bottom position in the pile by holding down the Command key while you drag.

Sometimes windows get buried. Unfortunately, there's no way to get a side view of the Mac desktop to see what windows might be hidden. But you can always move windows aside to uncover the ones underneath.

The Disappearing Window Trick

When you finish with a window, you can remove it from the desktop. Later, if you change your mind, you can recall it by once again opening its icon.

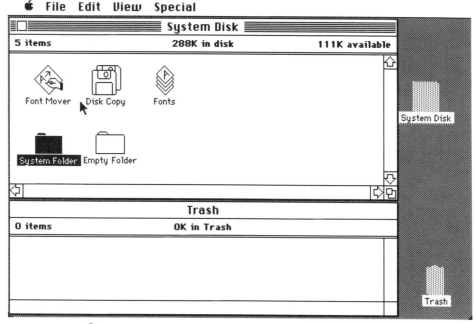

To remove the active window from the desktop, choose the Close command from the File menu.

When you close a window, the corresponding icon sucks the information back, the window disappears, and the icon resumes its normal appearance.

Buttons, Bars, and Boxes

You've seen elaborate stereo systems bristling with knobs, buttons, and dials. Imagine adding the controls of a television, phone, and calculator to that collection—pretty intimidating. But that's nothing compared with what a computer would look like if it had separate controls for everything it can do.

Most computers are controlled solely from the keyboard. In contrast, the Macintosh displays controls to suit the situation. You use the pointer and mouse button to push buttons or adjust knobs and levers displayed on the screen. Most windows, for example, have several built-in controls that the Mac displays when the window is active.

Big Windows, Little Windows

The small box displayed in the lower right corner of most active windows, called the *size box*, gives you control over the size of the window. To make the window narrower, use the mouse to drag this size box to the left. To make the window wider, drag the size box to the right. Drag the size box up and the window gets shorter; drag it down and the window gets taller. Drag the size box diagonally to change both height and width simultaneously.

Changing the window size does not change the size of what's displayed; it just changes the amount of information you can see at once.

Seeing More in Less

Sometimes a window doesn't show all the available information, even if it covers the whole desktop. The *scroll bars* let you scan back and forth over the information. Most windows have two scroll bars. One, located on the left edge of the window, controls up-and-down movement. The other, located at the bottom of the window, controls side-to-side movement.

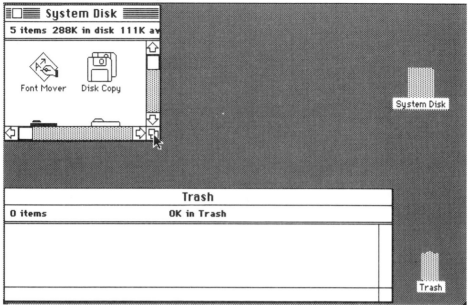

● *Change the size of the System Disk window by dragging its size box toward the top left corner of the screen.*

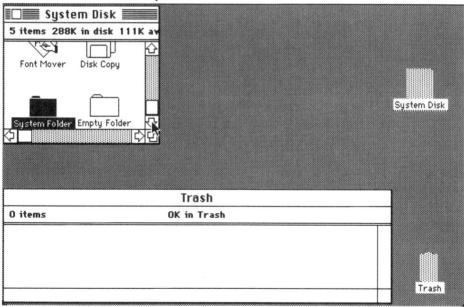

● *To bring other information into view, click or press the arrows at either end of the scroll bars.*

Of the many ways to use scroll bars, the simplest is to click the arrow that points in the direction you want the window to move over the information. (Actually, the window stays put on the screen and the information moves under it, but the effect is the same as if the window had moved in the direction of the arrow used.) If you press and hold the mouse button instead of just clicking it, the information keeps moving.

As the information moves, a small white box in the scroll bar, called the *scroll box*, moves too. Two scroll boxes, one in each scroll bar, gauge the window's position relative to the top and bottom, or left and right extents of the information. Click in the gray area on either side of a scroll box to scan by the windowful. Drag the scroll box along the scroll bar to move the window quickly to a different part of the available information.

Shutting the Window

The active window has one more control, a small box located at the left edge of the title bar. Called the *close box*, it is a shortcut for choosing the Close command from the File menu.

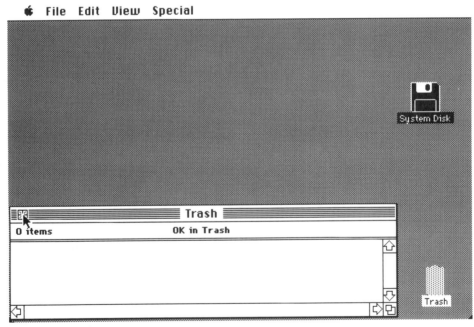

● *Close the System Disk window by clicking on its close box. Then close the Trash window by clicking on its close box.*

Dialog and Alert Boxes: More After These Messages

The Mac takes the unexpected in stride. When something unusual happens, it displays a special window to inform you of the exceptional circumstances. You may have to click some buttons, manipulate some other controls, and occasionally do some typing inside that window. These special windows are called *dialog boxes* when they appear only for the purpose of getting supplemental information from you, information needed to proceed with the task at hand. Special windows that contain warning messages (such as when you try to open too many windows) are called *alert boxes*.

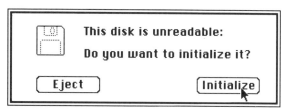

● *A dialog box appears when the Mac needs additional information to proceed.*

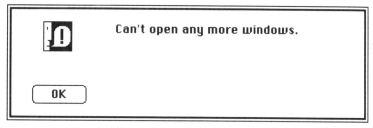

● *An alert box warns of an impossible or potentially dangerous situation.*

Desk Accessories: Things You Need for Work and Play

A real desk generally has a few pieces of equipment on it, such as a clock, a note pad, or a calculator. Electronic versions of these desk accessories and others are available on the Mac desktop, too. The available accessories are listed in the Apple (🍎) menu at the left end of the menu bar.

● *To put a desk accessory on the desktop, choose it by name from the Apple menu.*

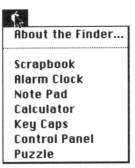

The Apple menu contains a list of desk accessories, not a list of commands, but you choose from it the same as you would any other menu. You place the pointer over the Apple logo in the menu bar, press and hold the mouse button, slide the pointer down the list of choices, and release the mouse button when the desk accessory you want is highlighted.

About the Finder...

The first item on the Apple menu, About the Finder..., displays a small window with information about the *Finder*, the program that manages and organizes disks.

● *About the Finder... reports the version number of the Finder program.*

To close the information window, place the pointer anywhere on it and click the mouse button.

Scrapbook

Each Macintosh disk can keep excerpts from pictures, writing, or calculations that have been clipped from one place for possible use in another place later. The method for doing this is described later in this book.

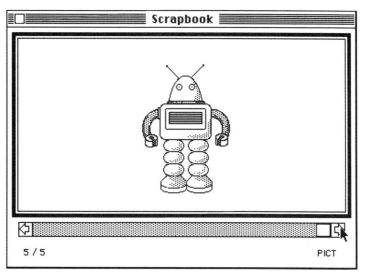

● *The Scrapbook allows you to view, add to, or extract from the collection of clippings stored on the disk.*

The Scrapbook window shows one clipping at a time. The size of the window is fixed and there are no scroll bars to move the window around over a large clipping. If the clipping is larger than the window, you will not be able to see all of it. There is a scroll bar, but you use it to leaf through the clippings.

Two numbers in the bottom left corner of the window report the total number of clippings in the Scrapbook and the number of the clipping currently visible. A notation in the bottom right corner of the window identifies the kind of information in the clipping; for example, text (TEXT) or picture (PICT). To put the Scrapbook away, click the close box in its title bar or choose Close from the File menu.

Alarm Clock

The Macintosh has a built-in alarm clock and calendar. The clock is accurate to within a second or so each day. The calendar is accurate through the 21st century, including leap years. The clock keeps running when the Macintosh is switched off, thanks to a self-contained, long-life battery.

● *The Alarm Clock reports the time of day, the date, whether the alarm is set to ring, and the time at which it will ring. It also enables you to set and adjust those items.*

Initially only the top part of the Alarm Clock appears, show-ing just the time of day. Clicking the small lever to the right of the time drops the other two parts of the Alarm Clock into view. The middle part is used for viewing and setting the date, or for setting the time. The bottom part of the Alarm Clock contains three icons that control the function of the middle part.

● *To set the time, first select the clock face by pointing at it and clicking the mouse button.*

A second digital clock appears, keeping time below the first one. Move the pointer over the lower digital clock, where it will change from an arrow to a cross (large plus sign).

● *Next, click any element in the lower digital clock and change it by clicking or pressing the dis-played adjustment button.*

When you select any part of the lower clock—hours, minutes, seconds, or AM/PM—an adjustment button appears and the lower clock stops keeping time. The upper digital clock con-tinues to keep time while you set the lower one.

To adjust a selected number upwards, place the pointer on the up adjustment arrow and click or press the mouse button. Click to bump the number up by one; press to spin ahead rapidly.

Use the down adjustment arrow to decrease the number. For AM and PM, clicking anywhere on the adjustment button switches back and forth between them.

● *When the time on the lower digital clock is correct, click the clock face.*

Clicking on the highlighted clock face, or anywhere on the upper digital clock, resets the upper clock so that it matches the lower clock. To reset the lower clock instead, click the mouse button with the pointer between the adjustment button and the AM/PM indicator.

● *To view or change the date, select the calendar icon. Use the same method to set the date as to set the time.*

● *To check the alarm, select the alarm-clock icon. Set the alarm time the same way that you set the time of day.*

When you click the alarm-clock icon, the time at which the alarm will ring appears, with an on/off button to its left. Clicking the on/off button alternately arms and disarms the alarm.

When the alarm goes off, the Mac beeps once, then starts flashing the Apple logo in the menu bar. If the alarm goes off while the power is off, the next time you switch the machine on, the Mac beeps once and flashes the Apple logo. To stop the Apple logo flashing, choose Alarm Clock from the Apple menu and disarm the alarm by clicking on the displayed on/off button.

Tuck the middle and bottom parts of the Alarm Clock away by clicking a second time on the lever next to the time of day. Put the whole Alarm Clock away by clicking on its close box or choosing Close from the File menu.

Note Pad

The Macintosh stores eight pages of typewritten notes on disk and the next chapter will show you how to create, review, and revise the notes.

● *The Note Pad provides an eight-page typing scratch pad.*

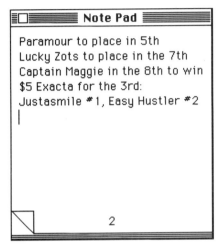

Turn the pages of the Note Pad by clicking on the dog-eared bottom left corner. Click above the diagonal line to turn ahead; click below the diagonal line to turn back. Put the Note Pad away by clicking on its close box or by choosing the Close command from the File menu.

Calculator

The Macintosh can display a working model of a pocket calculator. You enter numbers or operations on it by clicking on its displayed keys or by typing on the keyboard.

● *The Calculator can add, subtract, multiply, and divide just like a real pocket calculator.*

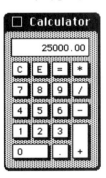

Numbers that are larger than one trillion or smaller than one hundredth are displayed in exponential notation. For example, the number 0.001 will appear as 1E-3 and the number 9000000000000 as 9E12.

Put the Calculator away by clicking on its close box or choosing Close from the Apple menu.

Key Caps

In addition to the characters printed on the keytops, you can use the Macintosh keyboard to type many symbols and foreign letters. The Key Caps desk accessory tells you which keys generate what characters.

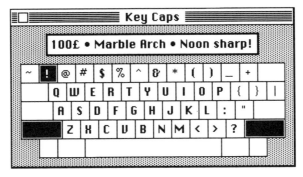

● *Key Caps shows a mockup of the keyboard. Each key is labeled with the character it will generate when pressed.*

As you press a key on the keyboard, the matching displayed key cap is highlighted and its character appears in the Key Caps window. You can also "type" by clicking the displayed keys. Keys such as Option, Shift, and Caps Lock do not generate characters themselves, but they do change the characters that other keys generate. Press them on the keyboard and watch the displayed key-cap labels change. To put the Key Caps window away, click its close box or choose Close from the File menu.

Control Panel

Many system functions can be adjusted on the Macintosh to suit individual preferences.

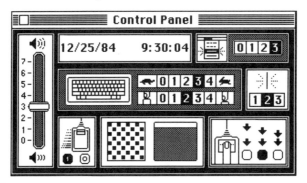

● *The Control Panel lets you adjust speaker volume, date and time, command flashing, keyboard sensitivity, text insertion point blink rate, mouse-pointer coupling, desktop background, and double-click rate.*

The speaker volume (on the left) can be set at any of eight levels, from off (0) to loud (7). Point at the volume control lever, press the mouse button, and drag the lever to the level you want. When you release the mouse button, the speaker beeps once to demonstrate the level you chose.

The date and time are adjusted using the same method as for the Alarm Clock. Note, however, that the Control Panel clock reports the time in 24-hour format.

The control in the upper right corner determines the number of times a menu command flashes after you choose it. Your options are zero (no flashing) to three times.

Two adjustments in the middle of the Control Panel affect the keyboard sensitivity. One determines the rate at which characters repeat when you hold down a key, from fewer than one per second (0) to more than eight per second (4). The other adjustment affects how long you much hold down a key before characters start repeating, from forever (0) to a split second (4).

To the right of the keyboard adjustment is a control that lets you choose among three speeds for flashing the text insertion point. The next chapter describes the insertion point in detail.

Mouse-pointer coupling is adjustable too, at the bottom of the Control Panel next to the volume control. In most situations you want the pointer to zip across the electronic desktop if you move the mouse quickly; click the 1 button for this effect. The other choice, the 0 button, makes the distance the pointer travels independent of mouse speed.

At the bottom of the Control Panel, near the center, is a swatch of the background pattern of the desktop. You can choose among 38 predefined patterns or design your own. Clicking on the white bar atop the swatch changes the swatch to another predefined pattern, and clicking on the swatch itself chooses that pattern. Next to the swatch is a piece of the desktop pattern magnified to show the individual dots that comprise it. To design your own pattern, move the pointer into the magnified area. Clicking on a white space there turns the space black; clicking on a black space turns it white. As you change the magnified pattern, watch the swatch next to it, and then click the swatch when it looks the way you want.

Buttons in the lower right corner give you three choices of mouse-button double-click interval. The middle choice means two clicks must occur within about one second to be considered a double-click. The choice on the left allows more than a second to elapse; the one on the right allows less than a second.

Puzzle

No desktop, real or model, would be complete without some way to while away five minutes here and there. The Macintosh offers the familiar numbered-tile rearrangement game.

● *The Puzzle offers a bit of inno-cent diversion.*

The object of this game is to arrange the tiles in numeric order. Any tile next to the vacant space can move into that space; click the tile you want to move there. A new game begins every time you choose Puzzle from the Apple menu.

The End of the Quick Tour

This concludes the tour of the Macintosh model desktop. You were introduced to icons, pointers, the mouse, commands, menus, shortcuts, displayed controls, dialog boxes, alert boxes, and desk accessories. You should know how to point, press, click, drag, double-click, select, shrink, stretch, scroll, choose, open, and close. If you like, take a break now from reading and review and experiment with your new knowledge. Don't worry if you can't yet figure out how to apply this knowledge; the second and third parts of the book explore that realm thoroughly. When you feel comfortable with your mastery of the skills presented in this chapter, proceed to the next chapter, where you'll learn some more advanced skills.

If you want to switch off your Mac and leave it for awhile, eject the disk from the drive first. On the Macintosh, you don't use a mechanical lever or button to eject a disk. Instead you choose a command with the mouse or press a couple of keys.

● *To eject the disk that's currently inserted, choose Eject from the File menu or press Command-E.*

If the Eject command is dimmed, you cannot eject the disk. To undim the Eject command, select the disk icon (point at it and click the mouse button).

After ejecting a disk, its icon turns gray to show that the disk is no longer in the drive. Go ahead and switch off the Mac.

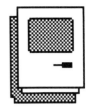

Mastering
The Macintosh

● *In this chapter, you'll learn important Mac skills, including how to cut-and-paste information; enter and edit text; name, remove, and copy icons; and initialize disks.*

A washing machine can be programmed to launder work clothes or lingerie by pushing buttons and rotating knobs to different settings. A food processor can be programmed to slice french fries by installing a certain blade or to knead bread by installing a kneading hook. The Macintosh can be programmed to process words, pictures, numbers, or other kinds of information by installing the appropriate *application program*.

The washing machine produces clean clothes, the food processor prepares dinner, and the Macintosh creates *documents.* Documents are nothing more than processed information. For example, the MacPaint application program lets you prepare illustrations and draw pictures. The MacWrite application program lets you write letters, memos, reports, and such. The Multiplan application program lets you manipulate rows and columns of numbers.

Although application programs specialize in the kinds of information they handle, there is some overlap. Some amount of text, for example, exists in almost every document, so every application program can do some text editing. Where such common functions occur, application programs for the Macintosh tend to use consistent methods. Thus, if you learn how to type and edit text using MacWrite, you can expect the same basic techniques to work when you type in MacPaint and Multiplan. Of course, MacWrite, being a word processor, lets you do more things with text than MacPaint or Multiplan do, but all Mac applications take the same approach to such fundamental tasks.

Exploring a new application on the Mac is not intimidating or frustrating, because you can apply the methods you already know from working with other applications. You may start by writing a letter or report using MacWrite. To take a break, you may doodle with MacPaint for a while and surprise yourself by producing something useful, such as a map to your house or a letterhead for your stationery. Because that was so painless, you'll brave Multiplan to do an expense account or personal net-worth statement.

This chapter takes a look at some of the operations that are common to most Macintosh application programs. It gives you enough information for you to be able to move on to the projects in Part Two, and will serve as a reference if, later, you need to remind yourself how to do something. It describes methods for moving information within and between documents, typing and editing text, organizing and manipulating the electronic desktop, and managing disks.

● *If you wish to try the examples firsthand and have not already started up your Mac with a System Disk, do so now. Close any windows that may be open by choosing Close All from the File menu.*

Moving Information: Cut and Paste

All Mac applications share common methods for moving or copying information from one place to another. The methods, called *cut-and-paste* and *copy-and-paste*, transfer any kind of information within or between documents, even if the documents were created by different applications. Cut-and-paste removes the information to a new location; copy-and-paste puts a duplicate of the information in another location. It doesn't matter whether you transfer text to text, text to a picture, a picture to a picture, or a picture to text. However, information transferred between applications generally loses something in the translation. Later chapters describe exactly what happens. In addition, some applications completely reject certain types of information. For example, MacWrite can handle information from MacPaint but Multiplan cannot.

You do the whole cut-and-paste or copy-and-paste job with the mouse; no typing is ever required. Some experiments with a couple of desk accessories will demonstrate and compare cut-and-paste and copy-and-paste.

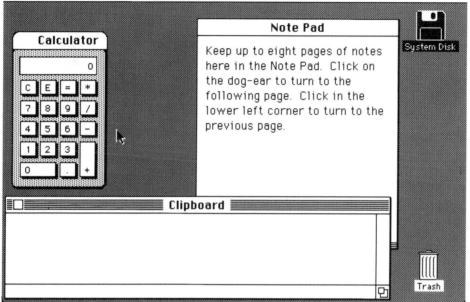

● *Pull down the Apple menu. Get out first the Note Pad and then the Calculator. Drag them by their title bars to opposite sides of the desktop. Then choose Show Clipboard from the Edit menu.*

The *Clipboard* is a special holding area in the Mac's memory. Choosing Show Clipboard opens the Clipboard window and displays the holding area's current contents.

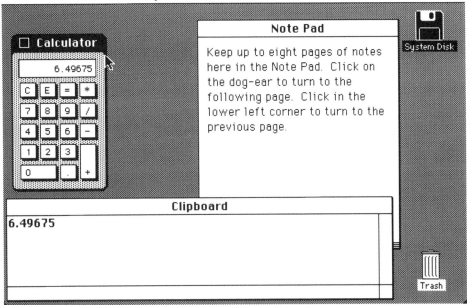

● *Select the Calculator (click it)
and punch in a number. Choose
Copy from the Edit menu and
watch as the number appears in
the Clipboard window.*

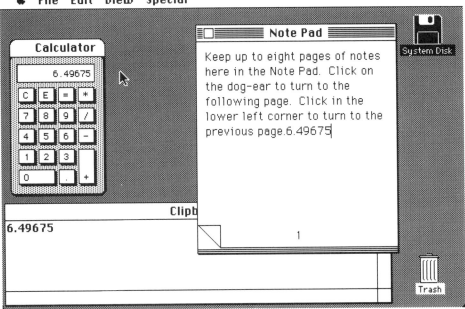

● *Select the Note Pad. Then choose
Paste from the Edit menu to
copy the information from the
Clipboard to the Note Pad.*

When the Calculator is active, choosing either Copy or Cut from the Edit menu puts the number from the Calculator onto the Clipboard. Cut also clears the Calculator to zero, but Copy leaves it untouched.

Suppose you change your mind, or make a mistake. Many commands are reversible if you act promptly.

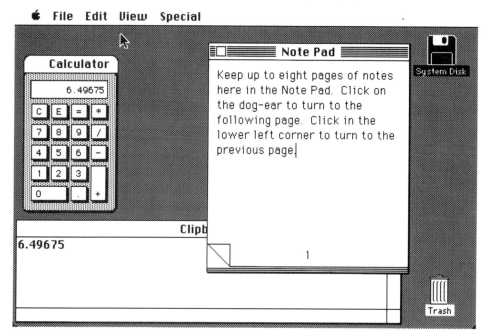

*To reverse your most recent com-
mand, choose Undo from the
Edit menu before typing or
choosing any other command.*

The Undo command usually reverses the effect of the most recent command, but you must choose it before doing anything else. So if you cut when you meant to copy, you can undo the cut and then do the copy as you intended. Choosing Undo twice consecutively undoes and then redoes the previous command. However, Undo does not always work. For example, you cannot undo a Cut or Copy from, or a Paste to, the Calculator. Most of the time the Undo command is dimmed when it will not work, but there are a few exceptions. In those exceptional cases, choosing Undo simply has no effect.

Try using the Cut, Copy, and Paste commands in different ways with the Calculator and Note Pad. Select the Note Pad and choose the Paste command several times in succession. Each time, the same number is copied from the Clipboard to the Note Pad, without removing the number from the Clipboard.

Select the Calculator again and punch in another number. Then use the Cut command to move it to the Clipboard and clear the Calculator to zero. The new number replaces the old number on the Clipboard because the Clipboard can only contain one item. With the Calculator still selected, use the Paste command to copy the number from the Clipboard back to the Calculator.

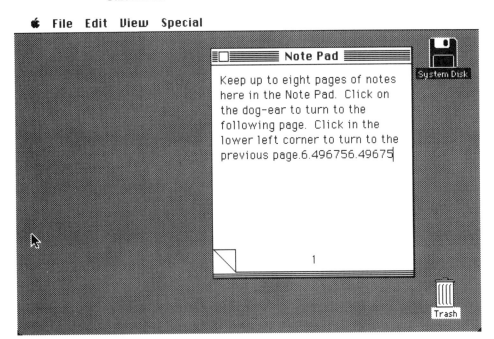

● *Put away the Clipboard window and Calculator by clicking their close boxes, leaving the Note Pad alone on the desktop.*

The opportunities for moving information between the Calculator and Note Pad are limited and not terribly useful. The cut-and-paste and copy-and-paste methods excel at making changes to text. And text editing is a pastime you will certainly pursue if you go very much further with the Macintosh—unless you never make a mistake or change your mind. The next section describes standard text editing methods using examples in the Note Pad.

Editing Text

In spite of the Mac's extensive use of icons and other graphic devices, you will have plenty of opportunity to type on the Macintosh keyboard. There are icons to name, letters to write, pictures to caption, numbers to enter, formulas to specify, and more.

When you type, you just may make a typographical error or two. After you type, you may want to make changes. You are in luck, because you can remove, insert, replace, move, and copy individual characters, words, phrases, sentences, paragraphs, and more, all with ease and efficiency. The mouse and the Cut, Copy, Paste, and Clear commands do the work. The same mouse editing methods work with only minor variations everywhere you must type text on the electronic desktop.

The Text Pointer

The mouse-controlled pointer assumes a special shape when it points at a place where you can type or edit text. It looks like an I-beam viewed from one end.

The pointer has this I-beam shape when you position it over most parts of the Note Pad. But when positioned over some parts, like the dog-ear in the bottom left corner, the pointer is shaped like an arrow. The dog-ear is for turning pages on the Note Pad. You cannot enter or edit text there, so the pointer has an arrow shape. Elsewhere on the desktop—in the menu bar, near the Trash icon, over a directory window, and so on—the pointer takes an arrow shape too. You cannot type or edit text in any of those places while the Note Pad is active.

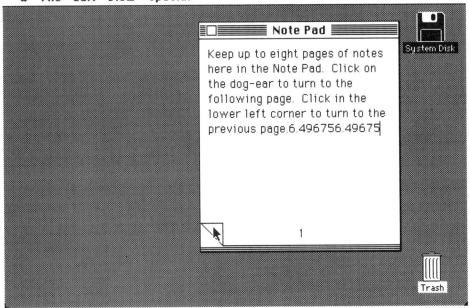

● *When you place the pointer over text in the Note Pad, it has an I-beam shape. But move it down to the dog-ear in the corner and it changes back to an arrow.*

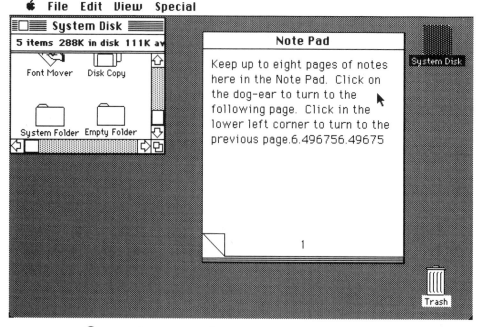

● *Open the System Disk icon by pointing at it and double-clicking the mouse button. Then move the pointer back over a visible part of the Note Pad.*

Activating another window, such as a directory window, inactivates the Note Pad. You cannot type or edit text in an inactive Note Pad, so the pointer stays arrow-shaped when you move it over the Note Pad.

The Insertion Point

Before you can type text on the Note Pad or anywhere else, you must establish the point where the text will go. The I-beam pointer itself does not establish that location. A separate *insertion point*, represented by a thin flashing vertical line, marks the spot. To select an insertion point, move the I-beam pointer to the place you want your typing to go and click the mouse button. The insertion point fits between characters to show exactly where the next text you type will appear.

Inserting New Text

To insert text, just click an insertion point and type. You can put the insertion point, and hence the text you type, anywhere: before or after any paragraph, sentence, word, letter, number, blank space, punctuation mark, or special symbol. You can use the Backspace key to correct mistakes you notice while typing.

⬤ *Try inserting text on the Note Pad. First, close the System Disk window. Then turn to a new page in the Note Pad by clicking above the diagonal line in the dog-ear.*

The insertion point automatically appears at the beginning of a blank page. Try clicking a new insertion point elsewhere on the page (remember, point and click). You can't, because there are no characters to put the insertion point in front of or behind. The mouse can only move the insertion point around in text, not in vacant parts of the page.

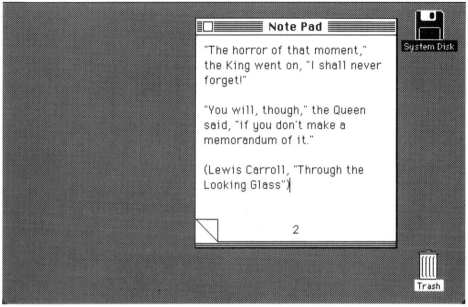

● *Type something and watch
the insertion point move as
you type.*

As you approach the end of a line, just keep typing. Do not
press the Return key. When you type a word that won't fit at the
end of a line, the Note Pad puts that word on the next line for
you. Compare that to a typewriter, where you must judge
whether the next word will fit on the line and must manually
return the carriage to the next line (by pressing its Return key,
for example) if it won't. When typing on the Note Pad, you
press the Return key only at the end of a paragraph, or to create
a blank line.

Selecting Text for Change

There is a very simple rule for correcting or changing text on
the Macintosh. Select the text you want to edit, then choose
what you want to do with it. You use the mouse to select text,
and the commands in the Edit menu to determine what will
happen to the selected text.

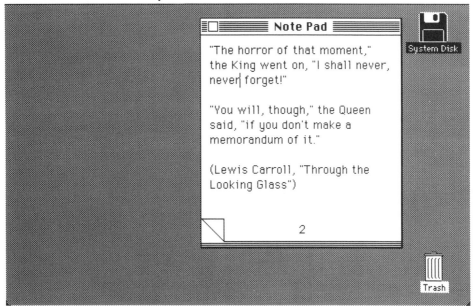

● *Suppose you inadvertently omitted some words or characters. No problem; just select an insertion point where the omissions go, and type away.*

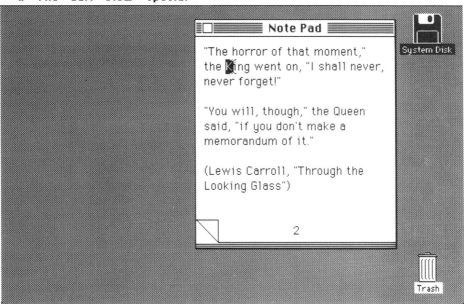

● *To select a single character, point at the character or just to its left, press the mouse button, and drag the pointer slightly to the right.*

Text you select is highlighted. Notice that when you select text, the insertion point disappears. The highlighted text does the same job of showing where the next text editing will occur, so the insertion point isn't needed.

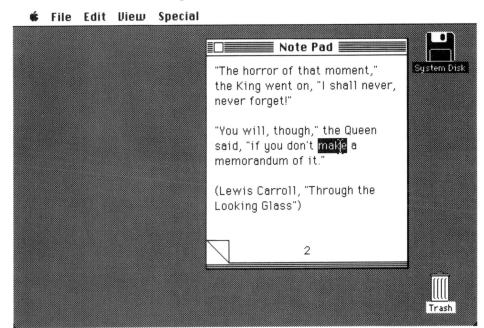

● *To select a word, point anywhere in the word and double-
click the mouse button.*

Placing the pointer on a word and double-clicking the mouse button selects every character in the word. Highlighting starts just after the nearest blank space on the left and ends just before the nearest blank space on the right. Blank spaces are not high-lighted. The Note Pad does not highlight adjoining punctuation marks, symbols, and special characters either.

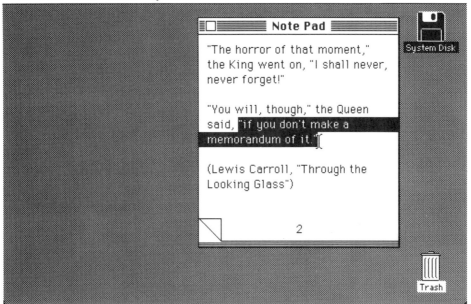

● *To select a phrase, sentence, paragraph, or more, point at the first character you want to select, press the mouse button, and drag the pointer to the last character you want to select.*

When you press the mouse button, you establish a starting point for a selection. As long as you continue to hold down the mouse button, you can change the size and shape of the selection. No matter where you drag the pointer—right, left, up, down—all the characters between it and the starting point are highlighted. The selection is not finally defined until you release the mouse button.

Be careful about clicking or pressing the mouse button after you have made a selection. Ordinarily, clicking the mouse button cancels the selection and selects an insertion point, while pressing the mouse button and dragging the pointer selects a new piece of text. In fact, the way you correct an inaccurate selection is by redoing it (point, press, drag, and release).

You can lengthen or shorten a selection instead of canceling it by pressing the mouse button while holding down the Shift key.

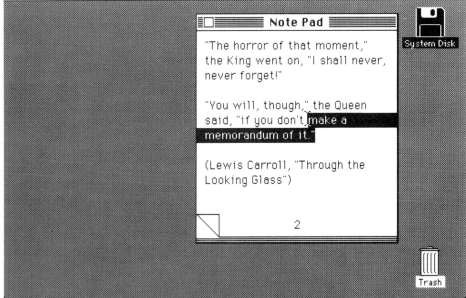

● *To change a selection, hold down the Shift key, press the mouse button, and drag the pointer. When the selection is right, release the mouse button.*

Removing Text

To remove text, select it and choose either the Cut or Clear command from the Edit menu. The Clear command erases the selection without a trace. The Cut command removes the selection but, as you've seen, puts it on the Clipboard, from which you can later retrieve it. Either way, the Note Pad re-forms the paragraph so that each line is as wide as the margins will allow.

As a shortcut for the Clear command, you can press the Backspace key. As a shortcut for the Cut command, press Command-X.

Moving Text

Moving text is a two-step procedure. First, cut it from its present location (select it and choose Cut from the Edit menu). Second, paste it at its new location (select an insertion point where you want the text to go and choose Paste from the Edit menu). The Note Pad automatically adjusts both the source and destination paragraphs to compensate for the loss and addition of the text.

Copying Text

To copy text from one location to another, first select it, then choose Copy from the Edit menu. This puts a copy of the selected text on the Clipboard without removing it from its original location. After that, click an insertion point where you'd like the copy to go and choose the Paste command from the Edit menu. Since pasting text does not remove it from the Clipboard, you can click additional insertion points and paste copies of the same text at those places. Wherever you paste text, the Note Pad re-forms paragraphs to fit within the margins.

Replacing Text

You can replace text with fresh characters typed at the keyboard or with text from the Clipboard. First, select the characters to be replaced. Then you can replace the selected characters with text previously cut or copied to the Clipboard by choosing Paste from the Edit menu.

To replace characters you have selected with completely new ones, simply type the new text on the keyboard. As soon as you type the first character, the selected text vanishes, leaving nothing but the character you typed and a flashing insertion point. Each character you type appears just ahead of the insertion point.

The replacement text need not be the same length as the original text. The Note Pad will automatically readjust the paragraph so that all lines fill out the margins.

Organizing Your Work

What do you do with something once you have written and corrected it? At a real desk, working with real papers, you might grab a file folder, scribble a name on it, cram it with papers, and stuff it in a drawer. Need one of the papers you "filed"? Rummage around until you find it. Perhaps you keep your desk clean, neatly type your file folder labels, and alphabetize your files. If you're lucky, someone else files and retrieves your papers for you. One way or another, you need some system for organizing and finding your work. You also need places to store different types of paper, pens, pencils, erasers, rulers, and the other tools you use for writing, drawing, and figuring.

So it is with the work you do on a Mac. Since all the tools (desk accessories and applications) you will use and papers (documents) you will create can't possibly fit at one time on the electronic desktop, you must be able to put some of them aside in such a way that you can easily find them again. The Macintosh stores desk accessories, applications, documents, and its own equivalent of file folders on disks until you need them. You may have heard the disk spin when you got out desk accessories or put them away. The Macintosh was retrieving or storing the desk accessories on disk.

You can hear the disk spin when you put a desk accessory away, because it is stored on disk. But the disk directory is usually stored in the Macintosh memory, so the disk is usually silent when you open or close a disk icon.

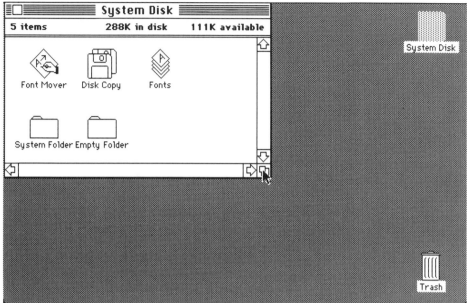

● *Listen carefully to the disk drive as you close the Note Pad. Then open the System Disk icon and enlarge its window.*

The Finder

A special built-in program, called the Finder, knows how to locate and retrieve applications and documents from disks so you can use them. When you insert a disk, the Finder quickly scouts for documents and applications. Later, when you open the disk icon, the Finder displays the icons that represent the applications and documents it found on the disk.

With the Finder, you can name, save, duplicate, copy, move, rename, and remove both applications and documents, or organize them in folders. The Finder can also eject, copy, erase, and initialize whole disks. In short, the Finder helps you organize and manage disks and the documents and applications on them.

Identifying Icons

Every icon has a name centered immediately below it. The name must be at least one character long. Disk and application icon names can be as long as 26 characters; document and folder icon names can be 63 characters long. For example, you can change the name of the Fonts document to Standard Auxiliary Fonts. Simply click an insertion point in front of the letter "F" and type the additional words.

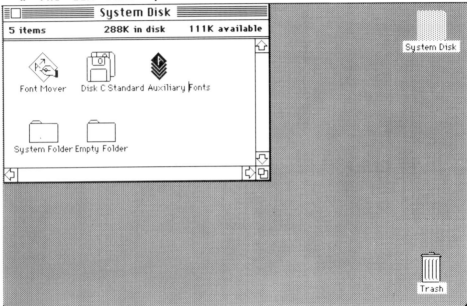

● *To change an icon name, move the pointer over it until the pointer's shape changes from an arrow to an I-beam. Then use the standard editing methods described earlier.*

Even though long names are allowed, it's a good idea to label your icons succinctly. A long name extends to the right and left as far as necessary. If there are other icons close by, the name either overlaps and obscures them or is obscured by them.

Revise a long icon name, if possible, by removing words or abbreviating. But avoid vague acronyms or abbreviations; they will look like hieroglyphics after a few weeks. Use meaningful names that suggest the contents of the icon. For example, change the overly long "Standard Auxiliary Fonts" to "Aux. Fonts."

If you must use a long name, move the icon to a place in the window where it will not obscure important parts of other icons or icon names. You can stagger the icons so their names do not line up horizontally. After staggering them, avoid using the Clean Up command in the Special menu, since it will line icons up in neat rows and columns without regard to name overlap.

Clicking an icon selects the icon and its name. Remember that typing replaces selected text? If you type immediately after selecting an icon, you change its name to whatever you type. However, you cannot ever change the name of the Trash icon.

The Copy, Cut, Paste, and Clear commands are all available from the Edit menu for editing an icon name. The Undo command is not. But as long as you are still editing the name, you can change your mind and restore the old name. First, use the Backspace key to erase the new name. Second, move the pointer away from the name until the pointer changes shape from an I-beam to an arrow, then click the mouse button.

The Finder does not allow duplicate application, document, or folder names on the same disk. For example, a document cannot have the same name as another document on the disk, even if the two are in different folders. However, one disk can contain icons with the same names as icons on another disk, so you can make backup copies of your disks.

Duplicate disk names, which the Finder does allow, can be troublesome. The Finder differentiates between seemingly identical names by attaching different invisible characters to each one. It occasionally asks you to insert a disk it names, and it wants a specific disk, not any disk that has the requested name. You have to insert each like-named disk in turn, until the Finder recognizes the one it wants. Giving disks unique names avoids ambiguity and hassle.

Getting Information About Icons

An icon's name provides a limited amount of information about the disk, application, document, or folder that the icon represents. The Finder keeps track of even more information about the object the icon represents, including:

■ What kind of object it is.

■ How much space it occupies on the disk.

■ Which disk it's on and whether that disk is inserted in the internal or external drive or has been removed.

■ The date and time it was created and last modified.

■ Whether it is locked against changes.

■ An optional description you can write and edit.

● *To see additional information about any icon, select the icon (point and click), then choose Get Info from the File menu.*

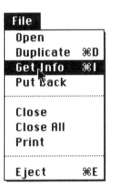

File	
Open	
Duplicate	⌘D
Get Info	⌘I
Put Back	
Close	
Close All	
Print	
Eject	⌘E

Information about Aux. Fonts

Aux. Fonts

Kind: Font Mover document
Size: 55808 bytes, accounts for 56K on disk
Where: System Disk, internal drive
Created: Wednesday, May 2, 1984 at 8:07 AM
Modified: Wednesday, May 2, 1984 at 8:08 AM

☐ Locked

The *comments box* at the bottom of an information window can hold a 150-word summary that describes the purpose or contents of the disk, application, document, or folder. By typing a carefully worded summary, you save the time it takes to open the icon to see what it does or what it contains.

▤□▤▤▤▤▤ Information about Aux. Fonts ▤▤▤▤▤

                                 Aux. Fonts

Kind:	Font Mover document
Size:	55808 bytes, accounts for 56K on disk
Where:	System Disk, internal drive
Created:	Wednesday, May 2, 1984 at 8:07 AM
Modified:	Wednesday, May 2, 1984 at 8:08 AM

☐ **Locked**

Contains these fonts: Cairo 18; Los Angeles 12 and 24; New York 36; San Francisco 18; Toronto 9, 12, 14, 18, and 24.

● *While the information window is active, you can type or edit the text in the comments box using the standard editing methods described earlier.*

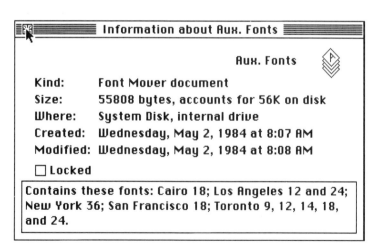

● *To put an information window away, click its close box or choose the Close command from the File menu.*

Locking Icons and Disks

You can lock individual applications, documents, and folders so that they cannot be removed, replaced, or changed in any way. Not even the icon name can be changed. The icons inside a locked folder cannot be removed, replaced, or changed either. A locked object and its contents can be copied and the contents of its comments box can be changed, however.

● *You lock and unlock an application, document, or folder in its information window. Place the pointer over the Locked box and click the mouse button.*

You can also lock a whole disk against change or erasure, preventing anyone from renaming it or saving anything on it. However, MacWrite and Multiplan cannot print from a locked disk, and MacPaint will not work at all. Some desk accessories work, others don't.

● *To lock a disk, slide the small tab (red on most disks) toward the edge of the disk. To unlock it, slide the tab away from the edge of the disk.*

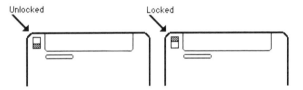

Alternate Directory Views

Icons usually represent applications, documents, and folders in a directory window, but the Finder can suppress the icons and display a written list instead. It can list disk contents in alphabetical order by name, in chronological order by date of last activity, in order by size, or in order by kind.

● *To change the directory window to a different view, choose one of the commands in the View menu. Widen the directory window to see the full listing.*

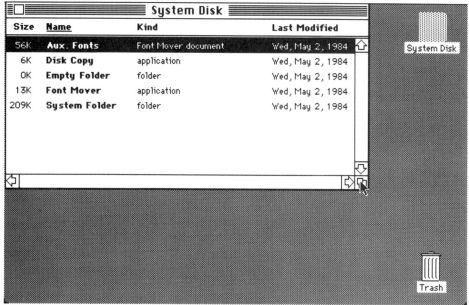

Printing a Directory Window

You will, of course, write a disk's name on an adhesive label and stick that on the disk. The name will remind you of the contents, but will not tell you specifically which documents and applications the disk contains. You may find room for the names of a dozen or so icons on the label, but some disks will have more than you can keep track of that way. What's worse, disk contents have a way of changing, and when they do, you must laboriously scratch old names off the label and squeeze in new ones.

One cure for Messy-Label-Syndrome is to write on a piece of paper the name and type of every icon on the disk. That gets old fast. Fortunately, the Finder can use your printer to print a copy of any window, including the directory window, on paper.

Size	Name	Kind	Last Modified
56K	**Aux. Fonts**	Font Mover document	Wed, May 2, 1984
6K	**Disk Copy**	application	Wed, May 2, 1984
0K	**Empty Folder**	folder	Wed, May 2, 1984
13K	**Font Mover**	application	Wed, May 2, 1984
209K	**System Folder**	folder	Wed, May 2, 1984

System Disk

● *To print a copy of the active window, press the Shift, Command, and 4 keys simultaneously. Your printer must be connected, switched on, and ready to print.*

Pressing Shift-Command-4 prints only the visible part of the active screen window. So before printing, use the size box in the lower right corner of the window to make the window big enough to show all the applications, documents, and folders. If they won't all fit, you will have to print the disk directory on more than one page. Use the window's scroll bars to bring fresh, unprinted applications, documents, and folders into view, then press Shift-Command-4 again.

You can also print the entire screen contents by depressing the Caps Lock key before pressing Shift-Command-4.

Using Folders

As long as you have only a few documents, you can get away with leaving them lying around the desktop. Eventually, though, you will want a way to group them. That is exactly what *folders* help you do. If you deal with many companies, for example, you might have a separate folder for each one. Inside those you might have other folders, one for each person or department you contact in the company. Actual documents related to your dealings with those people or departments go inside the inner folders. If you deal with just a few companies, you might prefer to have separate folders to collect each kind of document you create, such as letters, memos, purchase orders, invoices, and collections.

To illustrate the use of folders, try creating a new folder to hold the Font Mover application and Aux. Fonts document. Before you can use folders, your view of the directory window must be by Icon, so choose by Icon from the View menu.

To create a new folder, first se-lect the Empty Folder icon, then choose the Duplicate command from the File menu.

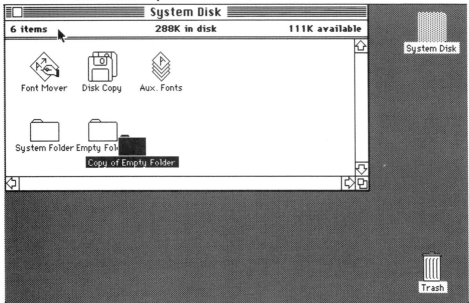

Choosing Duplicate (or pressing Command-D, the shortcut equivalent) duplicates the selected icon and automatically switches the selection to the duplicate icon. It also formulates an interim name for the duplicate icon by prefixing the name of the original icon with the words "Copy of."

The interim name is cumbersome and uninformative. Since the duplicate is already selected, you can change its name just by typing a new one.

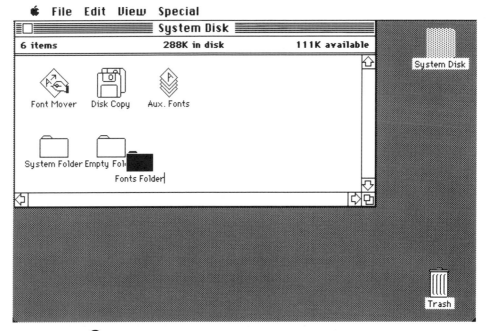

● *To change the interim name, type a new name immediately.*

It will be awkward using the new Fonts Folder icon, crowded as it is next to the Empty Folder icon. Drag the Fonts Folder to a clearing in the directory window before you try to put the Aux. Fonts icon in it.

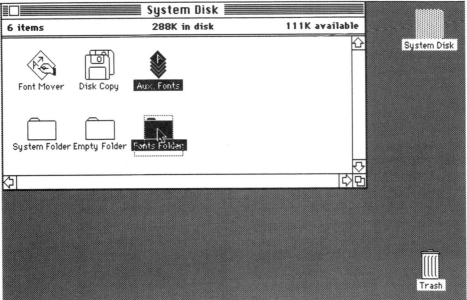

● *To put an icon in a closed folder, drag the icon over the top of the destination folder's icon. When the folder icon becomes high-lighted, release the mouse button.*

Remember, to drag an icon you point at it, press the mouse button, and slide the mouse. An outline of the Aux. Fonts icon breaks away and follows the pointer. When you move the pointer (and with it, the icon outline) over the closed Fonts Folder icon, the Finder highlights the folder icon. Release the mouse button while the folder icon is highlighted, and the Aux. Fonts icon moves into the Fonts Folder.

Next, try opening the Fonts Folder icon by double-clicking on it. Notice the Aux. Fonts icon in the folder window. Use the window's size box to make the window smaller, and then drag the window by its title bar so you can see the Font Mover icon in the System Disk window. Drag the Font Mover icon into the Fonts Folder window.

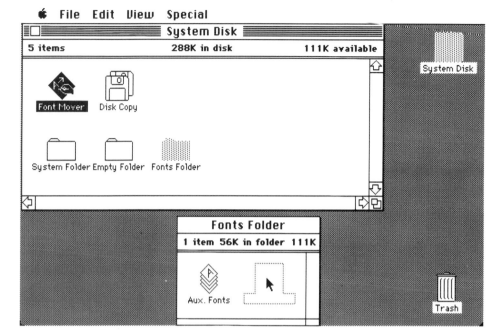

● *To put an icon in an open folder,
drag the icon into a clear space
in the folder window and release
the mouse button.*

When dragging an icon from one window into another, make
sure the tip of the pointer is inside the destination window before you release the mouse button. Otherwise the icon simply
moves to a new location inside the original window. If that happens and the icon seems to be lost, use the window's scroll bars
to see if the icon has merely moved out of sight. Use the pointer
and mouse button to grab the errant icon and move it again.

● *To close an active folder window, click its close box or choose
Close from the File menu.*

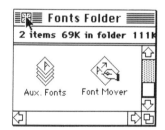

Selecting Several Icons at Once

Moving lots of icons one at a time can be quite a chore. You can expedite mass moves by selecting all the icons first, and then moving them collectively.

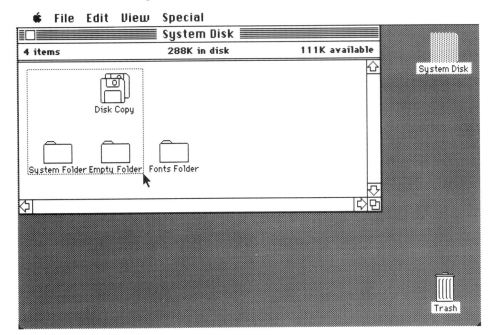

● *To select a group of adjacent icons, imagine a rectangle around them. Move the pointer to one corner of the rectangle, press the mouse button, then drag the pointer to the opposite corner. Release the mouse button there.*

When you drag the pointer from one corner of the imaginary rectangle to the opposite corner, the Finder actually displays a dotted-line rectangle. The rectangle changes size and shape as you drag the pointer around. All icons even partially inside the rectangle will be selected when you release the mouse button. If you accidentally select the wrong group, just redraw the selection rectangle by pointing and dragging again.

With the help of the Shift key, you can also select a group of nonadjacent icons. For each member of the group, hold down the Shift key, point at its icon, and click the mouse button. Be careful; if you forget to use the Shift key, the Finder cancels the group selection and you have to start over. You can use this same technique to add an icon to any existing group selection, including one made with a selection rectangle. If you click a highlighted icon while holding down the Shift key, you remove that icon from the selection.

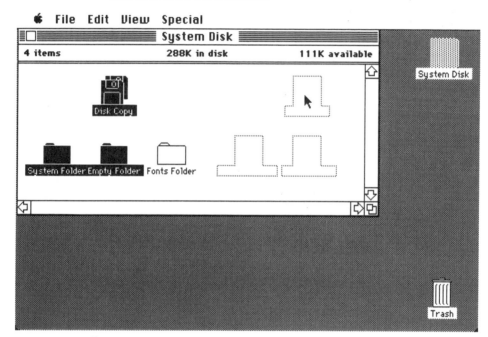

● *To drag a group of selected icons, point at any one of them, press the mouse button, and then drag the pointer.*

Putting Icons on the Desktop

You can drag any icon out of a window and leave it on the desktop. Putting a folder icon on the desktop, for example, facilitates gathering documents into it from the far reaches of a large directory. Once on the desktop, the folder icon is visible, no matter which direction you scroll the directory window.

To move an icon from the desktop back into the directory window, select it and choose Put Back from the File Menu. If the icon you select came from a folder window, not a disk window, the Put Back command returns it to the folder. Furthermore, if you select an icon in a folder window and choose Put Back, the icon returns to the window it came from.

Juggling Disks

You can only do so much with a single disk such as the System Disk. Eventually you will want to use an application such as MacWrite, MacPaint, or Multiplan. These applications are on different disks, so you need a way to change disks. Using these applications, you will create new documents and store them on disks. The disks soon fill up, so you need a way to move some documents to another disk and get rid of others altogether.

The rest of this chapter describes how you can use the Finder to change disks, remove icons from disks, copy icons from disk to disk, duplicate an entire disk, erase a disk, and more.

Using More Than One Disk

The disk icon you first see on the desktop represents the disk you used to start up your Macintosh. If you need an application or document not on that disk, you can eject it and insert a different disk. If your Mac has an external as well as an internal disk drive, you can put the second disk in the external drive. Either way, the Finder keeps track of both disks.

Every time you insert another disk, its icon is added to the desktop. Any disk icon on the desktop can be opened, whether its disk is inserted or not, to show the directory window. An ejected disk's icon is dimmed to gray. When you open a gray disk icon, the icons in its directory window are gray too. You can open folders and move icons around in any disk's directory window, but you can only change the names of the icons in the directory window of a currently inserted disk.

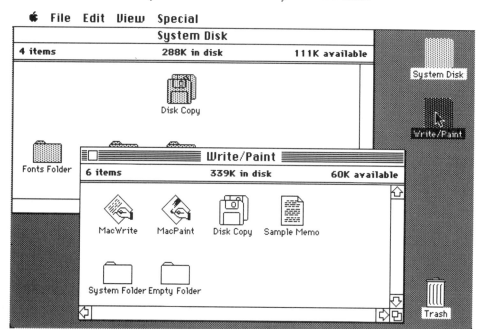

● *Close the System Disk window and choose Eject from the File menu to eject the System Disk. Insert the Write/Paint disk. Then open both disk icons.*

You can continue to eject disks and insert others, up to a point. For each different disk you insert, the Finder remembers the name of every application, document, and folder, as well as everything that appears in their information windows. The Finder has only a small part of the Mac's memory in which to keep track of all that. Three or four disks can easily use up the available memory; it all depends on the number of applications, documents, and folders that are stored on the disks you've inserted so far. The Finder advises you when it has too little memory left to keep track of a disk you just inserted or ejected. You can try inserting a disk with less on it, or you can remove an existing disk icon to make way for a new one.

Removing Icons from the Desktop

You can remove the icon of a disk that has been ejected by dragging it to the Trash. Moving a disk icon to the Trash removes it immediately. To get the icon back, reinsert its disk.

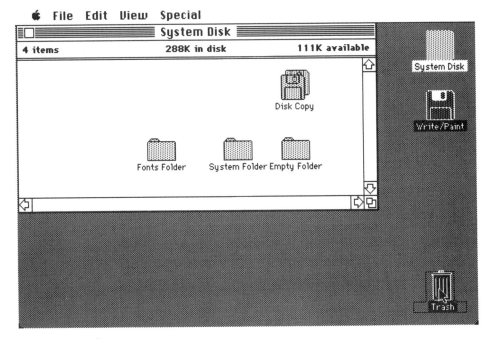

● *Close the Write/Paint window*
and eject the Write/Paint disk.
Then drag its icon to the Trash,
and watch it disappear.

You cannot remove the icon of the disk you used to start up the Macintosh.

When you no longer need an application, document, or folder, you also remove it by dragging its icon into the Trash. If you put an empty folder icon in the Trash, the Finder removes it immediately. All other icons you put in the Trash remain there until you choose Empty Trash from the Special menu, eject the disk, or start an application (as described in the next chapter). You can open the Trash icon, like a folder or disk icon, to check its contents and to retrieve icons from it.

If you drag an application or a document from the System Folder into the Trash, an alert box appears asking you to confirm or cancel its removal by clicking a displayed button. You cannot remove any applications, documents, or folders that are in use, locked, or contained in a locked folder or disk.

Initializing Disks

The first time you insert a brand new disk, the Finder will not be able to read it or display its icon. It must be initialized first. *Initializing*, sometimes called *formatting*, writes timing marks on a disk that help the Finder locate information later. Initializing completely obliterates any documents or applications that might have been on the disk before.

Other computers have explicit initialization or formatting commands. The Macintosh does not. The Finder recognizes a brand new (unreadable) disk when you insert it, and asks if you wish to initialize it.

● *To initialize a brand new disk, insert it and click the Initialize button in the dialog box that appears.*

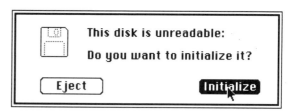

If the Finder ever wants to initialize a disk you think you've used before, eject the disk by clicking the displayed Eject button. Remove and inspect the disk. Does it belong to some other computer, such as an Apple Lisa? If it is a Macintosh disk, try reinserting it. Should the message persist, try other disks. If the Finder accepts them, the troublesome disk has become corrupted and must be initialized. If the Finder thinks all the disks you try need initializing, there is probably something wrong with your Macintosh.

After about one minute, the Finder finishes initializing the disk and asks you to name the disk.

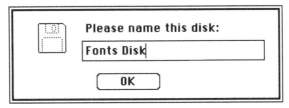

● *Enter a name for the disk.*

Anything you type, up to 26 characters, will appear under the icon on the desktop. If you type nothing, the Finder assigns the name Untitled. Although the pointer has an arrow shape inside the dialog box, you can edit your typing using the standard editing methods described earlier.

Erasing Disk Contents

After a period of time, disks have a way of becoming cluttered with stale documents, folders, and even applications. You can always dispose of such objects by dragging their icons into the Trash, either singly or in groups. But if the disk contains nothing of value, it is faster to erase everything at once.

● *To erase the entire contents of a disk, select its icon (point and click), then choose Erase Disk from the Special menu.*

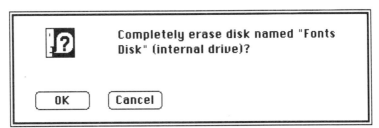

The Erase Disk command displays an alert box, giving you a chance to reconsider before it removes everything from the disk. If you are sure you want to lose forever all the documents and applications on the selected disk, click the OK button.

Start-up Disks and Applications

You cannot start up a Macintosh from a freshly initialized or erased disk, because such disks have nothing on them except an Empty Folder. In order to start a Macintosh, you have to insert a disk containing certain documents. Specifically, two special documents named System and Finder are required. Disks without those documents are called *nonstart-up disks;* disks with them are called *start-up disks.* The System Disk is a start-up disk. The MacWrite, MacPaint, and Multiplan applications also come on start-up disks.

Every start-up disk has a *start-up application,* which the Macintosh automatically starts as part of the start-up procedure. The Finder program is the start-up application on the System Disk and many other start-up disks. You can designate any other application on the disk as the start-up application with the Set Startup command. For example, on the System Disk you could make Font Mover the start-up application.

● *To designate a startup application, select its icon and choose Set Startup from the Special menu. In the alert box that appears, confirm or cancel this action by clicking the appropriate button.*

To make the Finder the start-up application again, select the Finder icon in the System Folder and choose Set Startup from the Special menu.

Copying and Moving Between Disks

There will be times when you need to move or copy information from one disk to another. You may want to organize your disks by moving related applications, documents, and folders to their own disks, rather than intermixing them. For example, you might put MacWrite, MacPaint, and Multiplan on three separate disks, each with documents you create and edit with that particular application. Those disks will eventually fill up, and you will have to move some of the documents off to other disks.

Also, it's a good idea to periodically make copies of important applications, documents, and folders on separate backup disks. That way, if the original disk gets damaged or lost, you have something to fall back on. And in order to create new start-up disks, you must copy the System and Finder documents from the System disk.

Before you can copy or move an application, document, or folder, the icons of both the source and destination disks must be on the desktop. If necessary, eject the current disk and insert the source and destination disks in turn. It does not matter what disk is inserted when you begin copying because the Finder will ask for the disks it needs by name. However, if you have an external drive, you will save time if both source and destination disks are inserted before you begin.

Dragging an icon to a new disk puts a copy of the application, document, or folder on the new disk. If you copy a folder, its entire contents are copied along with it. The copy's name is the same as that of the original.

Try copying the Fonts Folder icon from your System Disk to the disk you just initialized and named Fonts Disk. Since the Fonts Folder contains the Font Mover and Aux. Fonts icons, they will both be copied too. Though you can copy the Fonts Folder icon whether it is open or closed, close it to reduce the clutter on the desktop.

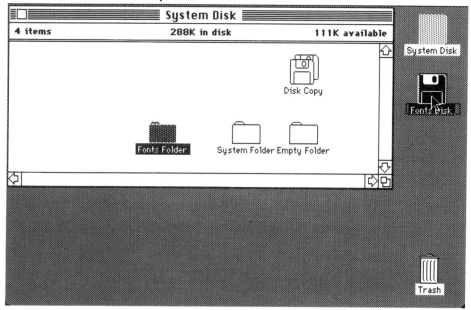

To copy an application, document, or folder to a closed disk icon, drag its icon over the destination disk's icon. When the disk icon is highlighted, release the mouse button.

Unless you have two disk drives, you will have to swap the source and destination disks back and forth. This involves inserting them in turn in the disk drive until the Finder has finished copying. When it's time to exchange disks, the Finder ejects the disk it has and asks for the other disk by name. If your Macintosh has two drives, you can put the source disk in one and the destination disk in the other, avoiding the disk swapping.

The Finder also displays a box in which it counts down the number of documents and applications (it calls them files) it has yet to copy. The number of files it reports does not correlate directly with the number of disk swaps, which is determined more by the total amount of information being copied. A folder full of documents requires much more swapping than a single document, for example. However, copying an entire folder takes less time than individually copying each icon in it.

Open the Fonts Disk icon to verify that the disk now contains a copy of the Fonts Folder icon. Notice the Fonts Disk lacks the Finder and System documents, which it needs to make it a start-up disk. You can copy them from the System Folder in the System Disk directly to the Fonts Disk directory window. First you must shrink the Fonts Disk window, drag it off to the right, and open the System Folder.

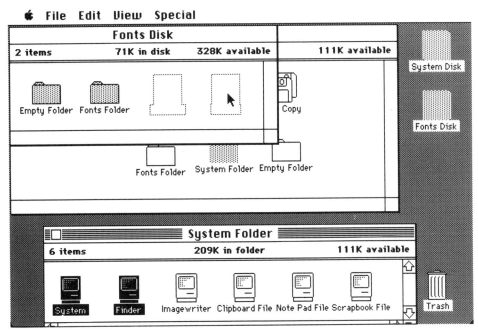

● *To copy an application, document, or folder to a directory window, drag its icon into the destination window and release the mouse button.*

If an icon on the destination disk has the same name as an icon you are copying from the source disk, the Finder displays an alert box. The box asks your permission to replace the old with the new. You click a displayed OK button to approve or a displayed Cancel button to cancel the copy.

The original application, document, or folder (and its contents) remains on the source disk. If you wanted to remove it, you would drag its icon from the source disk's directory window to the Trash. Removing an icon from the source disk after copying effectively turns the copy operation into a move operation.

Copying Entire Disks

Not only can you copy applications, documents, and folders from one disk to another, you can copy the entire contents of one disk to another.

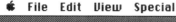

● *To copy everything on one disk to another, drag the source disk icon on top of the destination disk icon. When the destination disk icon is highlighted, release the mouse button.*

Both source and destination disk icons must be present on the
desktop before you can begin to copy. If necessary, insert one
disk, then the other, to achieve this. For an extra measure of
safety, lock the source disk before inserting it.

Because the contents of the destination disk will be completely
erased and replaced by the contents of the source disk, the
Finder asks you to confirm the disk copy operation before it
proceeds. If you have any doubts or second thoughts, cancel the
disk copy operation.

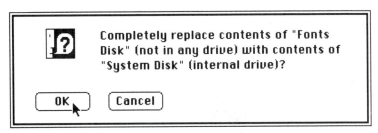

● *Double check that the disk* *you want before you click the*
names and the direction the *OK button to begin.*
Finder plans to copy are what

If you don't have an external drive, copying one disk to another involves switching disks many times. When the Finder
needs a different disk, it ejects the one it has and asks by name
for the one it needs. If you have an external drive, little or no
disk switching is required, assuming you put the source disk in
one drive and the destination disk in the other. A dialog box
counts down the number of files (documents and applications)
still to be copied.

The Disk Copy Program

The most efficient way to duplicate a disk using a single drive is
with the Disk Copy program. It copies an entire 400K disk in
four swaps (eight insertions), about half the number required by
the icon-dragging method. To start the Disk Copy program,
double-click on its icon. A large dialog box full of information
about the program fills the screen. Read it and click the displayed OK button to continue.

The Disk Copy program automatically initializes the destination
disk. Unless the destination disk is new, the program asks for
your permission before erasing the disk.

During the copy operation, the Disk Copy program appropriates most of the Macintosh memory, including the memory normally dedicated to the screen display. The whole screen fills with meaningless static, except for one message line at the bottom. That line gives you instructions and status reports. Follow those instructions. The message line always includes a Quit or Cancel button so you can stop the copy at any time.

The resulting duplicate disk is an exact copy of the original. It even appears to have the same name. However, the Finder can tell the two disks apart even if you can't. You may want to rename the duplicate to avoid confusion.

Copy Protection and Software Piracy

Do not construe the Mac's ability to copy disks and applications as license to enter the software distribution business. Virtually all software developers copyright the applications they develop. This makes copying—except for personal use—highly illegal. It is against the law to copy and distribute MacWrite, MacPaint, Multiplan, and other copyrighted applications to family, friends, fellow club members, business associates, or anyone else.

In spite of its illegality, software piracy is common enough that some developers have devised schemes to combat it.

Multiplan, for example, can be copied using the icon-dragging method, but copies cannot be used without the original application disk, which is named Multiplan Master. The Disk Copy program will not copy disks that have been copy-protected.

Creating Separate MacWrite and MacPaint Disks

If you received MacWrite and MacPaint on a single Write/Paint disk, you will have to separate them in order to do any useful work. Follow these steps:

1 Make two copies of the original Write/Paint disk.

2 Put the original Write/Paint disk in a safe place.

3 Remove MacWrite from one copy; rename the disk Paint.

4 Remove MacPaint from the other copy; rename the disk Write.

5 Optional: Remove from the new Write and Paint disks the Disk Copy, Font Mover, and Fonts icons, if present.

Moving On

By now you should be thoroughly familiar with things Macintosh, and be chafing at the bit for some productive work or fun. The next part of the book tells you how to use the MacWrite, MacPaint, and Multiplan applications—three tools for fun and profit with the Mac.

Before going on, make sure you know how to select, insert, remove, move, copy, and replace pieces of text. You also need to know how to cut and paste information, name icons, remove icons from the desktop, initialize new disks, lock disks and icons, eject disks, copy documents from one disk to another, and copy whole disks. Your work (or play) on the Mac will be easier if you can print a directory, create folders, make a start-up disk, and erase a whole disk. And for maximum effectiveness, you should know how to view a disk's contents by name, date, size, and kind, as well as by icon; select and move icons in groups; and put icons on the desktop and get them back.

Three Projects in Detail

Part Two

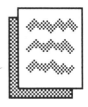

Writing a Report with MacWrite

● *Follow the detailed descriptions of this MacWrite project and learn how to type and edit paragraphs and tables, change margins and tabs, mix type fonts, and print a report.*

Spray cans, pens, pencils, typewriters, and MacWrite all have one thing in common: You can write with them. Some writing tools are better suited to one type of writing than another. Spray cans scrawl graffiti under overpasses, pens dash off postcards from Florida, pencils mark carpenters' measurements on lumber, and typewriters fill out loan applications. MacWrite doesn't do any of those writing jobs well. However, it is handy at most everything else: letters, memos, résumés, outlines, articles, essays, reports, briefs, contracts, pamphlets, press releases, circulars, menus, advertising copy, or you-name-it.

MacWrite is an application program that turns a Macintosh into a word processor. Like all word processors, MacWrite allows you to type text on the keyboard, correct typing mistakes, make modifications, adjust the page appearance, print a copy of your work on paper, and save a copy on disk. MacWrite has some features you won't find in many other word processors. For example, it can freely mix different fonts, sizes, and styles of type for a typeset, not typewritten, effect.

To illustrate what you can do with a word processor, this chapter investigates how you might use MacWrite to write a business report. It does not explain how to choose your words; for that, you need experience and a book or two on writing style. It does describe how to enter, edit, and format your words.

The sample report analyzes a quarter's sales for one suburban location of Mr. Shoe, a mythical shoe-store chain. The full report runs eight pages, but only the first four are shown here. The four sample pages, which include regular paragraphs, an indented list, a table, page headers and footers, and a title page, are shown in Figure 1.

By showing you how to create the four sample report pages, this chapter covers nearly all of MacWrite's features. The only topic not covered here is pasting pictures into a MacWrite document; the next chapter explains how you do that.

Mr. Shoe

Sunset Valley Mall

Top-Selling Shoes Report

First Quarter 1985

prepared by

Bernie Myerson

Figure 1. Four sample pages from the Mr. Shoe report

This promises to be another year of high growth for Mr. Shoe's Sunset Valley Mall store. Sales figures for the first quarter of this year are now in, and they show a 23 percent increase over the first quarter sales of a year ago. First quarter has always been our weakest, so we expect the rest of the year to look even better. Also, we are about to start the Fashion Footware Fling promotion that has been so successful at other Mr. Shoe stores. The Sunset Valley location is ideal for such a promotion because people around here are extremely fashion conscious. We expect it to boost our sales significantly.

To help focus the Spring buying trip and assist the advertising group with its fall promotional plans, this report correlates computer reports with our salespeople's feedback, identifying our top sellers by manufacturer and product type. It also describes top-selling styles, profiles typical customers, and lists top manufacturers. Also discussed are advertising and promotion results and a comparison of first quarter '84 sales with first quarter '85 sales.

The first and most important question is always the same: What were our top sellers? Have they changed since last year? What's hot, what's not? Who are the top manufacturers? The accompanying table, culled from reports generated by the new computerized point-of-purchase sales system, details Sunset Valley's top sellers by department. Our salespeople had several observations about the results.

Women's Shoes

Women's shoes continue to be our strongest department by a ratio of three to one. With the increasing number of European designers we carry, the average cost per pair has also increased 19 percent. Our sales research indicates women's sales also contribute substantially to our dramatic increase in multiples. That is, when a woman comes in to shop for herself, she will most likely buy a pair for her kid. The reverse is also true. In the first quarter of this year our top-of-the-line women's shoes have experienced the biggest jump. Calfskin and leather shoes are becoming increasingly popular. Canvas and plastic styles are dropping. Both low- and high-heeled styles remain popular.

Sunset Valley Top Sellers
by Department [1]

Manufacturer	Style	Product Code [2]	Number Sold
Alberto Amante	Black leather pump	WD	32
Alberto Amante	Navy leather sling-back	WD	30
Caresso	Red spectator	WD	26
Caresso	Gray wedgie [3]	WC	20
First Court	White canvas court	WC	20
Bandino Boot	Brown lace-up boot	WC	9
Bandino for Men	Black wingtip	MD	14
Dali	Black tassel slip-on	MD	12
Kodiak	Gray jazz oxford [3]	MD	9
Poindexter	Cordovan penny loafer	MC	13
Off Balance	880 trainer	MC	12
Clerk's	Kangaroos	MC	9
Little Folk	Girl's runner	CH	14
Little Folk	Boy's saddle oxford	CH	12
Play Rite	Red Mary Jane	CH	10

[1] Top three sellers are listed for each product code; slippers are not included.
[2] WD=Women's Dress; WC=Women's Casual; MD=Men's Dress; MC=Men's Casual; CH=Children's.
[3] Gray has been increasingly popular for both men's and women's styles.

Alberto Amante is a brand new line for us and is doing phenomenally well. Our salespeople report brand recognition is very high. Women are coming into the store in droves specifically for Amante shoes. According to the Amante rep, seven new styles will be added this spring and a new line of men's shoes will be introduced at the Milan Shoe Show in June. Alberto Amante now accounts for 19 percent of our women's department sales, surpassing Caresso as the top manufacturer.

Men's Shoes

Sales of our men's shoes remain strong primarily because of their high unit cost. We are selling 12 percent fewer pairs this quarter; however, the cost per pair has increased 27 percent. The black wingtip continues to be our top seller at 14 pairs a quarter. This is only because of the IBM plant located in Lawndale. The black tassel slip-on is the next best-selling shoe and at $150.00 a pair is contributing substantially to the department's sales. Amante will introduce a fall loafer in cordovan; it would be great to have a full run of this style.

Children's Shoes

In the children's department, sales have dropped markedly since last year, as the graph on the next page shows. This is due primarily to increased competition. Nickel's department store has added a beautiful new children's shoe department on their third floor. Our salespeople were certain we were losing more and more customers to Nickel's, so for two weeks in February we asked customers in our children's department what they liked about the new Nickel's children's shoe department. These are the most common responses:

- Convenience of one-stop shopping.
- Able to use store charge.
- Sales in children's department heavily advertised and promoted through store statement stuffers.
- Conveniently located between the children's clothing and toy departments.

Because so many of our competitors are carrying the same children's lines, it may be advantageous to investigate a new line of European kid shoes. They must be high quality and very trendy. We've had some higher than average returns with Little Folk; the soles seem to split. This hasn't helped our image with concerned parents; a more durable brand is in order.

Skills You Need

Before starting MacWrite, you should have mastered some basic Macintosh skills, namely how to:

- Click, select, and drag with the mouse.
- Choose commands and features from pull-down menus.
- Open icons.
- Move, scroll, and resize windows.
- Perform cut-and-paste and copy-and-paste editing.
- Insert, eject, and handle disks.

These techniques are covered briefly in this chapter. If you need more detailed explanations, consult the first two chapters of this book or your Macintosh owner's manual.

Starting MacWrite

When you switch on a Macintosh, it only knows how to do one thing: read instructions from a disk. It waits patiently until you insert a start-up disk from which it can get the instructions that tell it how to manage the electronic desktop and how to start applications. When you start an application, the Finder (the built-in program that locates and retrieves information on the disk) finds the application program and gives it control of the Macintosh. The application furnishes you with commands especially suited to working with one kind of information. MacWrite, a word-processing application, facilitates writing, editing, formatting, and printing text.

The MacWrite Desktop

Starting MacWrite clears the desktop. The directory window vanishes along with the disk icon, the Trash icon, and any open windows. The menu bar is erased and replaced briefly by the name of the application, MacWrite. The pointer assumes a wrist-watch shape, letting you know you must wait while the Finder transfers the MacWrite program from disk to memory. About 30 seconds after opening the MacWrite application icon, the desktop assumes the standard look for MacWrite.

If the MacWrite application icon is dimmed, it means the MacWrite program resides on a disk you inserted some time

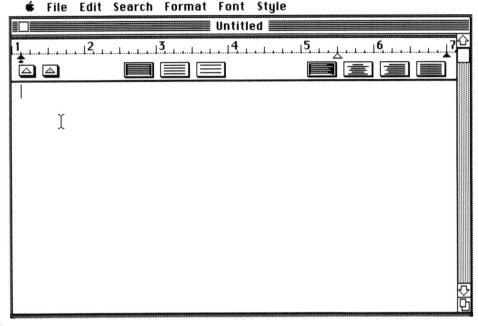

To start MacWrite, insert a disk that contains the MacWrite application program. Open that disk's icon. Then find the MacWrite application icon and open it.

MacWrite

ago but ejected. When you open the dimmed icon to start the application, a dialog box appears telling you to switch disks. Insert the disk named in the dialog box so the Finder can locate the MacWrite program.

The Menu Bar

Across the top of the screen is a menu bar with seven titles. The Apple menu lists desk accessories. The File menu lists commands that act on an entire document at once. The Edit menu lists cut-and-paste and copy-and-paste editing commands. The Search menu assists you in finding every place a particular word or phrase appears in your document, and in changing whichever occurrences of it you designate. The Format menu provides the commands for adjusting the appearance of text on a page. The Font menu lets you choose a text font. The Style menu enables you to embellish and resize selected text.

The Document Window

An untitled, almost-empty document window occupies most of the screen. It's up to you to create written text in the window and to name the document. MacWrite provides the tools, but you must furnish the formats and the facts.

You can drag the document window around on the desktop by its title bar. The title bar has a close box, which you can use to put away the document window along with the document it contains. The window has a size box, which you can use to shrink or enlarge the window.

With the scroll bar at the right edge of the document window, you can scroll a lengthy document up and down. MacWrite does not allow scrolling from side to side, even though the window may be narrower than the document inside it. The only way you can see all of a wide document is by dragging the window to the left, widening it, and then dragging it back and forth, from left to right.

Inside the Document Window

At the top of the document window is a *formatting ruler*. It sets the margins, paragraph indentation, tabs, line spacing, and line alignment for all the text you type below it. A ruler marked in inches runs across the middle of the formatting ruler. On it are two black triangles that set the left and right margins, a black arrow that sets paragraph indentation, and a white triangle that sets one tab.

In the bottom left corner of the formatting ruler are two tab wells. One is labeled with a white triangle, the symbol for regular tabs. The other is labeled with a triangle with a decimal point in the middle, the symbol for decimal tabs.

Near the tab wells are three icons for selecting either single-spaced, space-and-a-half, or double-spaced formats. In the bottom right corner are four other icons for setting the line alignment for ragged-right, centered, ragged-left, or justified at both margins.

You'll learn how to use formatting rulers as you create the Mr. Shoe report.

Creating Regular Paragraphs and Indented Lists

Most people attack a report by typing the straight text first, leaving tables, page headings, title page, and other extensively formatted material for last. As they type along, they mark the approximate location of a table in the first draft with a slug such as " + + +Insert Top Sellers by Department table + + + ." A first draft is also likely to need corrections—words changed, paragraphs restructured, and so forth.

This section shows you how to type the first draft of the Mr. Shoe report shown in Figure 2. You'll also learn how to save the new report on disk, and then how to review and correct the work you've done so far.

This promises to be another year of growth for Mr. Shoe's Sunset Valley Mall store. Sales figures for the first quarter of this year are now in, and they show a 23 percent increase over the first quarter sales of a year ago. First quarter has always been our weakest, so we expect the rest of the year to look even better.

Also, we are about to start the Fashion Footware Fling promotion that has been so successful at other Mr. Shoe stores. The Sunset Valley location is ideal for such a promotion because people around here are extremely fashion conscious. We expect it to boost our sales significantly.

To help focus the Spring buying trip and assist the advertising group with its fall promotional plans, this report correlates computer reports with our salesmen's feedback, identifying our top sellers by manufacturer and product type. It also describes top-selling styles, profiles typical customers, and lists top manufacturers. Also discussed are advertising and promotion results and a comparison of first quarter '84 sales with first quarter '85 sales.

The first and most important question is always the same: What were our top sellers? Have they changed since last year? What's hot, what's not? Who are the top manufacturers? The accompanying table, culled from reports generated by the new computerized point-of-purchase sales system, details Sunset Valley's top sellers by department. Our salesmen had several observations about the results.

+++ Insert Top Sellers by Department Table +++

Women's shoes continue to be our strongest department by a ratio of three to one. With the increasing number of European designers we carry, the average cost per pair has also increased 19 percent. Our sales research indicates women's sales also contribute substantially to our dramatic increase in multiples. That is, when a woman comes in to shop for herself, she will most likely buy a pair for her kid. The reverse is also true. In the first quarter of this year our top-of-the-line women's shoes have experienced the biggest jump. Calfskin and leather shoes are becoming increasingly popular. Canvas and plastic styles are dropping. Both low- and high-heeled styles remain popular.

Alberto Amante is a brand new line for us and is doing phenomenally well. Our salesmen report brand recognition is very high. Women are coming into the store in droves specifically for Amante shoes. Alberto Amante now accounts for 19 percent of our women's department sales, surpassing Caresso as the top manufacturer.

Sales of our men's shoes remain strong primarily because of their high unit cost. We are selling 12 percent fewer pairs this quarter; however,

● *Figure 2. First draft of the*
Mr. Shoe report

the cost per pair has increased 27 percent. The black wingtip continues to be our top seller at 14 pairs a quarter. This is only because of the IBM plant located in Lawndale. The black tassel slip-on is the next best-selling shoe and at $150.00 a pair is contributing substantially to the department's sales. Amante will introduce a fall loafer in cordovan; it would be great to have a full run of this style.

In the children's department, sales have dropped markedly since last year, as the graph on the next page shows. This is due primarily to increased competition. Nickel's department store has added a beautiful new children's shoe department on their third floor. Our salesmen were certain we were losing more and more customers to Nickel's, so for two weeks in February we asked customers in our children's department what they liked about the new Nickel's children's shoe department. These are the most common responses:

- Convenience of one-stop shopping.
- Able to use store charge.
- Sales in children's department heavily advertised and promoted through store statement stuffers.
- Conveniently located between the children's clothing and toy departments.

Because so many of our competitors are carrying the same children's lines, it may be advantageous to investigate a new line of European kid shoes. They must be high quality and very trendy. We've had some higher than average returns with Little Folk; the soles seem to split. This hasn't helped our image with concerned parents; a more durable brand is in order.

Typing Regular Paragraphs

MacWrite, like the Note Pad desk accessory and most word processors, watches the right margin for you. You can type straight through to the end of the paragraph without pressing the Return key.

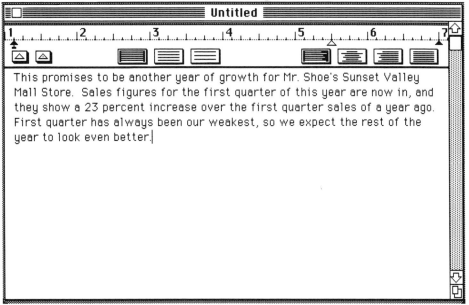

● *Type the first paragraph of the Mr. Shoe draft without pressing the Return key.*

Don't worry about typing the paragraph perfectly. You can go back and correct it later, using the standard editing methods described in the last chapter. *p. 34*

The Return Key's Role

Pressing the Return key puts an invisible character, called a *Return* character, in the document to mark the end of a paragraph. The Return character occupies the same amount of space in the document as a regular character, such as the letter F or the digit 7.

You do not see the Return character itself. You see its effect: advancing the insertion point to the beginning of the next line. If you type nothing but just press the Return key, MacWrite still puts a Return character in the document and advances to the next line. The result is a "paragraph" with no text—in other words, a blank line.

In a MacWrite document a paragraph can be any length, from one blank line to many lines of actual text. This somewhat unconventional notion becomes important when you make changes that affect the length of a line.

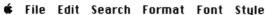

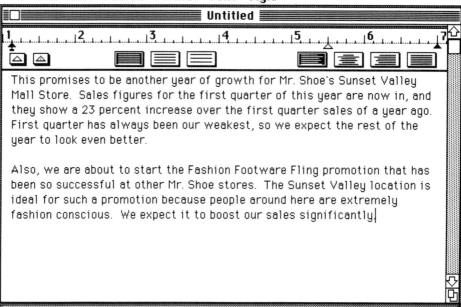

● *Press the Return key to end the paragraph. Press it again to leave a blank line. Type the next paragraph of the first draft.*

Re-forming Paragraphs

If you make changes to the text, MacWrite automatically re-arranges the words in the paragraph to fill out the lines and stay within the margins. This process, often called *paragraph re-forming*, happens whenever you add or remove text. You can see how paragraph re-forming works by adding some text to the first paragraph.

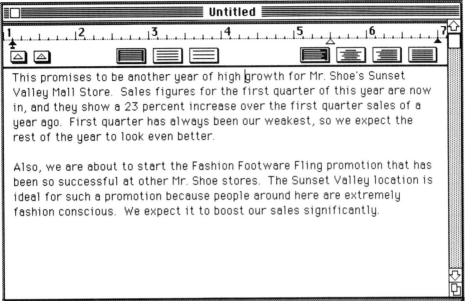

● *For a demonstration of paragraph re-forming, add the word "high" ahead of the word "growth," in the first line of the first paragraph.*

Adding just one word to the first line has a domino effect. MacWrite bumps a word from the end of the first line to the start of the second line, a word from the end of the second line to the start of the third line, and so on. The domino effect stops when MacWrite encounters a Return character marking the end of the paragraph. Subsequent paragraphs are not affected.

Suppose you had pressed the Return key at the end of every line and then added a word to the first line. The text would look exactly the same before the addition, but afterwards it would look like this:

This promises to be another year of high growth for Mr. Shoe's Sunset
Valley
Mall Store. Sales figures for the first quarter of this year are now in, and
they show a 23 percent increase over the first quarter sales of a year ago.
First quarter has always been our weakest, so we expect the rest of the
year to look even better.

In MacWrite's eyes, the first paragraph would have ended at the Return character at the end of the first line, and it would stop re-forming there. Again, subsequent "paragraphs" would not be affected.

Combining Adjacent Paragraphs

By removing a Return character, you effectively join two paragraphs together. If you wish to join two paragraphs that are separated by blank lines, you have to remove the Return character responsible for each blank line.

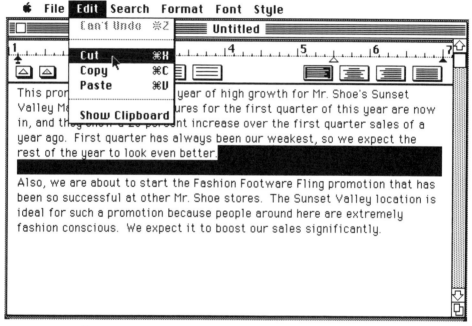

● *To join two paragraphs, select all the blank space between the end of the first and the start of the second paragraph. Then choose Cut from the Edit menu.*

Once the paragraphs are combined, you may have to insert a couple of blank spaces to separate what was the last sentence of the first paragraph from what was the first sentence of the second paragraph.

Typing More Paragraphs

Now type in the next six regular paragraphs in Figure 2, up to the indented list. Include the slug for the table, but don't worry about the missing headings. You'll put them in later. Scroll back to the beginning of the document.

Justifying Both Margins

The formatting ruler at the top of the Mr. Shoe report sets both the left margin and the paragraph indentation at 1⅛ inches, the right margin at 7 inches, one regular tab at 5½ inches, and single-spaced ragged-right lines. You can change the alignment to produce a more professional-looking report.

● *For lines justified at both margins, click the icon at the far right of the formatting ruler.*

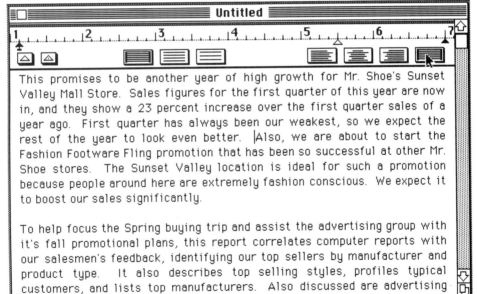

Creating an Indented List

Any time you list names, topics, steps, ingredients, features, and so forth on separate lines, you have to press the Return key after each item on the list. How else would you start a new line for the next item?

Suppose you want the list to be indented from the left margin. Futhermore, if any item is long enough to wrap around to additional lines, you want those lines indented even more. An example of just such an indented list appears near the end of the Mr. Shoe report.

Inserting a Formatting Ruler

You set up this format, called *hanging indentation,* on a newly inserted formatting ruler. Without the new ruler, you would have to set up hanging indentation on the ruler that formats the text above the indented list. The text above the indented list would end up with hanging indentation too! In contrast, a new ruler affects only the text below it, leaving the format of the text above unchanged.

● *Click an insertion point at the spot where you want to insert a formatting ruler and choose the Insert Ruler command from the Format menu.*

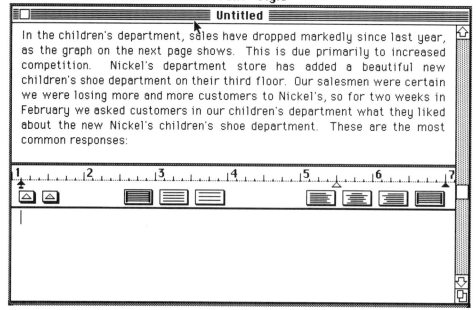

In the children's department, sales have dropped markedly since last year, as the graph on the next page shows. This is due primarily to increased competition. Nickel's department store has added a beautiful new children's shoe department on their third floor. Our salesmen were certain we were losing more and more customers to Nickel's, so for two weeks in February we asked customers in our children's department what they liked about the new Nickel's children's shoe department. These are the most common responses:

The Insert Ruler command inserts—at the insertion point—an exact copy of the formatting ruler used most recently in the document. The settings for margins, indentation, tabs, spacing, and alignment are identical until you change them.

In addition to the Insert Ruler command, you can use your copy-and-paste skills to generate new formatting rulers. Select an existing ruler by clicking anywhere on its upper half. Use the Copy command from the Edit menu to copy the selected ruler to the Clipboard. Click an insertion point where you want to put the copy and choose Paste from the Edit menu.

Setting Indentation and Margins

The indentation marker designates how far from the left edge of the paper the first line of a paragraph will start. The left-margin marker determines how far from the left edge the rest of the paragraph will start. Positioning the two markers in the same spot on the ruler results in no paragraph indentation, as in the regular paragraphs of the Mr. Shoe report. When the indentation marker is positioned to the right of the left margin, the result is conventional paragraph indentation. When it is positioned to the left, the result is hanging indentation.

All lines in an indented list must start to the right of the regular left margin. So both the paragraph indentation and left-margin markers must be moved to the right in the new formatting ruler. To get hanging indentation, the left margin must be further right than the indentation marker.

The indentation marker is often partially hidden beneath the left-margin marker. To extricate it, point at its tail, not its head, then press the mouse button and drag it away. If you accidentally get the left-margin marker or a tab (from a tab well), release the mouse button and try again.

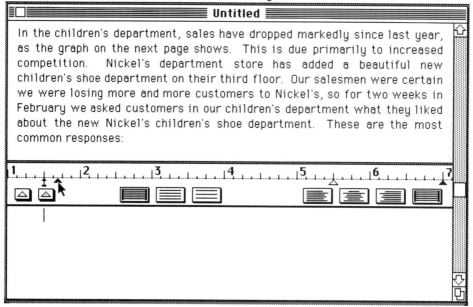

Use the pointer to drag the
indentation marker to the 1½-
inch mark. Use the pointer to
drag the left-margin marker to
the 1^{11}/$_{16}$-inch mark.*

Setting margins in MacWrite is simply a matter of dragging the
margin markers into place in a formatting ruler. If there is text
below the ruler, MacWrite re-forms it, paragraph by paragraph,
until it encounters the next ruler (or the end of the document).

Typing the List

Because you want each item on the list to start at the indentation marker, you must treat each item as a new paragraph and
end it by pressing the Return key. If you do not, only the first
line with start at the indentation marker, and the rest will start
at the new left margin to the right of the indentation mark.

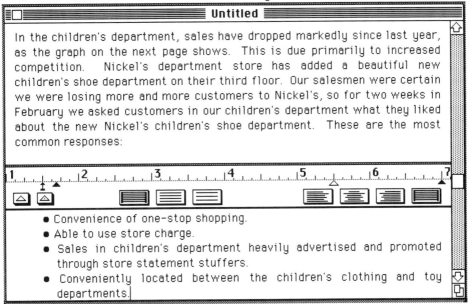

● *Type the list. Press the Return key at the end of each item on the list.*

The large dot (bullet) that begins each item on the list in the Mr. Shoe report can be typed by pressing the Option and 8 keys simultaneously. For a rundown of the special characters you can type with the Option key, use the Key Caps desk accessory.

With justified alignment selected in the formatting ruler, the bullet characters will line up but the rest of the list may not. To rectify the situation, select ragged-right alignment.

When you finish typing the whole list, you must insert another ruler to reset the left margin, paragraph indentation, and alignment for the regular paragraphs that follow.

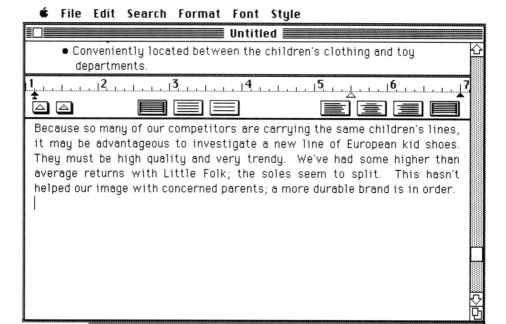

ⓦ File Edit Search Format Font Style

▤□▤▤▤▤▤▤▤▤▤▤▤▤ **Untitled** ▤▤▤▤▤▤▤▤▤▤▤

• Conveniently located between the children's clothing and toy
  departments.

|1....|....|....|2....|....|....|3....|....|....|4....|....|....|5....|....|....|6....|....|....|7|

Because so many of our competitors are carrying the same children's lines,
it may be advantageous to investigate a new line of European kid shoes.
They must be high quality and very trendy. We've had some higher than
average returns with Little Folk; the soles seem to split. This hasn't
helped our image with concerned parents; a more durable brand is in order.

● *Insert another ruler and set the
margins, indentation, and alignment for a regular paragraph.
Type the last paragraph in
Figure 2.*

Saving a New Document

After you invest half an hour of your time in creating a new
document, you should save your work on disk. Any power
outage will erase your document from the Macintosh memory.
This would mean losing a new document that has never been
saved plus all the time and effort spent creating it. A power
outage will not affect a copy of the document stored on disk.

● *To save a new document in its current state on a disk, choose Save or Save As. . . from the File menu. Type the document name. Click the Save button.*

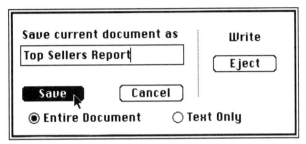

The first time you save a new document, or whenever you choose Save As. . . from the File menu, a dialog box appears asking for the name you wish to give the document. (For new documents, choosing Save or Save As. . . produces the same dialog box.) The Eject button in the dialog box lets you swap the current disk for another disk before saving the document. If your Macintosh has both an internal and an external drive, the dialog box includes a Drive button, which lets you switch between the drives.

Before you click the Save button, double-check the name you typed for the document. You can use standard editing methods to edit the name, if necessary. Also, check the name of the disk, which is displayed directly above the Eject button, to make sure the document will be saved on the correct disk. If not, swap disks or switch drives.

When you click the Save button, the Finder checks the name you typed against the names of documents and applications on the disk. If it finds a match, it displays a small dialog box asking whether you wish to replace the existing document or application. You answer by clicking a displayed Yes or No button.

MacWrite Save Options

MacWrite includes the option of saving the entire document or only the text. Entire Document is the most common choice. Choose Text Only and the characters alone are saved in a standard font, size, and style (12-point plain Geneva). Formatting rulers and their margin, tab, line spacing, and paragraph alignment settings are omitted, as are page breaks, headers, footers, or pictures you might have pasted into the document. (You'll find out how to paste in pictures in the next chapter.)

Reviewing and Correcting

Asked to name the greatest advantage of a word processor such as MacWrite, most people would mention how quickly and easily they can make the corrections and changes that turn a rough draft into a polished composition. You can scroll through the document, looking for errors and awkward phrases. When some solecism glares at you, you can dispatch it with the editing methods described in the previous chapter.

Misspell a word, use the wrong verb tense, or hit the wrong keys? Select the mistake and type a replacement.

Omit a word, forget a comma, or think of another topic to discuss? Click an insertion point and type the additional text or punctuation.

Would moving a word clarify an obscure sentence, juggling sentences illuminate a murky paragraph, or reordering paragraphs better organize a disjointed document? Select the text you want to move, choose Cut from the Edit menu, click an insertion point where you want to put the text, and choose Paste from the Edit menu.

Discover a leftover letter, a worthless word, a spurious sentence, or a pointless paragraph? Eliminate it by selecting it and choosing Cut from the Edit menu.

Finding Text

Suppose you're re-reading your work and suddenly remember a point you forgot to make about some topic. How will you find the place where you discussed the topic so you can add your new thought? You can scroll the document up and down until you see the place you're seeking. Or you can think of a key phrase, word, or syllable and use the Find. . . feature of the Search menu to search for it. In the Mr. Shoe report, for example, you might search for the word "Amante" so you could add a thought concerning Amante brand shoes.

● *Choose Find. . . from the Search menu. In the window that appears, type the word "Amante" and select the Partial Word option.*

Choosing Find. . . from the Search menu presents a special window in which you enter the syllable, word, or phrase you want found. You can type what you want found, or you can get it from another window by the copy-and-paste method. The text you're looking for can be up to 44 characters long, including blank spaces and punctuation. The text you enter in the Find window can be edited using standard editing methods.

You can instruct MacWrite to show you only whole words that match, or to show you matches embedded in larger words as well. You mark your preference in the Find window by clicking the Whole Word or Partial Word option. For example, MacWrite will match "Amante" to "Amante's" only if you select Partial Word.

MacWrite starts at the current insertion point or selection and scans down the document, looking for a match. It ignores capitalization, fonts, sizes, and styles when it searches. When MacWrite finds a match, it scrolls the surrounding part of the document into view and highlights the match. The Find window can be dragged around by its title bar so you can see any parts of the document window that were underneath it. If the highlighted match is not the one you want, click the Find Next button in the Find window to have MacWrite search for the next match.

● *Click the displayed Find Next button to locate the next occurrence of the word "Amante."*

Find Next

 File **Edit** Search Format Font Style

Find

Find what │Amante│

[Find Next] ○ **Whole Word** ● **Partial Word**

first quarter of this year our top-of-the-line women's shoes have experienced the biggest jump. Calfskin and leather shoes are becoming increasingly popular. Canvas and plastic styles are dropping. Both low- and high-heeled styles remain popular.

Alberto **Amante** is a brand new line for us and is doing phenomenally well. Our salesmen report brand recognition is very high. Women are coming into the store in droves specifically for Amante shoes. Alberto Amante now accounts for 19 percent of our women's department sales, surpassing Caresso as the top manufacturer.

Sales of our men's shoes remain strong primarily because of their high unit cost. We are selling 12 percent fewer pairs this quarter; however, the cost per pair has increased 27 percent. The black wingtip continues to

 File **Edit** Search Format Font Style

Find

Find what │Amante│

[Find Next] ○ **Whole Word** ● **Partial Word**

first quarter of this year our top-of-the-line women's shoes have experienced the biggest jump. Calfskin and leather shoes are becoming increasingly popular. Canvas and plastic styles are dropping. Both low- and high-heeled styles remain popular.

Alberto Amante is a brand new line for us and is doing phenomenally well. Our salesmen report brand recognition is very high. Women are coming into the store in droves specifically for **Amante** shoes. Alberto Amante now accounts for 19 percent of our women's department sales, surpassing Caresso as the top manufacturer.

Sales of our men's shoes remain strong primarily because of their high unit cost. We are selling 12 percent fewer pairs this quarter; however, the cost per pair has increased 27 percent. The black wingtip continues to

● *Click the Find Next button until you find the right occurrence of the text you're searching for.*

If MacWrite reaches the end of the document while searching, it circles around to the top of the document and continues from there. The search stops when MacWrite reaches the spot you originally selected as a starting point. Clicking the Find Next button after that results in a Not Found message unless you change what you want found or select a new starting point.

When MacWrite finds the spot you are looking for, you can get rid of the Find window and make any changes you like to the document.

**   File   Edit   Search   Format   Font   Style**

Top Sellers Report

average cost per pair has also increased 19 percent. Our sales research indicates women's sales also contribute substantially to our dramatic increase in multiples. That is, when a woman comes in to shop for herself, she will most likely buy a pair for her kid. The reverse is also true. In the first quarter of this year our top-of-the-line women's shoes have experienced the biggest jump. Calfskin and leather shoes are becoming increasingly popular. Canvas and plastic styles are dropping. Both low- and high-heeled styles remain popular.

Alberto Amante is a brand new line for us and is doing phenomenally well. Our salesmen report brand recognition is very high. Women are coming into the store in droves specifically for Amante shoes. According to the Amante rep, seven new styles will be added this spring and a new line of men's shoes will be introduced at the Milan Shoe Show in June. |Alberto Amante now accounts for 19 percent of our women's department sales, surpassing Caresso as the top manufacturer.

Sales of our men's shoes remain strong primarily because of their high

● *Click anywhere in the main document window to activate it. Then edit the document to reflect your new thoughts.*

Clicking in another window, such as the document window, deactivates the Find window, bringing the newly activated window to the front. To reactivate the Find window, click any visible part of it or choose Find… again from the Search menu. You can get rid of the Find window completely by clicking the close box in its title bar or, when the Find window is active, by choosing Close from the File menu.

Changing Text Repeatedly

Suppose you are reviewing your work and halfway down the first page you realize you used a socially unacceptable term. You wonder, "If I made that mistake somewhere else in the report, will I notice it?" In the Mr. Shoe report, for example, you discover that you have often used the archaic term "salesmen" instead of the preferred "salespeople." Sometimes you got it right, but usually you didn't. How embarrassing to miss even one mistake! Well, worry not, because the Change... feature of the Search menu can help you find and correct repeated errors.

● *Choose Change... from the Search menu. Type the word "salesmen," press the Tab key, and then type the word "salespeople." Choose the Partial Word option.*

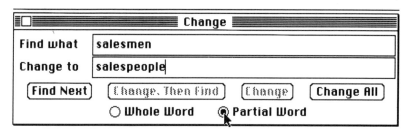

Choosing Change... from the Search menu presents a special window in which you enter the syllable, word, or phrase you want found and a second syllable, word, or phrase with which you want to replace it. Pressing the Tab key switches from one entry to the other.

You use the Change... feature and the Change window the same way you use the Find... window. You can type the replacement text or copy-and-paste it from another window. The replacement can be up to 44 characters long. The replacement can also be null, which means you can effectively delete text by replacing it with nothing.

The Change window has four buttons that tell MacWrite what to do when it finds a match. At first, only two buttons are available. You can click Change All if you want MacWrite to automatically change all occurrences in the document. If you do click Change All, MacWrite warns you it cannot undo the changes once they are made and waits for your go-ahead before proceeding. Your other initial choice is Find Next. If you click it, MacWrite finds the next match and waits for your instruction to change it or move on to the next match.

● *Click the Change All button. After reading the warning, click the Go Ahead button to change "salesmen" to "salespeople" throughout the document.*

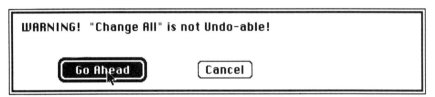

If you choose the Find Next option instead of Change All, MacWrite searches the document as described earlier for the Find. . . feature and highlights the next match. Once MacWrite finds a match, two additional buttons become available: Change and Change, Then Find. If you click the Change button, MacWrite changes the highlighted text, leaves the replacement highlighted, and waits for another command. If you click the Change, Then Find button, MacWrite changes the highlighted match and automatically goes on to find the next match.

After making a change throughout the document, you should think about whether there are any similar phrases, words, or syllables that should also be changed. For example, if you change "salesmen" to "salespeople," you should also change "salesman" to "salesperson."

Saving an Existing Document

The changes and additions you make to a document are lost unless you save them on disk. The more often you save the document, the less you stand to lose in the event of a surprise power outage.

● *To save an existing document on disk, choose the Save command from the File menu.*

The Mac always keeps track of which disk a document belongs on. So if that disk happens not to be inserted when you choose Save from the File menu, a dialog box tells you to insert it before the Mac saves the document.

If you have saved this document before, the document as it now exists replaces the previous version on the disk. That previous version is gone forever. MacWrite does not automatically save the last version as a backup the way some other word processors do.

Preserving the Previous Version

You can save the document displayed in the document window under a new name or on a different disk with the Save As. . . command from the File menu. Everything works just as if you were saving the document for the first time. A dialog box appears, in which you must type the new document name. Buttons displayed in the box allow you to eject the current disk and to switch between internal and external drives.

After you save the document under its new name, that name replaces the former name in the title bar of the document window. If you subsequently save the document with the Save command from the File menu, it will be saved under that new name. The old version of the document still exists on disk under the old name, of course. You can go back to the old version at any time with the Open. . . command.

Creating Tables

It's time to replace the slug you left between the third and fourth paragraphs in the Mr. Shoe report with the actual Top Sellers by Department table. The next section shows you how to do that.

Typing Tables

Like indented lists, tables call for additional formatting rulers. Tables often have wider margins than regular paragraphs and always require extra tabs to align entries in columns. Tables may use different font sizes and styles to set them apart from the rest of the document.

Inserting Formatting Rulers

Before typing anything, it's a good idea to insert a formatting ruler for the table. In fact, you may as well insert two rulers at once. The first ruler goes above the place-holding slug to format the table. The second ruler goes after the slug to reset the format for regular paragraphs.

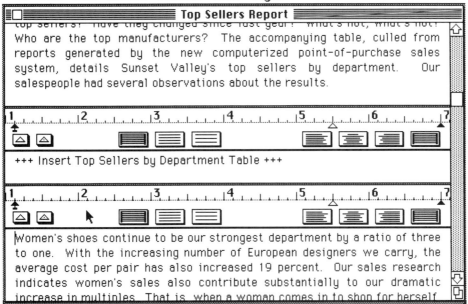

● *Click an insertion point at the left edge of the table slug and choose Insert Ruler from the Format menu. Then click an insertion point below the slug and choose Insert Ruler again.*

Typing Column Headings

You type the table between the two rulers, in place of the slug. First come the column headings.

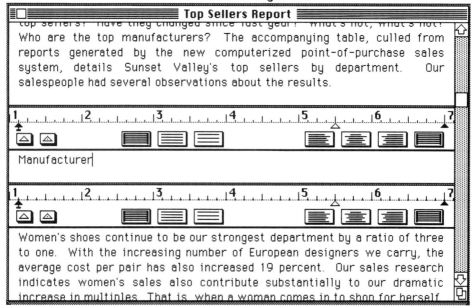

● *Select the table slug and replace it by typing the first column heading.*

The first column lines up at the left margin. All other columns line up at tabs.

Setting and Removing Tabs

MacWrite offers two types of tabs: regular and decimal. Setting either type of tab on a ruler determines the position of a column on the page. A regular tab aligns the column entries on the left. A decimal tab aligns the entries in a column of numbers on the decimal points or, if they have none, aligns them on the right. Markers for the two types of tabs are stored in separate wells in the bottom left of each formatting ruler.

● *Position the pointer over the regular tab well. Press the mouse button and drag a triangular tab up to the ruler line, somewhere to the right of the first column heading. Release the mouse button.*

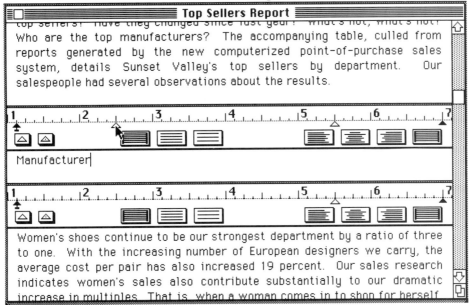

You must drag a tab within ⅛-inch of the ruler line before releasing the mouse button. Otherwise, the tab jumps back into the tab well.

Don't worry for now about the precise position of the tab on the ruler line. You can adjust it later to accommodate any entries in the first column of the table that turn out to be wider than the space you've allowed.

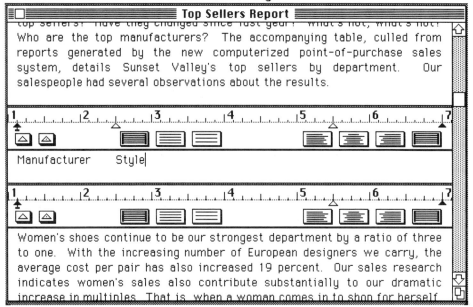

● *Press the Tab key to advance the insertion point to the first tab and type a heading for the second column.*

● *In the ruler above the table, put another regular tab to the right of the second column heading.*

The position of the second tab, like that of the first, is not critical because you can easily adjust it later when you type entries in the table.

The headings for the third and fourth columns occupy two
lines. In each case, you type the bottom half on the same line as
the headings for the first two columns.

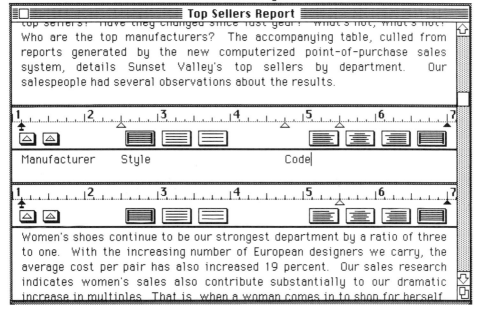

● *Press the Tab key to advance to
the third column and type the
bottom line of its heading.*

MacWrite presets one tab at the 5½-inch mark on the first formatting ruler of every document. However, you cannot use it
for the fourth column of the table because it is a regular tab.
The fourth column needs a decimal tab to align the numbers in
it on the right. Therefore, you must remove the preset tab before dragging a decimal tab into place.

To remove a tab, drag its triangular marker away from the ruler
until the triangle becomes bold. Then release the mouse button.

● *Remove the tab at the 5½-inch mark. Drag a tab from the decimal tab well and position it near the right-margin marker. Press the Tab key and type the bottom line of the fourth column heading.*

 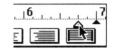

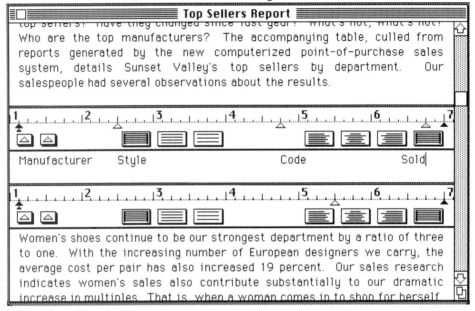

If you have spaced the tabs too far apart, there may not be enough room for the fourth column. You can move the existing tabs to the left a bit with the pointer. Text that is aligned with a tab is repositioned automatically, making room.

Setting Text Attributes

MacWrite allows you to change the typeface, type size, and type style anywhere in the document. The Font menu lists your choice of typefaces. You can add or remove fonts from the list; use the Font Mover application described in the reference section of this book. The reference section also has typeface samples.

The Style menu lists the size and style variations that can be applied to every font. The look of a style choice in the menu suggests the effect it has on text.

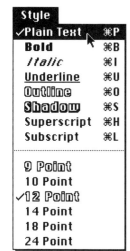

Type size is measured—in units called *points*—from the tops of the tallest letters (capitals or lowercase letters such as "h" and "k") to the bottoms of lowercase letters such as "p" and "q." One point is approximately 1/72-inch. MacWrite offers a choice of six point sizes. For any font you choose, at least one size is listed in outlined letters on the Style menu. The font looks better in a size listed in outlined letters than it does in a size listed in plain letters.

The regular paragraphs in the Mr. Shoe report are 12-point plain Geneva, the font, style, and size MacWrite uses by default. The column headings you just typed for the table are presently in that font, too. However, reducing the text in the table to a 10-point size would make the table more compact, and making the column headings bold would cause them to stand out. You can go back and change the font, size, and style of the headings or any other text without retyping.

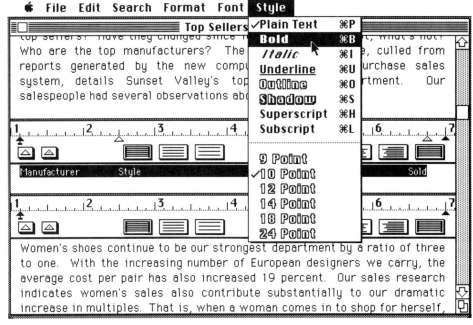

● *To change the font, size, or
style of existing text, select the
text and choose features from
the Font and Style menus.*

If text is selected when you change attributes in the Font and
Style menus, the changes affect the selected text. If an insertion
point is selected when you change attributes, the changes will
affect whatever you type next, unless you move the insertion
point before you type. If you move the insertion point and then
start typing, the new text will have the same attributes as the
character to the left of the new insertion point.

MacWrite uses checks (√) in the Font and Style menus to mark
text attributes that are in effect. If you are about to insert text at
an insertion point, you can look at the Font and Style menus
to see what attributes the text will have. You can also select a
piece of text and look at the Font and Style menus to see what
attributes the selection has. Should the selection encompass more
than one font or style, only the attributes that the whole selection shares are indicated. For example, a selection that encompasses both 10-point and 12-point type will not have a point size
checked in the Style menu.

Some attributes can be combined and others cannot. For instance, only one font can be used at a time, and only one point size. Choosing a different font or point size automatically cancels the existing choice. Likewise, you can choose either Superscript or Subscript from the Style menu, but not both.

In contrast, you can choose any assortment of ornamental attributes—Bold, Italic, Underline, Outline, and Shadow—or you can choose Plain Text. Choosing an ornamental attribute that is not active (is not checked on the Style menu) adds the attribute but does not remove other ornamental attributes that are active. Choosing an ornamental attribute that is active (is checked on the Style menu) removes the attribute. Choosing Plain Text from the Style menu automatically cancels all ornamental attributes, and also cancels Subscript or Superscript style if either of them is active.

Inserting Another Heading Line

Two of the column headings in the Mr. Shoe table occupy more than one line. You must insert a blank line above the existing headings to create space for the top heading line.

Anything you type on the new blank line will have the currently selected font, style, and size attributes (10-point bold Geneva) and will match the existing line of headings.

As you type the upper column-heading line, you may have to adjust the tabs slightly so that the additional words fit in the third and fourth columns. Notice how the words in the third column line up on the left at the regular tab, but the words in the fourth column line up on the right at the decimal tab.

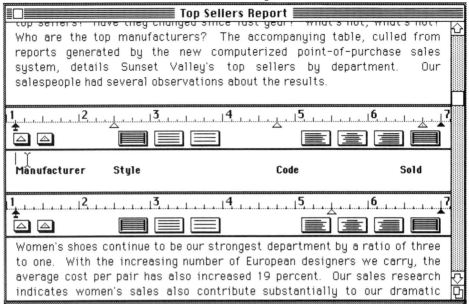

top sellers? Have they changed since last year? What's hot, what's not?
Who are the top manufacturers? The accompanying table, culled from
reports generated by the new computerized point-of-purchase sales
system, details Sunset Valley's top sellers by department.   Our
salespeople had several observations about the results.

Manufacturer	Style	Code	Sold

Women's shoes continue to be our strongest department by a ratio of three
to one. With the increasing number of European designers we carry, the
average cost per pair has also increased 19 percent. Our sales research
indicates women's sales also contribute substantially to our dramatic

● *Click an insertion point at the beginning of the existing heading line. Press the Return key to insert a blank line. Then click an insertion point at the beginning of the new blank line.*

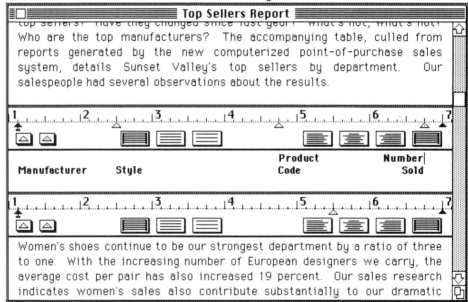

top sellers? Have they changed since last year? What's hot, what's not?
Who are the top manufacturers? The accompanying table, culled from
reports generated by the new computerized point-of-purchase sales
system, details Sunset Valley's top sellers by department.   Our
salespeople had several observations about the results.

Manufacturer	Style	Product Code	Number Sold

Women's shoes continue to be our strongest department by a ratio of three
to one. With the increasing number of European designers we carry, the
average cost per pair has also increased 19 percent. Our sales research
indicates women's sales also contribute substantially to our dramatic

● *Press the Tab key twice to advance to the third column. Type the additional part of its heading. Press the Tab key again to advance to the fourth column and type the additional part of its heading, too.*

Typing the Table Entries

With the tabs set and the column headings in place, you can type the table itself. It will be somewhat rough in appearance until you have a chance to fine-tune the tabs and margins.

After moving the insertion point to the blank line below the column headings, a quick check of the Font and Style menus shows MacWrite plans to use 12-point plain Geneva when you start typing. You must choose 10 Point from the Style menu to reset the font size before you start typing.

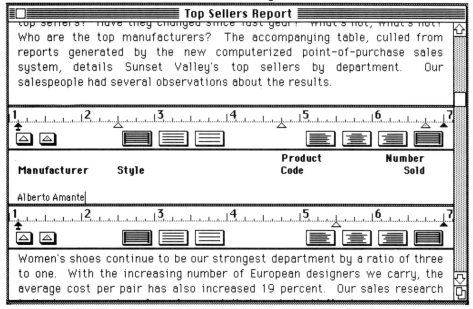

● *Click an insertion point at the beginning of the blank line below the headings and press the Return key. Choose 10 Point from the Style menu. Then type the first entry for the first column.*

Pressing the Tab key advances the insertion point to the next tab, and tells MacWrite to put an invisible character, a Tab character, in the document. Pressing the Return key after the last entry on a line advances the insertion point to the start of a new line.

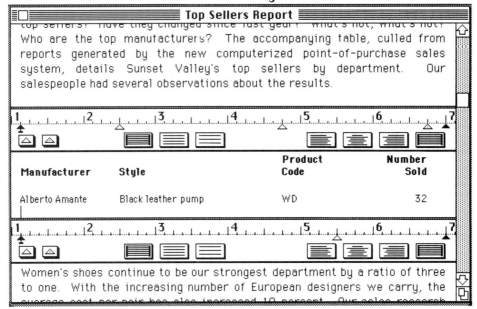

** File   Edit   Search   Format   Font   Style**

Top Sellers Report

top sellers? Have they changed since last year? What's hot, what's not?
Who are the top manufacturers? The accompanying table, culled from
reports generated by the new computerized point-of-purchase sales
system, details Sunset Valley's top sellers by department. Our
salespeople had several observations about the results.

Manufacturer	Style	Product Code	Number Sold
Alberto Amante	Black leather pump	WD	32

Women's shoes continue to be our strongest department by a ratio of three
to one. With the increasing number of European designers we carry, the

● *Using the Tab key to advance from one column to the next, type the first entries for the remaining columns. Press the Return key after the last entry.*

** File   Edit   Search   Format   Font   Style**

Top Sellers Report

Manufacturer	Style	Code	Sold
Alberto Amante	Black leather pump	WD	32
Alberto Amante	Navy leather sling-back	WD	30
Caresso	Red spectator	WD	26
Caresso	Gray wedgie	WC	20
First Court	White canvas court	WC	20
Bandino Boot	Brown lace-up boot	WC	9
Bandino for Men	Black wingtip	MD	14
Dali	Black tassel slip-on	MD	12
Kodiak	Gray jazz oxford	MD	9
Poindexter	Cordovan penny loafer	MC	13
Off Balance	880 trainer	MC	12
Clerk's	Kangaroos	MC	9
Little Folk	Girl's runner	CH	14
Little Folk	Boy's saddle oxford	CH	12
Play Rite	Red Mary Jane	CH	10

● *Enter values for each column on additional lines. Use the Return key to advance from line to line and the Tab key to advance from column to column.*

Some of the entries you type may spill over into the next column to the right. If that happens, move the tabs or shorten the entries to eliminate the encroachment.

You can improve the readability of the table by inserting blank lines occasionally.

Adjusting Margins and Tabs

The table is accurate but hard to read because it is so spread out across the page. You can improve its looks and readability by widening the page margins and rearranging the tabs. MacWrite will automatically move the table in response.

** File   Edit   Search   Format   Font   Style**

Top Sellers Report

Manufacturer	Style	Product Code	Number Sold
Alberto Amante	Black leather pump	WD	32
Alberto Amante	Navy leather sling-back	WD	30
Caresso	Red spectator	WD	26
Caresso	Gray wedgie	WC	20
First Court	White canvas court	WC	20
Bandino Boot	Brown lace-up boot	WC	9
Bandino for Men	Black wingtip	MD	14
Dali	Black tassel slip-on	MD	12
Kodiak	Gray jazz oxford	MD	9
Poindexter	Cordovan penny loafer	MC	13
Off Balance	880 trainer	MC	12
Clerk's	Kangaroos	MC	9

● *Move the left margin and indentation markers to the 1¾-inch mark. Move the two regular tabs to the 3⅛-inch and 4⅞-inch marks. Move the decimal tab to the 6¼-inch mark.*

Drawing Horizontal Rules

Horizontal rules are common at the top and bottom of a table and under the column headings. These three rules always extend the full width of the table.

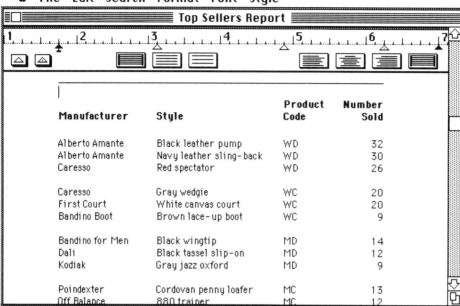

● *To draw a horizontal rule, click an insertion point and type Underscore characters.*

When you type the rule, don't forget about the keyboard's repeat feature. Instead of peck, peck, pecking at the Underscore key, hold it down and it will automatically repeat the character.

A rule composed of Underscore characters appears at the bottom of the space allowed for the line, very close to the line below it. The table will look better if you insert an extra blank line below each horizontal rule. You could use hyphens to draw the rule instead of underscores. Hyphens appear in the middle of the line, making a blank line below the rule unnecessary. However, hyphens create a broken rule, not a solid one like underscores, and don't look as polished as a solid line.

You could type every horizontal rule, but it's easier to type one and then copy-and-paste it in other places. To do that, select one rule and choose Copy from the Edit menu. Then, at the beginning of a line where you want another rule, click an insertion point and choose Paste from the Edit menu.

Adding a Table Title

The table needs a brief but specific title above the top horizontal rule. The title can be set in a larger type size. By adding another formatting ruler, you can also center the title over the table.

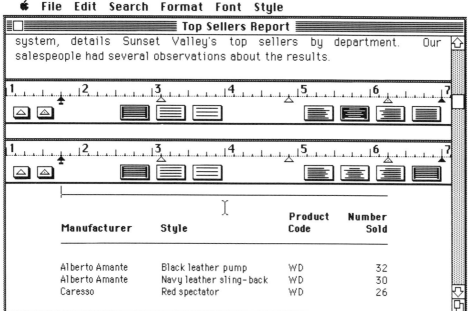

● *Click an insertion point at the left edge of the top horizontal rule and press the Return key. Choose Insert Ruler from the Format menu. Click the alignment icon in the upper formatting ruler for centered lines.*

MacWrite will center the title between the indentation and the right-margin markers. The title will not appear centered over the table unless the indentation marker lines up with the left edge of the table and the right-margin marker lines up with the right edge of the table. The indentation marker is OK, but the right-margin marker will have to be moved.

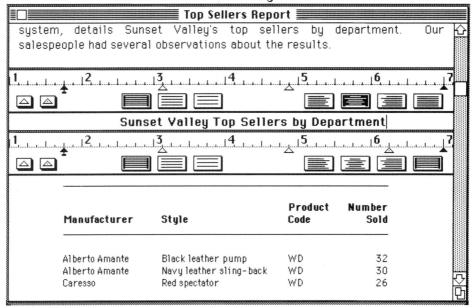

● *Move the insertion point between the formatting rulers, choose 12 Point from the Style menu, and type the title.*

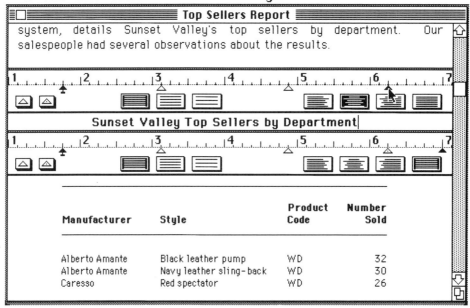

● *In the formatting ruler above the title, remove the decimal tab at the 6¼-inch mark and drag the right margin to that point.*

Splitting Paragraphs

A paragraph of any length, one line or many, can be split in two by inserting a Return character ahead of the character you want to lead off the new paragraph. The table title, for example, is a one-line paragraph that would look better on two shorter lines, both centered above the table.

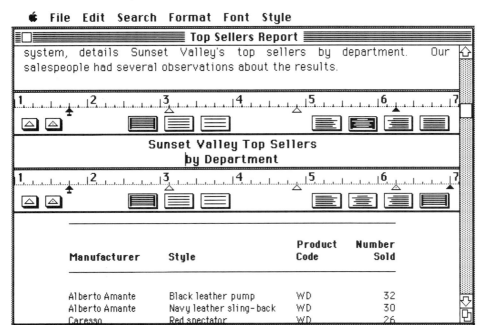

● *To split any paragraph, click an insertion point where you want it split and press the Return key.*

Adding Footnotes

Table footnotes are set directly below the table. They are keyed to the relevant part of the table by symbols such as an asterisk, or by small superscript italic numbers.

● *To insert a numeric footnote reference, click an insertion point, and choose Italic, 9 Point, and Superscript from the Style menu. Then type the appropriate number.*

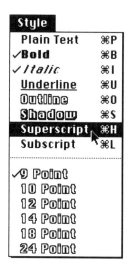

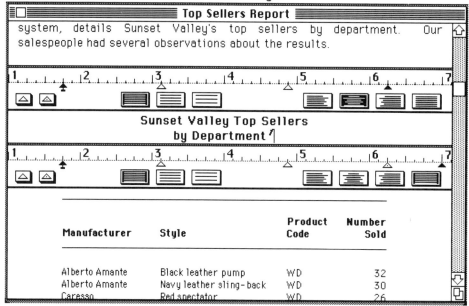

A footnote reference picks up attributes from the character next to it, unless you explicitly set other attributes in the Font and Style menus. For example, you do not have to set the bold attribute for footnote references in the title or headings; Bold is already checked in the Style menu.

The same footnote may appear more than once in the same table. For example, footnote number 3 appears twice in the

Mr. Shoe Top Sellers table. Instead of typing repeated references, use your copy-and-paste skills. Select the first reference, which you typed, and choose Copy from the Edit menu. Then click an insertion point where you want to repeat the reference and choose Paste from the Edit menu. Copy-and-paste preserves a footnote reference's special attributes without affecting the surrounding text.

After inserting all footnote references, be sure to type the footnotes themselves at the end of the table. Each footnote consists of the footnote reference in 9-point italic Geneva (but not bold) and the footnote text in 10-point plain Geneva. Treat each footnote as a separate paragraph; press the Return key only at the end of the footnote.

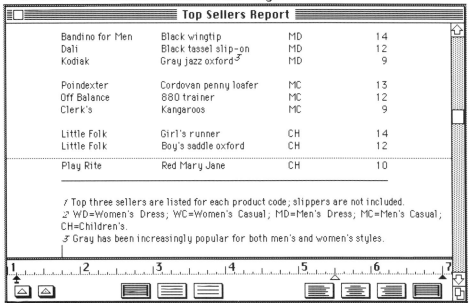

● *To type a footnote, click an insertion point below the table. Using the proper font, style, and size, type the footnote reference, a blank space, and the footnote text.*

The dotted line above the last item in the table marks a page break. MacWrite adjusts page breaks automatically as you insert, remove, and change text. Don't worry for now if a page break should fall in an awkward place. Later in this chapter you will learn how to adjust breaks manually.

A long footnote may extend all the way to the right margin before MacWrite wraps it around to the next line. Thus, some of the footnotes may be wider than the table, which does not extend all the way to the right margin. You can insert another formatting ruler to match the footnote width to the table width.

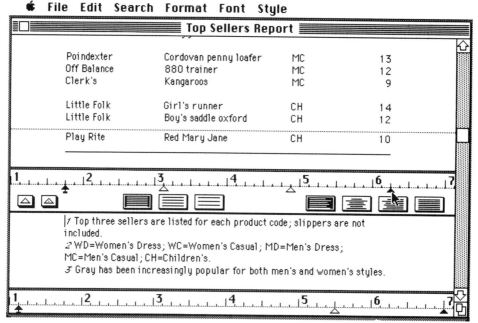

● *Insert a formatting ruler below the table. Select ragged-right alignment. Remove the decimal tab at the 6¼-inch mark and move the right-margin marker to that point.*

Hiding Rulers

Formatting rulers appear in the document window but not in the printed document. The rulers clutter up the document window, making it hard to get an accurate impression of how the table will look when you print it. MacWrite can hide the rulers from view but still keep them effective.

● *To conceal all formatting rulers, choose Hide Rulers from the Format menu. To reveal hidden rulers, choose Show Rulers from the Format menu.*

Format
Insert Ruler
Hide Rulers
Open Header
Open Footer
Display Headers
Display Footers
Set Page #...
Insert Page Break
Title Page

 File   Edit   Search   Format   Font   Style

Top Sellers Report

Who are the top manufacturers? The accompanying table, culled from reports generated by the new computerized point-of-purchase sales system, details Sunset Valley's top sellers by department.   Our salespeople had several observations about the results.

**Sunset Valley Top Sellers
by Department** [1]

Manufacturer	Style	Product Code [2]	Number Sold
Alberto Amante	Black leather pump	WD	32
Alberto Amante	Navy leather sling-back	WD	30
Caresso	Red spectator	WD	26
Caresso	Gray wedgie [3]	WC	20
First Court	White canvas court	WC	20
Bandino Boot	Brown lace-up boot	WC	9

Since the Hide Rulers and Show Rulers commands are mutually exclusive, they share the same spot on the Format menu. If rulers are visible, Hide Rulers is listed; if rulers are invisible, Show Rulers is listed instead.

Quitting MacWrite

You may write a report in one sitting, but it isn't likely. When the time comes to set the report aside for awhile, you can quit MacWrite and return to the directory window. From there you can open another application or eject the disk and switch off the Macintosh.

● *To return to the directory window, choose Quit from the File menu.*

If the document contains changes or additions made since it was last saved, a dialog box appears, suggesting you save the document again before quitting. You click a displayed Yes button to agree; the document is saved as if you had chosen Save from the File menu.

Upon return to the directory window, you will notice several changes. An icon for the new document now appears in the directory window and there is less space available on the disk because of it. Any desk accessories that were open are now closed. Usually only one disk icon remains on the desktop, no matter how many were there prior to opening the application. The remaining disk icon is the one from which you opened MacWrite, and it is now considered the start-up disk.

Finishing Touches

By now, most of the work is done. You've typed the whole report, reviewed it, corrected it, and gone back to fill in the table. All that remains is to add margins at the top and bottom of each page, adjust page boundaries, add topical headings, and create a title page.

Opening an Existing Document

When you are ready to resume work on the report, you must reopen MacWrite and the existing report document. You can open an existing document directly from a directory window, by selecting the document icon, and either choosing Open. . . from the File menu or double-clicking the icon.

Opening a document icon implicitly opens the application that created it. The Finder first tries to locate the application on the current disk. Failing that, it looks on the other disks whose icons are on the desktop. If it finds the application on a disk not currently inserted, it ejects the currently inserted disk and tells you to insert the disk it needs. You may have to swap disks several times before the document and application are both open.

If the Finder cannot find the application on any of the disks it knows about, a dialog box tells you so. In that event, you must eject the current disk with the Eject command and insert a disk with the sought-for application, thereby making it known to the Finder. Then you can try opening the document again.

After the Finder opens the application, it opens the document you selected.

The Mini-Finder

If you prefer, you can open existing documents from MacWrite instead of from the directory window. The MacWrite document window must be closed, which can be accomplished by choosing Close from the File menu or by clicking the close box in the title bar. Then you can use the Open... feature of the File menu to open another document.

● *To get a list of documents you can open from MacWrite, choose Open... from the File menu.*

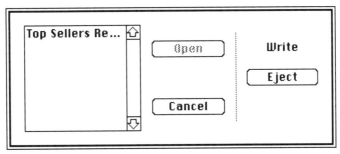

Choosing Open. . . from an application's File menu makes a dialog box appear. This dialog box, called the *Mini-Finder,* has the Finder's ability to locate and retrieve a document. A window inside the dialog box lists the names of up to seven documents on the disk that are available for the current application. If the disk has more than seven available documents, a scroll bar lets you scroll more names into view.

The Mini-Finder lists the documents on only one disk at a time. To see the names of documents on another disk, click the displayed Eject button and insert the other disk. If your Mac has an external drive, you can alternate between the internal and external drives by clicking the displayed Drive button. The disk name always appears in the Mini-Finder directly above the Eject button.

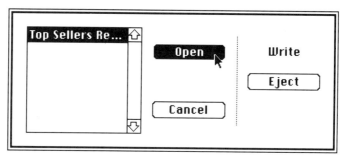

To open a document listed in the Mini-Finder, first select it by clicking its name, then click the Open button. As a shortcut, you can double-click the name.

Top Margins (Headers) and Bottom Margins (Footers)

MacWrite uses about 10 inches of an 11-inch page for your report unless you explicitly define larger margins at the top or bottom. The top margin is called a *header,* and the bottom margin is called a *footer.* The header and footer can contain blank lines and text. You create and edit each in its own window.

● *To see the Header window, choose Open Header from the Format menu. To see the Footer window, choose Open Footer from the Format menu.*

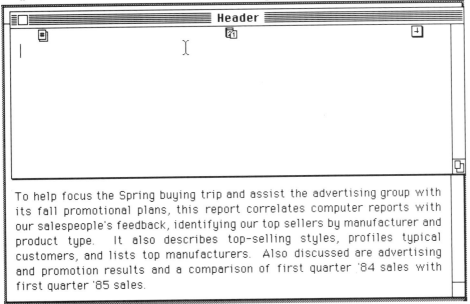

The Header and Footer windows look much like the main document window. Each has a title bar across the top, which you can use to drag the window around the electronic desktop. Inside the title bar is a close box for putting the window away. Below the title bar is the area in which you create and edit the header or footer. In the bottom right corner is a size box, but neither window has a scroll bar, so the header and footer are each limited in height to about a third of a page.

Formatting Rulers

The Header and Footer windows have their own formatting rulers, which work just like the ones in the main document window. This means the margins, indentation, tabs, line spacing, and alignment of the header and footer are completely independent of each other and of the main document. The ruler settings you make in the Header or Footer window affect the header or footer but not the main document. The Hide Ruler and Show Ruler commands from the Format menu conceal and reveal header and footer rulers along with main document rulers. Select Show Ruler so you can set margins and alignment in the Header and Footer windows.

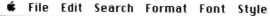

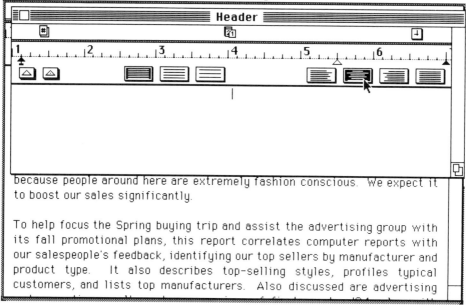

● *Set the header and footer formatting rulers for centered lines with margins at 1⅛ inches and 7 inches.*

Header and Footer Contents

Naturally, you can type text directly into the Header or Footer window; check the font and style attributes before typing. But you can also paste text, pictures, or anything else that has been cut or copied to the Clipboard, just as you can in the main document window. You can also have MacWrite automatically insert the current page number, the time, or the date anyplace in the top or bottom margin of each page.

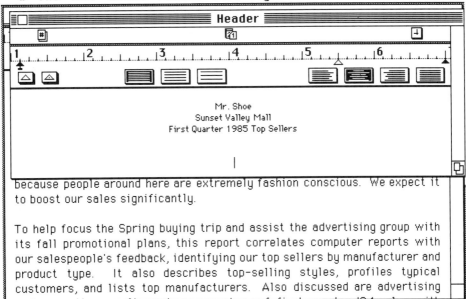

● *Type the text of the header in 9-point plain Geneva. Press the Return key once before the first line, at the end of each line, and two extra times after the last line.*

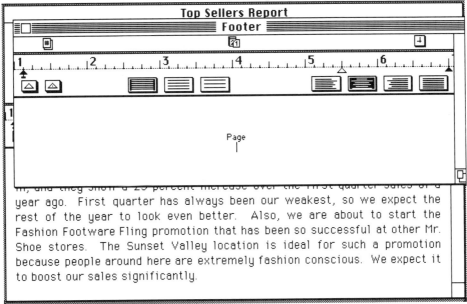

● *Type the text of the footer in 9-point plain Geneva. Press the Return key three times before the first line and once at the end.*

For short header and footer lines, you must press the Return key at the end of each line in order to advance to the next line. Pressing the Return key extra times puts blank lines in the header and footer, enlarging the top and bottom margins and positioning the header and footer text within those margins. For the Mr. Shoe report, the header is seven lines high, with one blank line above the header text and three blank lines below it. The footer is five lines high, with three blank lines above the footer text and one below it. You can press the Return key at most six times in the Header or Footer window.

Page Number, Date, and Time

Below the title bar are three icons that you can drag into the header or footer to mark the spot where MacWrite should place the current page number, date, or time.

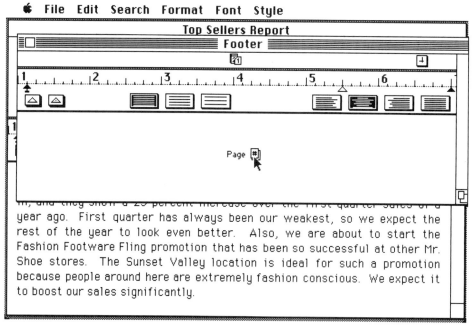

With the pointer, drag the page-number icon from its parking space below the title bar into place in the footer.

The page number, date, and time icons can go on any line you've typed in the header or footer. The icons appear in the Header and Footer windows, but MacWrite substitutes actual information in the top and bottom margins of each page. The font, size, and style of the actual page number, date, and time will be the same as the first character in the header or footer window, even if that character is a blank space or invisible Return character.

The time and date icons will be replaced by the time and date from the Mac's internal calendar/clock. To change the time and date, use the Alarm Clock or Control Panel desk accessories.

The page-number icon is replaced by the current page number. Normally, the first page of every MacWrite document is page 1. The Set Page #. . . command from the Format menu lets you specify a different starting page number for the document.

Placing an icon on a line does not allot space for the information that will replace it, however. MacWrite will start typing the information at the spot marked by the left edge of the icon and will use as much space to the right as it needs. If that means running over text you put on the same line or exceeding the right margin, that's what MacWrite will do. It is your responsibility to place the icons carefully so they do not interfere with each other or with other text in the margin.

Viewing Headers and Footers in the Document

Unless you have enlarged the Header or Footer windows to full size, the inactive main document window will still be visible underneath them. You can activate the document window by moving the pointer anywhere on it and clicking the mouse button. Then you can see how the header and footer look in the main document.

Instead of activating the document window directly, you can close the Header and Footer windows, activating the document window by default. To close the windows, click the close box in each title bar or choose Close from the File menu when each window is active.

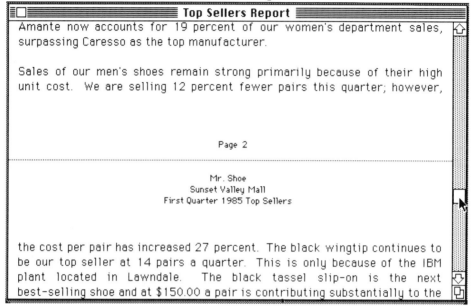

** File Edit Search Format Font Style**

Top Sellers Report

Amante now accounts for 19 percent of our women's department sales, surpassing Caresso as the top manufacturer.

Sales of our men's shoes remain strong primarily because of their high unit cost. We are selling 12 percent fewer pairs this quarter; however,

Page 2

Mr. Shoe
Sunset Valley Mall
First Quarter 1985 Top Sellers

the cost per pair has increased 27 percent. The black wingtip continues to be our top seller at 14 pairs a quarter. This is only because of the IBM plant located in Lawndale. The black tassel slip-on is the next best-selling shoe and at $150.00 a pair is contributing substantially to the

● *To see how headers and footers look in the document, activate the document window and scroll to the nearest page break.*

Some of the page breaks may make the report unsightly. Remember, you will adjust them later.

Hiding Headers and Footers

Closing the Header or Footer window does not remove the top or bottom margin from the main document. MacWrite has separate commands for that.

● *To hide headers in the document window, choose Remove Headers from the Format Menu. To hide footers, choose Remove Footers.*

Format
Insert Ruler
Show Rulers
Open Header
Open Footer
Display Headers
Remove Footers
Set Page #...
Insert Page Break
Title Page

 File   Edit   Search   Format   Font   Style

≡≡≡≡≡≡≡≡≡≡≡ **Top Sellers Report** ≡≡≡≡≡≡≡≡≡≡≡

Alberto Amante is a brand new line for us and is doing phenomenally well. Our salespeople report brand recognition is very high. Women are coming into the store in droves specifically for Amante shoes. According to the Amante rep, seven new styles will be added this spring and a new line of men's shoes will be introduced at the Milan Shoe Show in June. Alberto Amante now accounts for 19 percent of our women's department sales, surpassing Caresso as the top manufacturer.

Sales of our men's shoes remain strong primarily because of their high unit cost. We are selling 12 percent fewer pairs this quarter; however, the cost per pair has increased 27 percent. The black wingtip continues to be our top seller at 14 pairs a quarter. This is only because of the IBM plant located in Lawndale.   The black tassel slip-on is the next best-selling shoe and at $150.00 a pair is contributing substantially to the department's sales. Amante will introduce a fall loafer in cordovan; it would be great to have a full run of this style.

In the children's department, sales have dropped markedly since last year, as the graph on the next page shows. This is due primarily to increased

After you choose the Remove Headers command, it is replaced in the Format menu by Display Headers. Similarly, choosing Remove Footers changes the command to Display Footers. Whether the Header and Footer windows are open or closed, you can choose the Display Headers and Display Footers commands to make the headers and footers appear in the document window.

The commands Display Headers/Remove Headers and Display Footers/Remove Footers determine only whether you can see headers and footers in the document window. None of the four commands has any effect on the contents of the Header and Footer windows. To change the content of headers or footers, you must open the Header or Footer window and use standard text editing methods.

Adjusting Page Breaks

MacWrite decides where to break pages without regard to the look of the document. It may abandon the first line of a paragraph at the bottom of a page or it may isolate the last line of a paragraph at the top of a new page (these stranded lines are known as orphans and widows in publishing circles). Worse yet, MacWrite may split a table or an indented list between pages.

Inserting a Page Break

There are two cures for page-break ugliness: Juggle text or insert your own page breaks. Sometimes you must apply both cures for a satisfactory result. The Top Sellers table in the Mr. Shoe report, for example, can be kept on one page by forcing a page break between the table and the paragraph above it.

When you insert a page break, MacWrite draws a dotted line at the insertion point and adds enough empty space to the page above the line to fill up the page. Although the empty space looks like many blank lines, it is not. It is just a block of empty space. You can select the empty space in its entirety by pointing at it and clicking the mouse button; it will be highlighted so you can see how tall it is. If you insert text on a page that ends with one of these empty spaces, the empty space automatically contracts, just filling up that page. You can also remove the empty space, and the artificial page break with it, by selecting the empty space and choosing Cut from the Edit menu.

● *To force a page break, click an insertion point and choose Insert Page Break from the Format menu.*

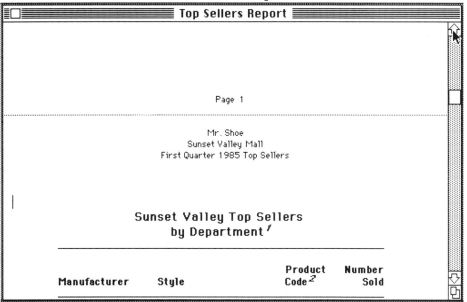

Juggling Text

Inserting a page break above the Top Sellers table keeps it on one page but leaves lots of unsightly blank space on the page before the table. To fill the gap, move some text as follows:

- Cut the paragraph that follows the table.
- Click an insertion point above the empty space to be filled.
- Paste the paragraph at the insertion point.

Moving the paragraph shrinks the empty space on the page above the table to an acceptable size. Take care to click an insertion point, not the empty space, or you'll end up replacing the page break with the text from the Clipboard. You may have to make minor adjustments by inserting and deleting blank lines here and there too.

Adding Topical Headings

Topical headings divide a lengthy composition into sections. Variations in text attributes—font size, capitalization, italic and boldface—can serve to distinguish different levels of headings. The Mr. Shoe report uses just one level of topical headings, set in 12-point bold Geneva. Each heading has two blank lines above it and one blank line below it. These are the steps for inserting a heading:

- Click an insertion point on the blank line above the first paragraph of a new section.
- Press the Return key to generate an extra blank line.
- Choose the text attributes from the Style menu.
- Type the section heading.
- Press the Return key at the end of the heading to leave another blank line.

Creating a Title Page

As a final touch, you might like to go back and insert a title page at the beginning of the report. You can expect to set up a special format for the title page, so you may as well insert another formatting ruler when you insert the page.

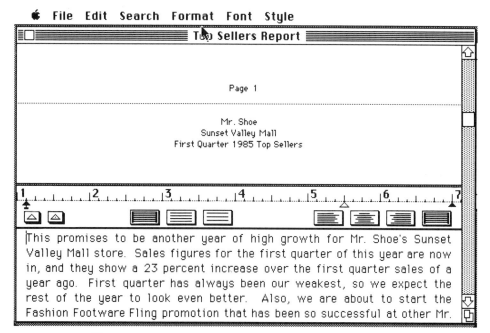

● *To insert a title page, click an insertion point at the beginning of the first paragraph in the document. Choose Insert Page Break, then Insert Ruler, both from the Format menu.*

If formatting rulers are hidden and you insert a ruler, all the rulers in the document reappear.

Omitting Title Page Header and Footer

The header and footer information you created for the other pages of the report does not usually appear on a title page. MacWrite can suppress header and footer text on the title page while retaining the top and bottom margins set up by the Header and Footer windows.

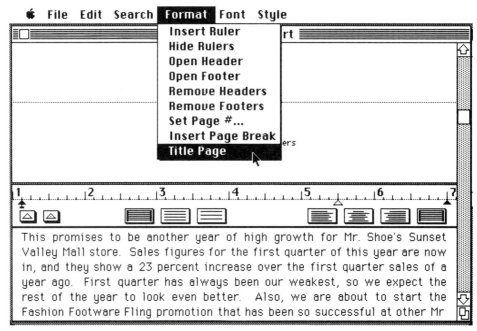

● *To omit the header and footer
text from the first page of the
document, choose Title Page
from the Format menu.*

Typing the Title Page

Text on the title page is frequently centered and is often set in
large, embellished type. The title page of the Mr. Shoe report
has centered, double-spaced lines with 18-point bold Geneva on
the first three lines, 14-point bold Geneva on the fourth line,
10-point plain Geneva on the fifth line, and 12-point bold
Geneva on the last line. There are two blank double-spaced lines
(12-point size) at the top of the page, two blank double-spaced

lines (18-point size) between the third and fourth lines of text, and four blank double-spaced lines (14-point size) after the fourth line of text.

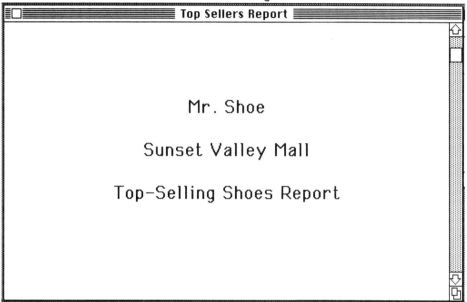

● *Select the double-spaced and centered icons in the first formatting ruler. Then type each line of the title page, choosing the appropriate text attributes from the Font and Style menus. Press Return to end every line and to insert blank lines.*

Printing the Report

In *Don Quixote de la Mancha,* Cervantes observed that "the proof of the pudding is in the eating." Well, the proof of writing done with a word processor is in the printing. MacWrite uses two dialog boxes full of options for tailoring your work to fit different paper sizes, page orientations, print qualities, page ranges, numbers of copies, and types of paper.

Before you choose any options, check that your printer is connected to the Macintosh printer port and is switched on. Insert a fresh sheet of paper or, if you are using continuous paper, set the paper at the top of a new page. With an Imagewriter, make sure the Select lamp on the printer control panel is lit.

Reviewing Page Setup

The Page Setup feature of the File menu displays a dialog box that enables review and change of page layout options. You only need to set the options once; the settings are saved on disk with the document the next time you save the document.

● *Choose Page Setup from the File menu. Select US Letter paper and Tall orientation, then click the displayed OK button.*

Paper

MacWrite can adjust the printed document to fit on any of the following four different sizes of paper:

Paper Size	Wide	×	Tall
US Letter	8½	×	11
US Legal	8½	×	14
A4 Letter	8¼	×	11⅔
International Fanfold	8¼	×	12

Continuous paper with sprocket holes is wider than single sheets with the same usable width, usually by 1 inch. For example, continuous US Letter measures 9½ inches wide by 11 inches tall, but after subtracting an inch for the sprocket holes on either side, the usable width is 8½ inches.

Orientation

Tall orientation provides normal upright printing, with the top line at the top of the page. But after you've learned to insert pictures in a document, you'll find that Tall makes the pictures appear somewhat narrower than when they are printed by MacPaint. Tall Adjusted orientation widens the printed document, printing truer pictures at the expense of slightly stretched text.

Wide orientation provides sideways printing, with the top line printed down the right side of the page and proportions similar to those obtained with the Tall Adjusted option.

Print Options

The Print. . . feature of the File menu offers a choice of print quality and lets you specify which pages to print, how many copies to make, and what style of paper you are using.

● *Choose Print. . . from the File menu. In the dialog box that appears, select High quality, All pages, 1 copy, and Continuous paper feed. Click the* OK *button to start printing.*

Quality:	◉ High	○ Standard	○ Draft	OK
Page Range:	◉ All	○ From:	To:	
Copies:	1			
Paper Feed:	◉ Continuous	○ Cut Sheet		Cancel

Draft quality is not available if you choose Wide orientation (sideways printing) during page setup.

Draft quality uses a high-speed font to quickly print a trial copy of a document. It prints in one font, two font sizes, and in plain, bold, underline, superscript, and subscript styles only. Unavailable styles such as italic and outline are printed plain. Most of the special letters and symbols that you type with the aid of the Option key cannot be printed in draft quality either, though the Imagewriter does make as many intelligent substitutions as possible.

Standard- and high-quality printing both reproduce a displayed document accurately and completely. Standard quality is about half as fast as draft quality and more than twice as fast as high quality. However, standard-quality characters are not nearly as dark and fully formed as high-quality characters.

Your choice of paper and the condition of your ribbon also affect print quality. A heavyweight, rag-content, rough-finish paper works best.

Interrupting Printing

Before MacWrite starts printing in standard or high quality, it takes a few seconds to copy the document into a scratch-pad area on disk. You cannot interrupt that process, but once printing begins you can cancel it by pressing the Command and Period keys simultaneously. When you do, MacWrite stops sending information to the Imagewriter, but printing does not cease immediately. First, the Imagewriter prints the residual information it has already received and stored in its own memory. This may take several seconds.

Printing from the Directory Window

You can print one or more MacWrite documents directly from a directory window. All you do is select their icons and choose Print... from the File menu. The documents are printed one after the other in a sequence determined by the arrangement of the icons in the directory window. The Finder starts with the document whose icon is located nearest the upper left corner of the directory window. After that one is printed, the Finder proceeds across the window, then down to the next row of icons, across it from left to right, and so on.

In order to print a MacWrite document, MacWrite must be present. If the Finder cannot locate it on the currently inserted disk, it checks the other disks whose icons are on the desktop. If MacWrite is on one of them, the Finder tells you to insert that disk. You may have to swap disks several times before printing is finished. If the Finder cannot locate MacWrite anywhere, it tells you so. In that event, you can eject the current disk, insert a disk with MacWrite, eject it, reinsert the document disk, and try printing again.

Before MacWrite begins printing the first document, the print-options dialog box appears, as if you had chosen Print... from the MacWrite File menu. You must choose the print quality, how many copies of which pages will be printed, and the style of paper you will use.

You can cancel the printing of the current MacWrite document by pressing the Command and Period keys at the same time. MacWrite advances the paper to the end of the page and begins printing the next document you selected, if any.

Saving the Finished Report

Be sure to save the finished document after printing it, even if you have made no changes since you last saved it. MacWrite saves all page setup options and most print options you choose along with the document. Saving the options means you don't have to reset them the next time you print the document, whether from the directory window or from MacWrite. The only exceptions are the page range and number of copies, which MacWrite always resets to print one copy of all pages.

Beginning a New Document

Once you're using MacWrite, you can start a new MacWrite document without returning to the directory window.

● *To open a new document from MacWrite, choose New from the File menu.*

The New command is dimmed and unavailable if the document window is already open. You have to close the existing document window before you can open a new one.

Summary

This chapter took a close look at one way of preparing a business report using the MacWrite word-processing application. In the process, the chapter covered most of MacWrite's features. You should now know how to:

- Start and quit MacWrite.
- Type regular paragraphs, blank lines, and indented lists.
- Use typography—fonts, font sizes, and styles—to enhance appearance and improve communication.
- Set margins.
- Set paragraph indentation.
- Set tabs, both regular and decimal.
- Change line spacing and paragraph alignment.
- Type and format tables of words and numbers, including footnotes.
- Split and combine paragraphs.
- Split and combine pages.
- Create new documents and open existing ones, and save them on disk.
- Quickly find any phrase, word, or syllable in the document.
- Replace every occurrence or just selected occurrences of one phrase, word, or syllable with another phrase, word, or syllable.
- Put a header in the top margin of every page, and a footer in the bottom margin.
- Create a special title page.
- Print the report on paper.

Other chapters in this book show samples of various MacWrite documents, including a letter and envelope with personalized letterhead, a personal telephone directory and address book, a restaurant menu, a wine-cellar inventory report, a get-well card, a party announcement, and a bulletin-board advertisement. For some of these projects, you need to know how to paste a picture into a MacWrite document; this topic is covered in the next chapter.

Designing a Letterhead With MacPaint

● *From the detailed descriptions of this MacPaint project, you'll learn how to draw, fill, letter, rearrange, overlay, erase, touch up a drawing, move it to a MacWrite document, and print it out.*

When it comes to business correspondence, you either shell out for printed stationery or use plain paper, typing your name and address along with the rest of the letter. Both choices have drawbacks. Printed stationery is expensive, and must usually be ordered in large quantities that are impractical for personal business or even for some small commercial firms. If you move, a common occurrence in today's mobile society, your old stationery is no better than yesterday's newspaper. The alternative, typing your name and address every time you write a letter, is tedious and error-prone, and doesn't look as professional or businesslike as printed stationery.

If you stop and think about the better-looking stationery that has crossed your desk, you'll realize that most of the letterheads had more to them than just type. The letters that made up the name might have been enlarged and shaded somehow. Maybe a thick line underscored the whole letterhead, separating it from the body of the letter. Perhaps a small picture or drawing suggested the letter writer's line of business. Someone spent extra time or money to impress you, and it probably worked.

To get your own personalized stationery, you could order one of the stock designs offered by a local stationer or you could hire a designer to create a custom letterhead. But you may do just as well experimenting with designs yourself, using MacPaint. For example, the two Phyllis Tien Gallery letterhead designs in Figure 3 can both be done in MacPaint using pretty much the same method; they differ only in size, type fonts, and background shapes.

MacPaint makes it easy to experiment with lines, shapes, patterns, positions, and fonts. You can draw, type, erase, outline, fill, blend, overlap, cut-and-paste, copy-and-paste, stretch, shrink, flip, rotate, and (most important) undo what you last did. This chapter describes many of MacPaint's features by showing one way to create one of the Phyllis Tien Gallery letterhead designs.

If your business or the company you work for already has printed stationery, try creating the Phyllis Tien Gallery sample anyway. Consider adapting the ideas and methods described here to create an informal letterhead for your personal correspondence. Unless you're already an expert with MacWrite and MacPaint, the exercise will surely uncover some valuable program features and methods that you will be able to apply to future projects of your own.

Skills You Need

Before starting to work with MacPaint, you should know some basic Macintosh skills, namely how to:

- Click, select, and drag with the mouse.
- Choose commands and features from menus.
- Open icons.
- Perform cut-and-paste and copy-and-paste editing.
- Insert, eject, and handle disks.

These techniques are covered briefly in this chapter. If you need more detailed explanations, consult the first two chapters of this book or your Macintosh owner's manual.

Much of the work you do with MacPaint involves judging the size and alignment of objects drawn on the screen. You may get satisfactory results gauging by eye. If not, get a small transparent plastic ruler that you can hold flat against the screen. Ideally, you should have two rulers: a shorter one for vertical measurements and a longer one for horizontal measurements.

Starting MacPaint

When you switch on a Macintosh, it only knows how to do one thing: read instructions from a disk. It waits patiently until someone inserts a start-up disk, from which it can get the instructions that tell it how to manage the electronic desktop and how to start applications. When you start an application, the Finder (the built-in program that locates and retrieves documents and applications from the disk) finds the application program and gives it control of the Macintosh. The application furnishes you with commands especially suited to working with one kind of information. MacPaint is an application for drawing and designing with free-form lines and shapes, geometric shapes, patterns, and decorative text.

Phyllis Tien Gallery
Phyllis Tien Gallery
Phyllis Tien Gallery

218 Evaro Avenue
Gunsight, New Mexico 65302
(602) 555-1212

February 25, 1985

Mr. Barney Stone
34 East Camelback Boulevard
Hercules, California 94355

Dear Mr. Stone:

The information you requested is contained in our enclosed brochure, "Sand Painters of Today." We are pleased to have this chance to spread the word about this fascinating art form. Sand painting is indeed a unique art form practiced only by natives of the Southwest.

I have also enclosed a flier about our upcoming one-artist show featuring Betsy Lone Eagle, who is widely acclaimed as one of the best sand painters of all time. She will be at the gallery every day during the show, demonstrating her skill and answering questions. Perhaps you can attend--the desert is lovely in Spring!

Yours truly,

Phyllis Tien

enclosures

● *Figure 3. Two sample letterhead*
designs created with MacPaint

Phyllis Tien Gallery
Phyllis Tien Gallery
Phyllis Tien Gallery

218 Evaro Avenue
Gunsight, New Mexico 65302
(602) 555-1212

February 25, 1985

Mr. Barney Stone
34 East Camelback Boulevard
Hercules, California 94355

Dear Mr. Stone:

The information you requested is contained in our enclosed brochure, "Sand
Painters of Today." We are pleased to have this chance to spread the word
about this fascinating art form. Sand painting is indeed a unique art form
practiced only by natives of the Southwest.

I have also enclosed a flier about our upcoming one-artist show featuring
Betsy Lone Eagle, who is widely acclaimed as one of the best sand painters
of all time. She will be at the gallery every day during the show,
demonstrating her skill and answering questions. Perhaps you can
attend--the desert is lovely in Spring!

Yours truly,

Phyllis Tien

enclosures

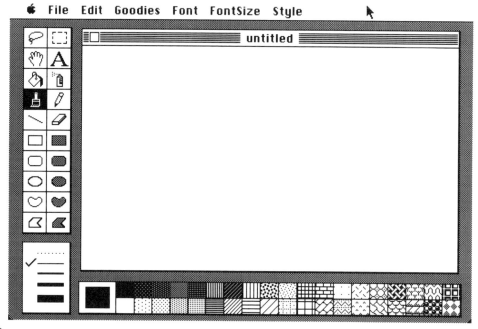

MacPaint

To start MacPaint, insert a disk that contains the MacPaint application program. Open that disk's icon. Then find the MacPaint application icon and open it.

If the MacPaint application icon is dimmed, it means the MacPaint program resides on a disk you inserted some time ago but ejected. When you open the dimmed icon to start the application, a dialog box appears telling you to switch disks. Insert the disk named in the dialog box so the Finder can locate the MacPaint program.

The MacPaint Desktop

Starting MacPaint clears the desktop. The directory window vanishes along with the disk icon, the Trash icon, and any open windows. The menu bar is erased and replaced briefly by the name of the application, MacPaint. The pointer assumes a wrist-watch shape, letting you know you must wait while the Finder transfers the MacPaint program from disk to memory. About 25 seconds after opening the MacPaint application icon, the desk-top assumes the standard look for MacPaint.

The MacPaint desktop has a conventional menu bar. It also has four unconventional windows: a drawing window, a tool rack, a pattern palette, and a line-thickness control panel. All these features are described briefly in the rest of this section, and most are described in detail later in this chapter.

The Menu Bar

Across the top of the screen is a menu bar with seven titles. The Apple menu lists desk accessories. The File menu lists commands that act on an entire drawing at once. The Edit menu lists cut-and-paste and copy-and-paste editing commands, plus some special commands for manipulating a selected part of your drawing. The Goodies menu provides drawing aids and hints for using MacPaint. The Font menu lets you choose a text font. The FontSize menu gives you a choice of text sizes, including two sizes that are larger than anything MacWrite offers. The Style menu enables you to embellish text and change its alignment.

The Drawing Window

An untitled, almost-empty drawing window occupies most of the screen. A drawing can be 8 inches wide by 10 inches tall, but you can only work on it a piece at a time. The piece you're working on appears in the drawing window.

The drawing window, unlike most windows, cannot be dragged around on the desktop by its title bar. The title bar has a close box, which you can use to put away the drawing window along with the drawing it contains.

The size of the drawing window is fixed; there is no size box for shrinking or enlarging the window. Scroll bars are absent as well. You move to a different part of the drawing with the Show Page command from the Goodies menu, as explained later.

You can use the drawing window to temporarily display a description of the MacPaint desktop.

● *For an on-screen description of the MacPaint desktop, choose Introduction from the Goodies menu. Click the displayed Cancel button to restore the normal drawing window.*

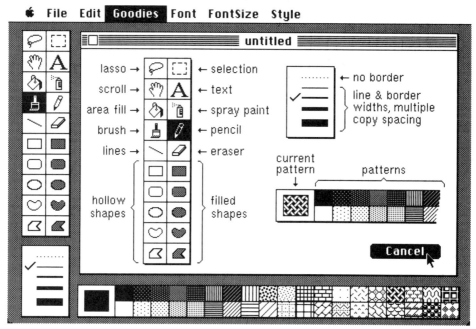

The Tool Rack

Tools hung on a pegboard are easier to get at than tools stored in a drawer. So MacPaint puts its tools out in the open, not in a pull-down menu. Pictures of 20 tools are displayed in a "tool rack" along the left edge of the screen.

You select a tool by clicking its icon in the tool rack. Selecting a tool makes it active; only one tool can be active at a time. MacPaint highlights the active tool in the tool rack so you can see at a glance which it is. The MacPaint tools table in Figure 4 identifies all 20 tools.

Icon	Name	Purpose
	Lasso	Select an object in the drawing window
	Selection rectangle	Select a rectangular region of the drawing window
	Grabber	Drag another part of the drawing into view
A	Text	Type text
	Paint can	Fill a bordered region, using the current pattern as "paint"
	Spray can	Spray paint using the current pattern as "paint"
	Brush	Freehand drawing in a variety of brush shapes and sizes, using the current pattern as "ink"
	Pencil	Draw black lines on white or vice versa
	Line	Draw a straight line
	Eraser	Erase
	Hollow rectangle	Draw hollow rectangles and squares
	Filled rectangle	Draw rectangles and squares filled with the current pattern
	Hollow rounded-corner rectangle	Draw hollow rectangles and squares with rounded corners
	Filled rounded-corner rectangle	Draw rectangles and squares with rounded corners and filled with the current pattern
	Hollow oval	Draw hollow ovals and circles
	Filled oval	Draw ovals and circles filled with the current pattern
	Hollow free-form shape	Draw hollow free-form shapes
	Filled free-form shape	Draw free-form shapes filled with the current pattern
	Hollow irregular shape	Draw hollow shapes with any number of straight sides
	Filled irregular shape	Draw shapes with any number of straight sides and filled with the current pattern

● *Figure 4. The MacPaint tools*

The Pattern Palette

A palette of 38 different patterns stretches across the bottom of the MacPaint screen. The large swatch at the left end of the pattern palette shows which pattern is currently selected. You pick a different pattern by clicking the swatch of it in the palette. You can also create your own pattern by modifying one of the existing 38; you'll learn how to do that later in this chapter.

Several tools always use the current pattern (the paint can, spray can, brush, and filled shape-drawing tools). You can draw in the current pattern with the line-drawing tool and hollow shape-drawing tools by holding down the Option key while you draw.

The Line-Thickness Control Panel

The small panel in the bottom left corner of the MacPaint screen controls the thickness of lines and borders drawn by the line- and shape-drawing tools. When you make multiple copies of a drawing (by dragging the drawing while holding down the Option and Command keys), the thickness setting also determines the amount of space between the copies.

The active thickness is marked with a check mark. You select a different thickness by clicking the sample of it in the control panel. The sample you see shows the thickness you get, with one exception: The dotted-line, when used with one of the filled shape-drawing tools, yields a shape with no border line—just pattern. It has the same effect as the thin line below it in the control panel with the other tools.

Pointer Shapes

Altogether, there are 42 different pointer shapes in MacPaint. When the pointer is outside the drawing window, it has the common arrow shape. Inside the drawing window, the pointer shape is determined by the active tool: the ten shape-drawing tools and the line-drawing tool share the same cross shape; the brush tool can assume any of 32 different shapes; and the other tools each have their own unique shapes. All this pointer information is summarized in the Reference section of this book.

Creating the Letterhead Logo

The Phyllis Tien Gallery logo you are going to create consists of the business name set in large outlined letters and repeated three times, with each line a shade darker than the line above it. To create this logo, you type one line of the text and set the font, size, and style attributes. Then you copy the line twice. Finally, you fill each duplicate line of outlined characters with a different pattern.

Typing the Logo Text

To type inside the MacPaint window, you must click the large capital A (the text tool) in the tool rack. Doing that changes the pointer to the standard Macintosh text pointer, the I-beam, whenever you move it inside the MacPaint window. Move the pointer to the upper left corner of the window and click an insertion point there. A blinking vertical bar appears, marking the place where characters you type will appear. The characters will be small and plain because you have not yet set any special size or style attributes.

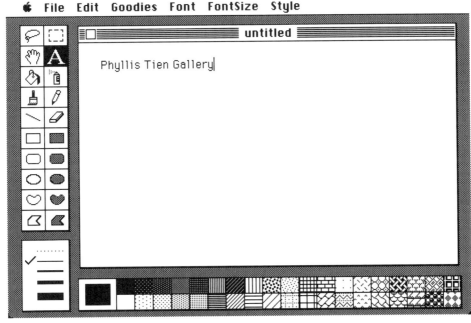

Select the text tool, click a text insertion point, and type the first line of the logo.

The exact position of the text is unimportant at this point since you will move the logo to another part of the drawing later.

Warning: As you type in MacPaint, always use the Backspace key to back up and correct mistakes. Be very careful not to use the mouse button until you finalize the font, size, and style of the text you just typed. You lose the ability to change those text attributes once you move the insertion point with the mouse or choose any of the commands from the Apple, File, Edit, or Goodies menus.

In fact, the MacPaint window does not allow you to insert, delete, or cut-and-paste text in the usual manner. If you click an insertion point between two characters with the intention of typing an insertion there, MacPaint responds by converting the existing text into a picture. Typing at the new insertion point writes over the "picturized" text instead of pushing the existing text aside as you hoped. If this seems unreasonable, remember that MacPaint is a picture processor, not a word processor.

Setting the Logo Text Attributes

Assuming you have made no changes in the Fonts, FontSize, or Style menus since you started MacPaint, the text you just typed is in Geneva font, 12 Point size, and Plain style. MacPaint uses checks ($\sqrt{}$) in the Font, FontSize, and Style menus to mark text attributes that are in effect. As long as the insertion point is still flashing at the end of the line of text, you can choose different attributes in those three menus.

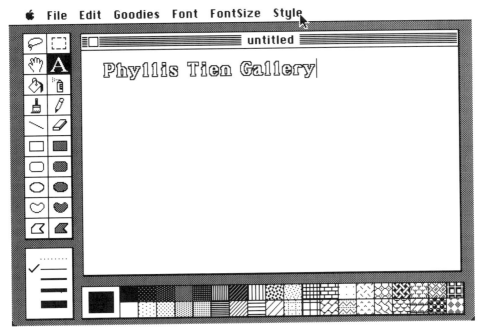

● *Change the text attributes by choosing the New York font from the Font menu, then 18 Point from the FontSize menu, and both Bold and Outline from the Style menu.*

Some text attributes can be combined and others cannot. For instance, only one font can be used at a time, and only one point size. Choosing a different font or point size automatically cancels the existing choice.

In contrast, you can choose any assortment of ornamental attributes—Bold, Italic, Underline, Outline, and Shadow—or you can choose Plain text. Choosing an ornamental attribute that is not active (is not checked on the Style menu) adds the attribute but does not remove other ornamental attributes that are active. Choosing an ornamental attribute that is active (is checked on the Style menu) removes the attribute. Choosing Plain text from the Style menu automatically cancels all ornamental attributes.

You can add or remove style attributes from the keyboard using the shortcuts listed in the Style menu. For example, pressing Command-B is the equivalent of choosing Bold from the Style menu.

There are no keyboard shortcuts for choosing a specific font name or font size from the Font and FontSize menus. However, you can use the keyboard to go consecutively up or down the list of fonts or list of sizes.

- Press Shift-Command-Period to advance to the next font.

- Press Shift-Command-Comma to back up to the previous font.

- Press Command-Period to advance to the next larger font size.

- Press Command-Comma to back up to the next smaller font size.

(Notice that the symbols < and >, the uppercase symbols on the Comma and Period keys, suggest direction.)

Duplicating the First Line

At this point, you could press the Return key and type the second line of the logo, then press it again and type the third line. Instead, you can duplicate the line you just typed. But before you can duplicate or move anything, you must select it.

Selecting an Object

Either of the tools at the top of the tool rack, the lasso or the selection rectangle, can select objects in the MacPaint drawing window. The selection rectangle is a little easier to use.

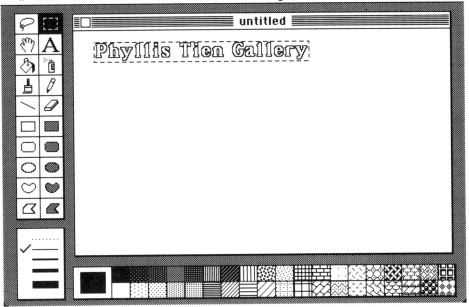

● *Click the selection rectangle in the tool rack. With the pointer, drag a selection rectangle around the line of text you just typed.*

When you click the selection rectangle and move the pointer into the drawing window, the pointer changes to look like cross hairs. Imagine a rectangle around the line you just typed, then move the cross hairs to any corner of that rectangle. Press and hold the mouse button; the cross hairs start to shimmer. Drag the shimmering cross hairs toward the opposite corner of the imaginary rectangle. As you drag, MacPaint draws a selection rectangle using dashes that move like a line of marching ants, or lights on a theater marquee.

As long as you hold down the mouse button, you can change the shape of the rectangle by dragging the pointer. When the selection rectangle just barely encloses the whole line of text, release the mouse button. If it turns out that the selection rectangle is the wrong shape, cancel it by clicking the mouse button in the drawing window anywhere outside the selection rectangle, and try again.

Duplicating a Selected Object

Move the pointer inside the selection rectangle and watch as the pointer changes shape from cross hairs to an arrow. Then press and hold both the Option and Shift keys with one hand and press the mouse button with the other. The Option key creates a duplicate of everything inside the selection rectangle. The Shift key constrains the movement of the duplicate to either exactly vertical or exactly horizontal, keeping the duplicate absolutely parallel to the original for you. You must press both these keys before pressing the mouse button to move the pointer.

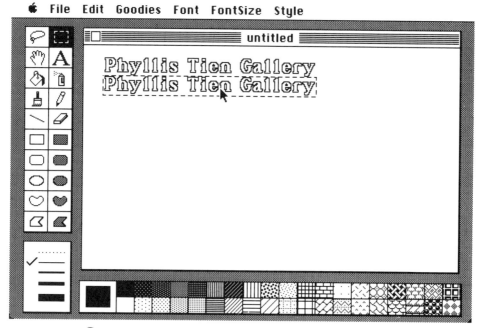

● *Holding the Shift and Option keys, point at the selected line of text, press the mouse button, and drag away a duplicate of it.*

The dashes that make up the selection rectangle stop marching while you press the mouse button. Slide the mouse toward you, dragging the pointer down the drawing window. A duplicate of the selected text tags along. Release the mouse button when the duplicate text is below the original. After duplicating, the top line is no longer selected. The selection rectangle surrounds the second line of text.

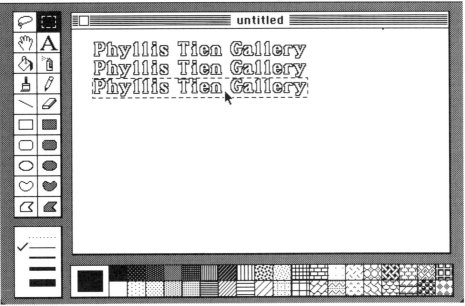

● *Use the selection rectangle,*
Option key, and Shift key to
duplicate the line of text again.

Use the selected second line to make the third line of the
logo. Place the pointer in the selected region, press and hold
the Option and Shift keys, press the mouse button, and drag the
pointer down the window. When the third line clears the second,
release the mouse button. Move the pointer away from the selected third line until the pointer changes to cross hairs, then
click the mouse button to remove the selection rectangle.

Shading the Second and Third Lines

The second line of the Phyllis Tien logo is medium gray and the
third line is black. To shade the outlined letters on the second
and third lines, you must fill each one with a pattern from the
palette displayed below the drawing window.

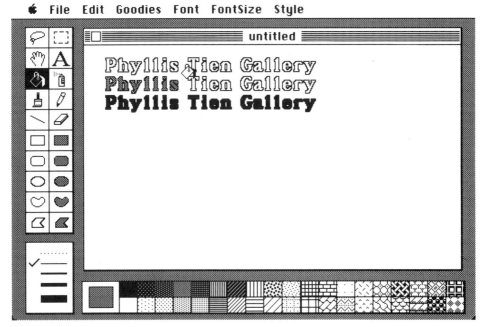

● *Click the paint can in the tool rack. Click inside each letter on the third line. Click the 50-percent gray swatch in the pattern palette and then click inside each letter on the second line.*

Each time you start MacPaint, the program picks the solid black pattern by default, so you may as well shade the third line first. When you finish the third line, you can pick another pattern to shade the second line by clicking the swatch of a lighter pattern in the pattern palette.

You use the paint can to fill in bordered areas with the current pattern. After clicking the paint can in the tool rack and moving the pointer into the MacPaint window, the pointer takes the shape of a paint can. The tip of the "paint" pouring out of the can points to the spot where MacPaint will start to fill an area with the current pattern as soon as you click the mouse button. MacPaint fills in every direction with the current pattern. It does not fill past a solid boundary line, but will leak through any gap in the boundary, filling to the next unbroken boundary.

If there are no unbroken boundaries, MacPaint fills the whole drawing window. If you miss with the paint can and inadvertently fill the whole screen instead of just inside a letter, you can undo that fill with the Undo command.

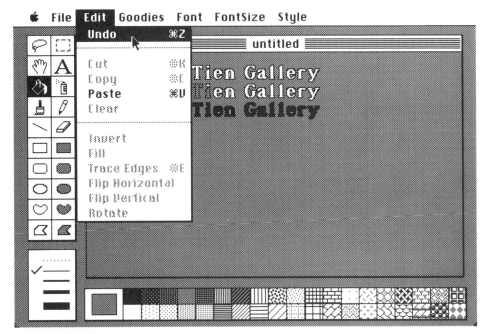

● *To clean up a paint spill, choose Undo from the Edit menu (or press the key in the upper left corner of the keyboard).*

The Undo command has two keyboard shortcuts: pressing the Accent/Tilde key (the one with the ` and ~ on it), or pressing Command-Z. After undoing the spill, adjust the paint can and try filling again.

Using the FatBits Magnifier

MacPaint can magnify any part of the drawing window to facilitate detail work. For instance, the whole pointer, no matter what its shape, fits inside most magnified outlined letters, making it easier to fill them accurately.

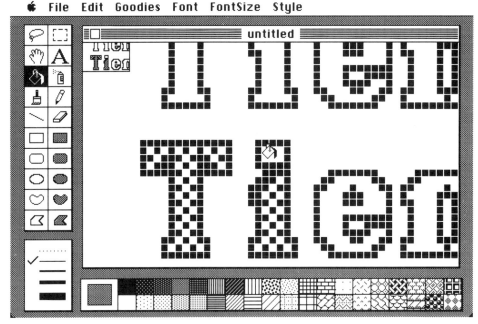

● *To make detail work easier, magnify the work area by choosing FatBits from the Goodies menu.*

Choosing FatBits from the Goodies menu instantly magnifies a small part of your work, usually the area where you were last working. You can easily see and manipulate the individual dots that make up an image; each dot appears as an enlarged square (a *fat bit*) in the magnified area. To help you keep your bearings, an inset window in the upper left corner of the drawing window lets you see the normal-size version of the magnified area.

To see a different part of your work through the FatBits magnifier, use the hand, or grabber, from the tool rack. Clicking the hand icon makes the pointer look like a hand whenever it is in the window. If you press the mouse button and drag the hand, your work follows as if the hand were grabbing it and pulling it along. Watch the inset window to see where you're going.

Instead of choosing FatBits from the Goodies menu, you can magnify part of the drawing window by double-clicking the pencil in the tool rack. To activate the FatBits magnifier over a particular part of the drawing window, use the Command key in conjunction with the pencil tool. First click the pencil in the tool rack. Then move the pointer, which will be pencil-shaped, into the area you want magnified, hold down the Command key, and click the mouse button.

There are four ways to put the FatBits magnifier away. If the pointer is pencil-shaped, just hold down the Command key and click the mouse button anywhere in the drawing window. Or, you can double-click the pencil in the tool rack, choose FatBits again from the Goodies menu, or click inside the inset window.

Retouching the Shaded Letters

You probably noticed that filling the "s," "e," and "a" characters with solid black makes them look like indistinguishable blobs. In addition, the "h," "i," "T," "n," and "r" characters could use some retouching. Use FatBits to magnify those letters and clean them up.

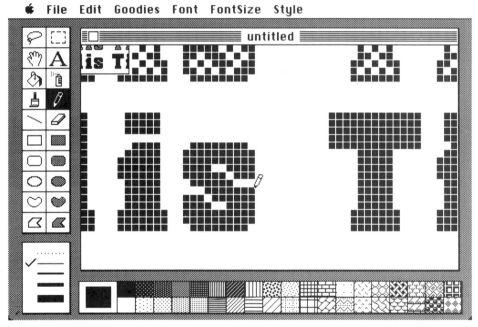

● *Touch up blotchy letters under the FatBits magnifier, using the pencil from the tool rack.*

Double-clicking the pencil in the tool rack is the fastest way to activate the FatBits magnifier. Click the hand in the tool rack and use it to scroll one of the offending letters into view.

Most people find the pencil the most convenient tool for touch-up work under the FatBits magnifier. It works by reversing the color of the squares that make up an image. If you click the pencil in a white space, a black square appears. Alternatively, if you click the pencil in a black space, a white square appears. And if you click and drag the pencil starting in a white space, you draw a solid black line composed of black squares. If you click and drag the pencil starting in a black space, you draw a solid white line composed of white squares.

Retouch the letters in the third line of the logo by reversing the color of the squares indicated in Figure 5.

When using the pencil under the FatBits magnifier, you can switch temporarily to the grabber (to scroll a new letter into view) just by pressing the Option key.

Saving a New Drawing

Having finished the parts of the logo, you may wish to put the Phyllis Tien letterhead project aside for now. If so, save your work before going on to another MacPaint project or quitting MacPaint altogether. It is a good idea to save your work at this point even if you intend to continue with the letterhead. Then, in the event of a sudden power failure, you will not have to start over from the beginning.

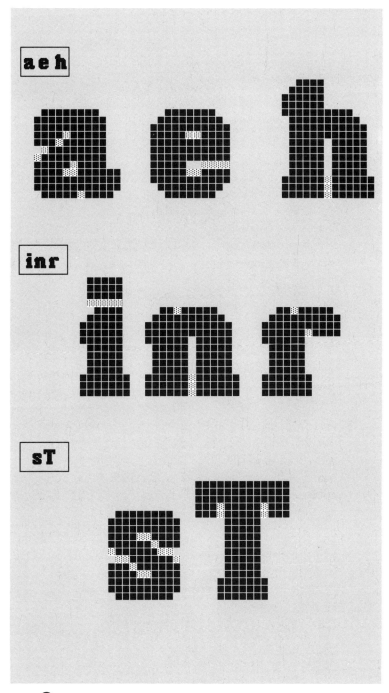

● *Figure 5. Letters to be retouched using the pencil and the FatBits magnifier*

● *To save a new drawing in its current state on a disk, choose Save or Save As... from the File menu. Type the drawing name. Click the Save button.*

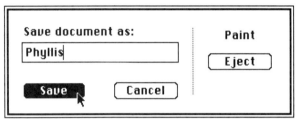

The first time you save a new drawing, or whenever you choose Save As... from the File menu, a dialog box appears asking for the name you wish to give the drawing. (For new drawings, choosing Save or Save As... produces the same dialog box.) The Eject button in the dialog box lets you swap the current disk for another disk before saving the drawing. If your Mac has an internal and an external drive, the dialog box includes a Drive button that lets you switch between the drives.

Before you click the Save button, double-check the name you typed for the drawing. You can use standard editing methods to edit the name, if necessary. Also, check the name of the disk, which is displayed directly above the Eject button, to make sure the drawing will be saved on the correct disk. If not, swap disks or switch drives.

When you click the Save button, the Finder checks the name you typed against the names of documents and applications on the disk. If it finds a match, it displays a small dialog box asking whether you wish to replace the existing drawing or application. You answer by clicking a displayed Yes or No button.

Typing the Name and Address

After typing and shading the logo in the upper left corner of the drawing window, you type the text for the address and telephone number in the lower right corner. This involves setting the proper font, size, and style, and typing the text.

Before typing, choose the New York font from the Font menu, 12 Point from the FontSize menu, and Bold and Align Right from the Style menu.

Font
Chicago
✓Geneva
New York
Monaco
Venice
London
Athens

FontSize
9 point
10
12
14
✓18
24
36
48
72

Style	
Plain	⌘P
✓**Bold**	⌘B
Italic	⌘I
Underline	⌘U
Outline	⌘O
Shadow	⌘S
✓Align Left	⌘L
Align Middle	⌘M
Align Right	⌘R

Set the text attributes for the name and address before you begin typing. Otherwise, your typing will have the same attributes as the logo and will not fit inside the window. Unless you have quit MacPaint or made changes to the font, size, or style since you typed the logo, the font is already New York, but the size is 18 Point, and the style is Bold Outline. Verify the font, and choose 12 Point from the FontSize menu. To cancel the Outline attribute, choose it again from the Style menu; the check mark disappears to show that Outline is no longer selected. Alternatively, choose Plain to clear all special style attributes (as if you had just started MacPaint), then choose Bold. Set right alignment by choosing Align Right from the Style Menu.

Choosing Align Right makes anything you type appear to the left of the insertion point, but the insertion point doesn't move as it does with left alignment. You can click an insertion point near the right edge of the drawing window and type a line of text all the way across the screen. As you type, each character is added to the end of the line (at the insertion point), and the beginning of the line moves across the window to the left (away from the insertion point). The text still reads normally (from left to right).

● *Click the capital A in the tool rack. Then click an insertion point near the right edge of the window, below the logo. Type the address and telephone number, pressing the Return key to end each line.*

Be sure the name and address clear the logo text, but don't worry about their exact placement. You are going to move them later, anyway.

If you notice mistakes on any of the three lines while you're typing, use the Backspace key to back up and correct them. Even if the mistake is on a line above the one the insertion point is on, pressing the Backspace key enough times will get you to it. Do not use standard text editing methods like those you might use in MacWrite. Remember, moving the text pointer with the mouse automatically turns the text into a picture, as does choosing commands from the Apple, File, Edit, or Goodies menus.

Creating the Background Shape

With the text typed, sized, and styled, it's time to create the background for the letterhead. The Phyllis Tien Gallery letterhead has a trapezoid-shaped background made with a custom grid pattern.

Moving to Another Part of the Drawing

The logo, address, and phone number take up most of the drawing window. Unless you draw over them, there's no place in the window to put the background trapezoid. But the drawing window shows less than one-third of the available drawing page. You can move the drawing window to a clear space on the drawing page and draw the trapezoid there.

● *Choose Show Page from the Goodies menu (or double-click the grabber in the tool rack).*

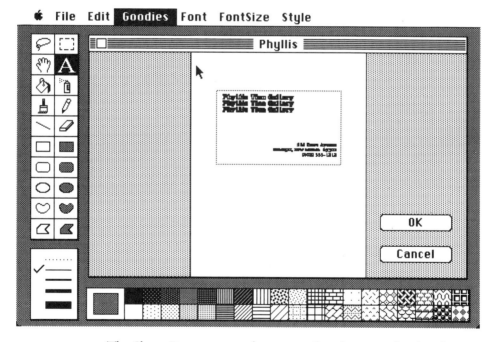

The Show Page command temporarily takes over the drawing window to show a miniature version of the whole drawing page. Everything on the page (the logo, address, and phone number, in this case) appears in shrunken form on the miniature page. Because everything is reduced in size, much of the detail is lost.

A rectangle made of dotted lines marks the current position of the drawing window on the page. When you click the displayed OK button, the Show Page command relinquishes control, and everything inside the dotted-line rectangle appears full-size in the drawing window.

Moving the Drawing on the Page

None of the tools or menus are available when the Show Page command is in control, so you cannot change anything on the page. However, you can slide everything on the page to a new position by placing the pointer outside the dotted-line rectangle, pressing the mouse button, and dragging the pointer around. Release the mouse button when the drawing is where you want it on the page.

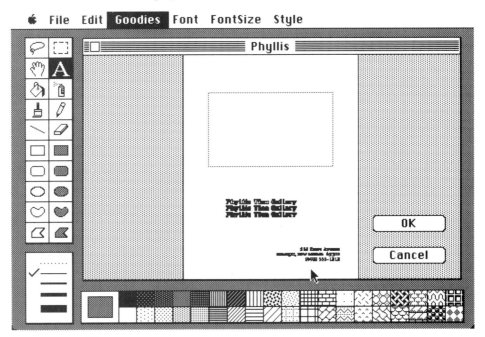

● *Use the pointer outside the dotted-line rectangle to move the logo, address, and phone number to the bottom of the page.*

If you hold down the Shift key before dragging the pointer, you restrict movement to either a horizontal or vertical direction—no diagonals.

Warning: You can actually slide part or all of the drawing off the page and then back on the page again. Any part of the drawing that is off the page when you click the OK *button will be erased. To avoid losing this part, click the Cancel button instead of the* OK *button.*

Moving the Drawing Window

In addition to moving the drawing on the page, you can move the drawing window by placing the pointer on or inside the dotted-line rectangle, pressing the mouse button, and dragging the rectangle to a new place on the page. Release the mouse button when the rectangle encloses the part of the page you want to see inside the drawing window and click the OK button to confirm the change and return to the normal drawing window.

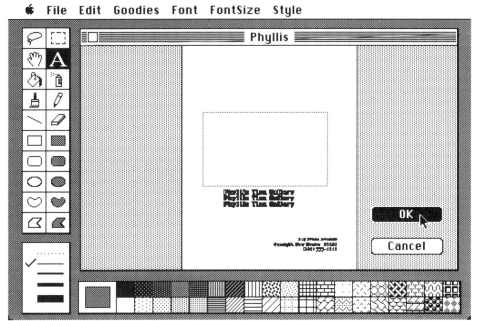

● *With the pointer inside the dotted-line rectangle, drag the rectangle down until it is just above the logo and then click the* OK *button.*

Pressing the Shift key while dragging the rectangle constrains movement to a vertical or horizontal direction.

Creating the Grid Pattern

MacPaint has 38 patterns in its pattern palette, but none of them quite matches the background in the Phyllis Tien Gallery letterhead. The background pattern was created by modifying one of the standard patterns, using techniques much like those used with the FatBits magnifier.

Each drawing has its own set of 38 patterns. It starts out with the 38 standard patterns, but you can change the patterns. Any changes you make stay with the drawing, so the patterns in one drawing can end up completely different from the patterns in another drawing.

The pattern in the center of the bottom row of the pattern palette closely matches the background for the Phyllis Tien Gallery letterhead. You need only remove the central black square to create the pattern you want.

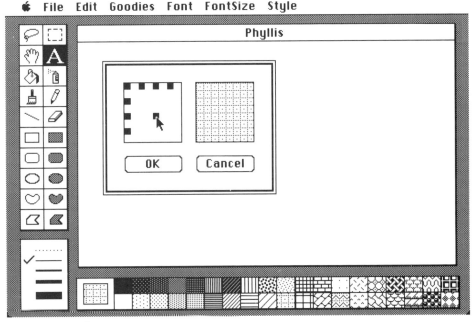

● *Create a pattern to match the Phyllis Tien Gallery background grid by editing the pattern that most closely resembles it.*

To edit the pattern, click its swatch in the pattern palette, then choose Edit Pattern from the Goodies menu. If you like short-cuts, simply double-click the pattern swatch. Either way, a dialog box appears showing the pattern magnified in one small window and the pattern life-size in another small window. To make changes, use the pointer in the magnifying window as you would use the pencil tool with the FatBits magnifier: Click the pointer in a white space to turn the space black, and vice versa. As you click, watch how the life-size sample of the pattern changes in the adjacent window. When the sample looks like the pattern you want, click the OK button.

If you click the pointer outside the pattern editing box in the drawing window, MacPaint picks up the pattern displayed at that point and copies it into the pattern editing window. For example, clicking in a white area of the drawing window blanks out the pattern editing box.

Drawing the Background Shape

MacPaint has a number of tools that help you draw regular shapes including rectangles, squares, rectangles with rounded-corners, squares with rounded-corners, ovals, and circles. There are two versions of all these tools: One draws a hollow shape; the other draws a shape filled with the current pattern.

The two tools at the bottom of the tool rack draw straight-sided irregular shapes. You can use the one on the right (the filled irregular-shape tool) to draw the trapezoid in the Phyllis Tien Gallery letterhead. From the panel in the bottom left corner of the screen, you can choose how thick the shape's border will be. You want the letterhead trapezoid to be bor-derless (the top selection).

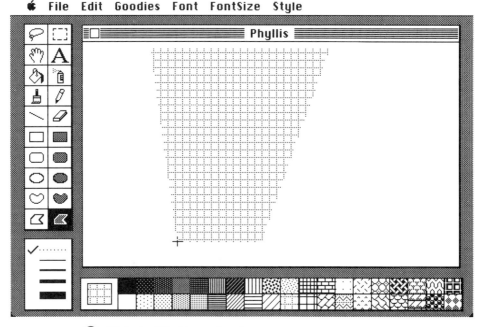

● *Click the filled irregular-shape
tool, the custom grid pattern,
and the no-border line thickness.
Then draw the trapezoid.*

To draw an irregular shape, click at each corner of the shape
in turn. As you move the pointer from one corner to the next,
a straight line stretches from the last corner you clicked to follow the pointer. The line acts like a rubber band attached
between the pointer and the last corner you clicked—shrinking,
expanding, and changing direction to follow the pointer.
Clicking again fixes the line in place and establishes another
corner. When you come to the last corner, double-click.
MacPaint automatically draws a line straight to the point where
you started.

Don't worry for now if the trapezoid is too small or too large.
Soon you will learn how to enlarge it here and trim it there.

Finishing the Letterhead

At one place or another on the drawing page, you have nearly
all the parts needed to assemble the Phyllis Tien Gallery letterhead. You are ready to copy and paste the logo, address, and

phone number onto the background trapezoid. Then you can draw the last part (the long, thin triangle) across the trapezoid between the logo and the address.

Putting the First Line in Place

The logo belongs on top of the trapezoid. Right now it is located just out of sight, below the trapezoid on the drawing page. You need to move the drawing window to bring the logo into view and copy it to the Clipboard. Then you can move the drawing window back to show the trapezoid again and paste the logo into place from the Clipboard. Since the lines of the logo are staggered in the final letterhead, you have to copy and paste each one separately.

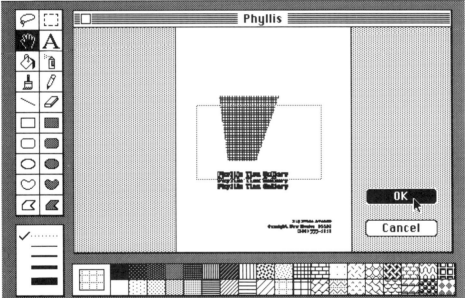

● *Choose Show Page from the Goodies menu. With the pointer inside the dotted-line rectangle, drag the rectangle down until the first logo line is just inside it. Click the OK button.*

Notice when you move the dotted-line rectangle down far enough to include the first line of the logo, the top part of the trapezoid is no longer inside the rectangle. Therefore, you should expect the top part of the trapezoid to be outside the drawing window after you click the OK button.

Selecting the First Logo Line

Once the first line of the logo is in the drawing window, you can select it. Then you can drag it to a new position, duplicate it, copy it to the Clipboard, and so on.

You could select the logo line by dragging a selection rectangle around it, as you did before. But, the selection rectangle selects everything inside it—text and white space. If you move the contents of the selection rectangle over the trapezoid, you will end up with a white shadow around the text. In contrast, the lasso, located just to the left of the selection rectangle in the tool rack, selects an object precisely. When you click the lasso in the tool rack and move the pointer inside the MacPaint window, the pointer changes to the shape of a lasso. You select an object by drawing a ring around it with the lasso-shaped pointer. To draw the ring, press the mouse button and slide the mouse. Release the mouse button and the ring automatically tightens around the encircled object, omitting any extra white space from around the edges.

Selecting an object with the lasso makes the object's outline shimmer, telling you at a glance whether you lassoed all of it. You can move only the part that you selected, so make sure the whole line of text is shimmering. If the lines of text are close together, you may have trouble drawing an accurate ring with the lasso. In that case, select the line you want with the selection rectangle, drag it away from its companions, and try again with the lasso.

Copying the Selected Text

You could now drag the selected line of text onto the trapezoid. But the text goes at the top of the trapezoid, which is outside the window. So you cannot position the text simply by dragging it. You must copy (or cut) it to the Clipboard, where it will be held while you move the drawing window again.

● *Use the lasso to draw a ring around the first line of the logo.*

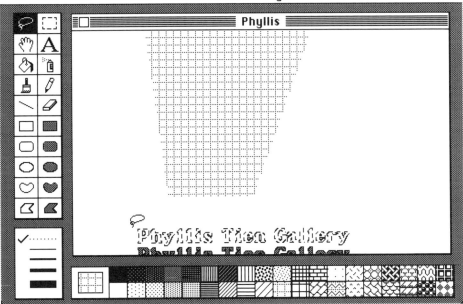

● *Release the mouse button to tighten the ring and select the encircled text.*

● *To copy the selected text to the Clipboard, choose Copy from the Edit menu.*

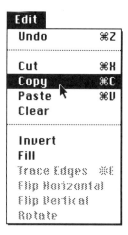

Moving the Drawing Window Again

Remember using the grabber to scroll the FatBits magnifier? You can also use the grabber to move the drawing around under the drawing window.

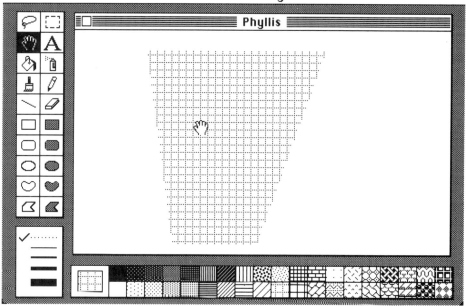

● *Click the grabber in the tool rack and move the hand-shaped pointer to the top center of the drawing window. Press the mouse button, drag the pointer* *down until the bottom of the trapezoid nears the bottom of the window, and then release the mouse button.*

Pasting the Selected Text

Scrolling the entire trapezoid back into view moves the text you copied to the Clipboard out of view. You can paste the text from the Clipboard into the middle of the drawing window by choosing Paste from the Edit menu.

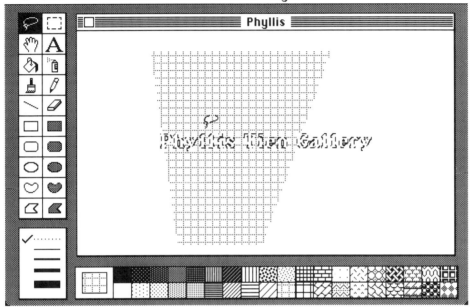

● *Paste the contents of the Clip-board into the drawing window.*

The text shimmers to show it is still selected by the lasso.

Enlarging the Trapezoid

You can see at a glance that the trapezoid was drawn too small. Fortunately, you can remove the pasted text with the Undo command and either redraw the trapezoid or enlarge it. Then you can paste the text back on top of the larger trapezoid.

To enlarge an object, you start by dragging a selection rectangle around one end. Next you choose Grid from the Goodies menu. Then, while pressing Command-Shift-Option, you drag the selected end away from the center of the object.

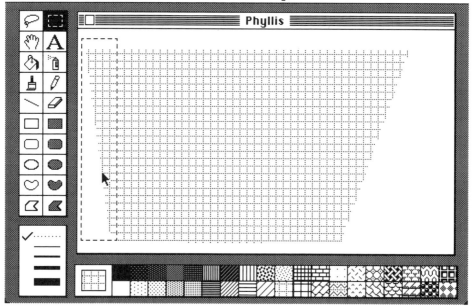

● *Using the selection rectangle, the Grid feature, and the Command, Shift, and Option keys, enlarge the trapezoid.*

Pressing the Command and Option keys while dragging a selected object creates continuous multiple copies of the selection. Pressing the Shift key at the same time restricts movement to a vertical or horizontal direction. Normally, if you drag continuous multiple copies of a patterned object, the pattern is ruined in the process. Choosing the Grid feature before dragging keeps the pattern intact.

You may have noticed when you were editing the pattern earlier that a pattern is defined by a grid eight squares high and eight squares wide. MacPaint fills an area with a pattern by laying the 8×8 grids end to end, like floor tiles. The Grid feature constrains the duplicating of a selection to the same eight-square intervals that the pattern grids are laid on. It's as if the drawing window were a piece of graph paper with lines representing multiples of eight; the pointer can only jump from line to line. The Grid feature only affects the following operations:

- Selecting, dragging, and duplicating with the selection rectangle.

- Selecting a text insertion point with the I-beam pointer.

- Drawing straight lines.

- Drawing rectangles, rounded-corner rectangles, ovals, and irregular, straight-sided shapes (but not drawing free-form shapes).

- Selecting with the lasso, but only after pasting something that was selected by the lasso, and then only until you click another tool.

- Dragging and duplicating an object that has been selected by the lasso.

Dragging the Pasted Text into Place

With the trapezoid enlarged, you can try pasting the first line of the logo from the Clipboard again. However, pasting when a selection rectangle is present crams the contents of the Clipboard inside the selection rectangle. You can prevent that by clicking anywhere in the drawing window to get rid of the selection rectangle before choosing Paste.

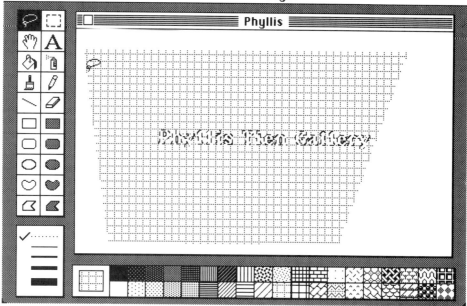

● *Remove the selection rectangle and once more paste the text from the Clipboard into the drawing window.*

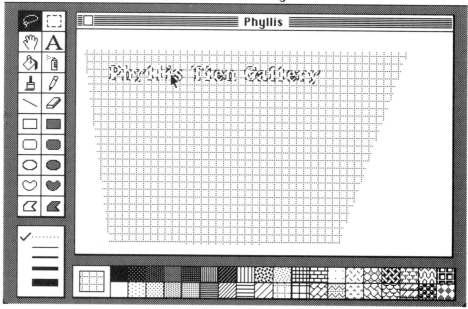

● *Choose Grid again to cancel it. Then drag the selection into place in the upper left corner of the trapezoid.*

The first line of the logo appears in the middle of the drawing window. You need to drag the lassoed selection into position about a quarter-inch from the top of the trapezoid and about a half-inch from the left edge. You can position the line by eye or measure with a small ruler held against the screen.

But before dragging the selection, cancel the Grid feature by choosing Grid again from the Goodies menu. The check mark disappears from the menu. Canceling the Grid feature leaves you free to drag the selection anywhere in the window, not just in eight-square intervals.

When you move the pointer inside the shimmering area, it changes shape from a lasso to an arrow. Do not press the mouse button to start moving the selection until the pointer shape changes. If you press the mouse button while the pointer is lasso-shaped, you cancel the selection. If that happens accidentally, choose Undo from the Edit menu. The pasted text disappears from the trapezoid and you can paste again.

Putting the Remaining Lines in Place

One by one, you can now copy and paste the remaining lines of text into place on the trapezoid background using the same method used to move the first line of the logo. Here is a step-by-step summary:

- Use the grabber to scroll the next line of text into view in the drawing window.

- Lasso the next line of text.

- Copy the selected text to the Clipboard.

- Use the grabber to scroll the trapezoid back into view.

- Paste the text from the Clipboard back into the drawing window.

- Drag the selected text into place.

The second line of the logo goes immediately below the first, indented about 1/16 inch on the left. The third line goes just below the second, indented another 1/16 inch on the left. The right edge of the first line of the address goes about 3/8 inch from the right edge of the trapezoid and ½ inch below the logo. The second line of the address falls right below that, indented about ⅛ inch on the right. The phone number goes below the second line of the address, indented another ⅛ inch on the right.

Erasing the Surplus Background

If the trapezoid ends up too tall, you need to erase the excess. The eraser from the tool rack (located below the pencil) will work, but it is inefficient for erasing large areas. Instead, try drawing a borderless white rectangle over the excess grid pattern at the top and bottom of the trapezoid.

● *Erase the excess grid background. Leave two grid lines showing at the top and bottom of the trapezoid.*

To erase from the bottom of the trapezoid with a white rectangle, first select the white pattern, the no-border line thickness, and the filled-rectangle tool. Then move the pointer, which is shaped like a cross, to the bottom left corner of the drawing window. Press and hold the mouse button, and then drag the pointer to the right edge of the window and up a bit toward the trapezoid. You are drawing a white rectangle that erases whatever it covers by replacing any black dots with white dots. As long as you continue to hold down the mouse button, moving the pointer changes the size and proportions of the white rectangle. Enlarge it to erase more; shrink it to erase less. When you have erased the right amount, release the mouse button. Repeat the procedure to erase from the top of the trapezoid.

Drawing a Triangle

The easy part is last. All that's left for you to do is draw the dark gray triangle between the logo and the address, using the filled irregular-shape tool, the no-border line thickness, and the gray pattern with diagonal white stripes.

● *Draw a thin, borderless, dark gray triangle to separate the logo from the address and phone number.*

Saving the Finished Letterhead

Save the finished letterhead on disk. You will use a copy of it whenever you write a letter.

● *To save an existing drawing on disk, choose Save from the File menu.*

The Mac knows which disk a drawing belongs on. If that disk is not inserted when you choose Save from the File menu, a dialog box tells you to insert it before the Mac saves the drawing.

Since you have saved this drawing before, the drawing as it now exists replaces the previous version on the disk. That previous version is gone forever. MacPaint does not automatically save the last version as a backup.

Preserving the Previous Version

You can save the drawing displayed in the drawing window under a new name or on a different disk with the Save As... command from the File menu. Everything works just as if you were saving the drawing for the first time. A dialog box appears, in which you must type the new drawing name. Buttons displayed in the box allow you to eject the current disk and to switch between internal and external drives.

After you save the drawing under its new name, that name replaces the former name in the title bar of the drawing window. If you subsequently save the drawing with the Save command from the File menu, it will be saved under that new name. The old version of the drawing still exists on disk under the old name, of course. You can go back to the old version at any time with the Open... command.

Using the Letterhead

You do the work of creating a letterhead just once, and save it on disk. When you want to write a letter, you copy the letterhead from the disk and paste it at the beginning of a MacWrite document. Then you use MacWrite to write and print the letter, at which time MacWrite prints the letterhead along with the body of the letter.

It takes more disk space to save a letter with a letterhead than without. Twelve such letters will chew up twelve times as much scarce disk space with carbon copies of the same letterhead. You may prefer to print the letterhead alone on several sheets of paper and use them like custom-printed stationery. In fact, many instant printing shops will accept a clean copy of your letterhead as a master for printing small quantities of stationery on their offset presses or photocopiers. Some shops can print in a color from your black-and-white master. A few can photographically reduce your Mac-designed letterhead so it will fit on an envelope, business card, notepaper, or mailing label.

Copying the Letterhead to the Clipboard

You may create a letterhead in MacPaint, but you will use it most often in MacWrite. To effect the transfer, you copy the letterhead from the MacPaint document to the Clipboard, and paste it from the Clipboard to the MacWrite document. If you expect to use the letterhead often, it pays to paste it into the Scrapbook on the MacWrite disk, too. Copying from the Scrapbook is easier than copying from another application.

Before choosing Copy from the Edit menu, you must first select the letterhead with the lasso or selection rectangle. The lasso is preferable because it automatically selects just the letterhead itself, with no extra white space around it. You want to avoid the extra white space because it prevents you from placing the letterhead itself flush against the MacWrite document's margins. And since MacWrite sees a whole picture—letterhead and surrounding white space—as an indivisible unit, you cannot remove the white space in MacWrite. If you select with the selection rectangle instead of the lasso, make the selection rectangle as small as possible, excluding excess white space.

Quitting MacPaint

Once you've copied the finished letterhead to the Clipboard, it's time to quit MacPaint.

● *To return to the directory window, choose Quit from the File menu.*

If you changed the drawing in any way since you last saved it, a dialog box appears, suggesting you save the drawing again before quitting.

Upon returning to the directory window, you will notice several changes. An icon for the new drawing now appears in the directory window and there is less space available on the disk because of it. Any desk accessories that were open are now closed. Usually only one disk icon remains on the desktop, no matter how many were there prior to opening the application. The remaining disk icon is the one from which you opened MacPaint, and it is now considered the start-up disk.

The letterhead stays on the Clipboard only until the next time you choose Cut or Copy from the Edit menu. Do not use either of these commands (or their Command-X and Command-C shortcuts) until you paste the letterhead from the Clipboard to the Scrapbook on a disk containing MacWrite, where it will remain until you need to use it.

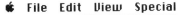

● *Choose Show Clipboard from the Edit menu to verify that the letterhead is there.*

Putting the Letterhead into a MacWrite Document

You used MacPaint to create the letterhead, but you need MacWrite to create a letter. The rest of this chapter tells you how to put a drawing such as the Phyllis Tien Gallery letterhead into a MacWrite document and how to manipulate and print the drawing as part of a MacWrite document. (The previous chapter covered writing with MacWrite.)

Starting MacWrite

To start MacWrite, you need to find the MacWrite application program. If the MacWrite icon is not in the directory window, you will have to eject the current disk and insert one that contains MacWrite. When you find the MacWrite application icon, double-click it to open it. If you switched disks, the Finder tells you to insert the MacPaint disk briefly so that it can copy the Clipboard, which contains the letterhead, to the MacWrite disk.

Pasting the Letterhead

Paste the letterhead into the Scrapbook now to make it more accessible in the future. Then, when you need the letterhead in MacWrite, you will be able to copy it from the Scrapbook; no need to quite MacWrite, open MacPaint, quit MacPaint, and reopen MacWrite.

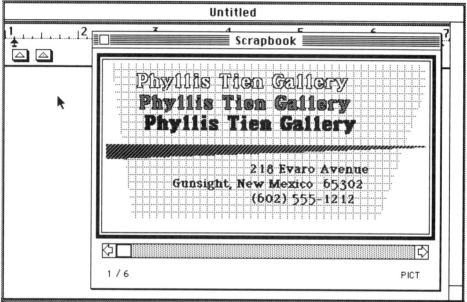

● *Paste the letterhead into the Scrapbook by choosing Scrapbook from the Apple menu, then choosing Paste from the Edit menu. Put the Scrapbook away by clicking the close box in its title bar.*

Warning: Unless MacWrite and MacPaint are on the same disk, do not paste the letterhead into the Scrapbook directly from MacPaint. Each disk has a separate Scrapbook, and an application like MacWrite or MacPaint only has access to the Scrapbook on its own disk.

The letterhead is still on the Clipboard, so you can go ahead and choose Paste from the Edit menu again to put the letterhead at the beginning of the new MacWrite document.

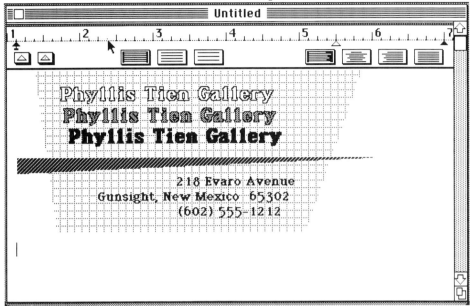

● *With the insertion point at the beginning of the document, paste the letterhead from the Clipboard into the MacWrite document. The letterhead is pasted at the left margin.*

Moving and Sizing the Letterhead

In a MacWrite document, you can move a picture such as the letterhead down the page, back up to the top, or right and left as far as the respective margins. MacWrite also allows you to change the size and proportions of a whole picture. You cannot type alongside the letterhead, only above it or below it. All other modifications to the letterhead must be made in MacPaint and copied to MacWrite as a new picture, via the Clipboard.

To move the letterhead down, insert blank lines above it by clicking a text insertion point just ahead of it and pressing the Return key. To move the letterhead up, remove lines above it by selecting the lines and choosing Cut from the Edit menu.

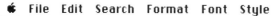

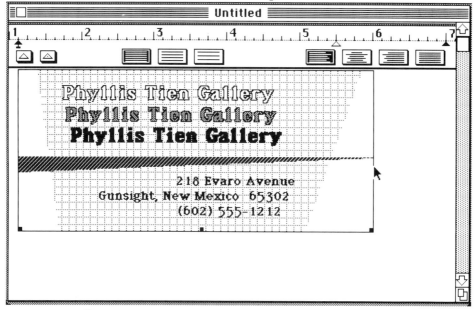

● *To move the letterhead sideways, first select it by clicking anywhere on it, then drag it by its selection box.*

When you select a picture such as the letterhead, MacWrite draws a selection box around it. The borders of the selection box define the extent of the picture. Place the pointer on the top or either side (but not the bottom) of the box, press the mouse button, and drag the rectangle right or left. When you release the mouse button, the letterhead jumps inside the selection box at its new location.

Warning: If you type anything while a picture is selected, the typing will replace the picture. Should this happen accidentally, immediately choose Undo from the Edit menu.

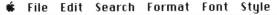

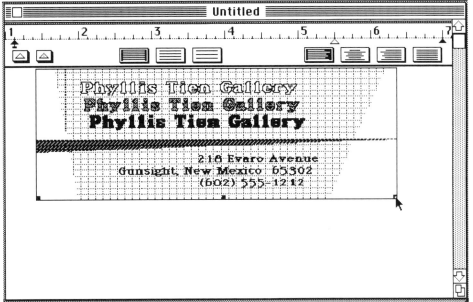

 *To stretch or shrink a selected
picture, drag one of the three
small black squares located on
the bottom border of the selection rectangle.*

There are three black squares on the bottom border of every
selection box. To use one, place the pointer over it, press the
mouse button, and drag the pointer. As you drag, the selection
box changes shape. When you release the mouse button, the picture changes its proportions to fit the new shape of the box.
You can undo the change to the shape by choosing Undo from
the Edit menu.

Writing a Letter

After copying the letterhead to a MacWrite document, you can
type a letter below it. When you print that letter, the letterhead
is printed along with it.

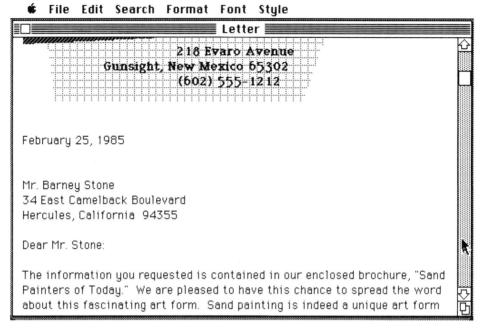

● *Type the letter.*

The letter will have the same left and right margins as the letter-head, unless you choose Insert Ruler from the Format menu to insert a new formatting ruler between them, and change the margins in that new ruler.

The minimum top and bottom margins on an 11-inch page total about ½ inch, leaving room for 47 lines of 12-point type, or 36 lines of 12-point type plus the Phyllis Tien Gallery letterhead.

Printing the Letter

Before you print a letter, you may need to set the paper size and orientation of the printing on the page.

Paper:	◉ US Letter	○ A4 Letter	OK
	○ US Legal	○ International Fanfold	
Orientation:	◉ Tall	○ Tall Adjusted ○ Wide	Cancel

● *Choose Page Setup from the File menu to set paper size and print orientation.*

The orientation you select affects the way MacWrite prints pictures. Tall orientation prints MacWrite text normally, but prints pictures about 13 percent narrower than MacPaint would. Tall Adjusted orientation compensates for the slight distortion, but in doing so, stretches MacWrite text sideways. Wide orientation prints sideways on the page, in the same proportions as Tall Adjusted.

Quality:	⦿ High	◯ Standard	◯ Draft	[OK]
Page Range:	⦿ All	◯ From:	To:	
Copies:	1			
Paper Feed:	⦿ Continuous	◯ Cut Sheet		[Cancel]

● *To print the letter, choose
Print... from the File menu.
Then select print options and
click the OK button.*

Your choice of paper and the condition of your ribbon affect printed picture quality, but your choices in the Print Options dialog box do not. The High and Standard options both print standard-quality pictures; only text typed in MacWrite varies. The Draft option does not print pictures at all.

Saving the Finished Letter

Be sure to save the finished letter after printing it. You may need to refer to it or print it again later.

● *Choose Save As... to save the
letter on disk.*

With the Save As... command, MacWrite requests confirmation before it replaces an existing document with the same name.

Summary

This chapter showed one method for creating a sample letter-head with MacPaint, and for using that letterhead in a MacWrite letter. In the process, it illustrated many of MacPaint's features, including:

■ Starting and quitting MacPaint.

■ Selecting part of a drawing to change.

■ Moving part of a drawing.

■ Constraining movement to vertical or horizontal.

■ Duplicating part of a drawing.

■ Setting text attributes.

■ Typing text.

■ Shading areas with patterns.

■ Creating custom patterns.

■ Using the FatBits magnifier.

■ Drawing shapes, with and without borders.

■ Undoing changes.

■ Viewing the whole page.

■ Scrolling the drawing in the window.

■ Copying a selection to another part of a drawing.

■ Erasing parts of a drawing.

■ Opening and saving drawing documents.

■ Enlarging a patterned selection.

■ Copying a drawing from MacPaint to MacWrite.

■ Pasting a drawing into the Scrapbook.

■ Printing a drawing with MacWrite.

MacPaint has many more features that you will want to explore on your own. They include:

- Reverting to the last saved version of a drawing.

- Printing drawings with MacPaint.

- Inverting, filling, tracing, flipping, and rotating a selection.

- Painting with the brush and changing brush shapes.

- Using the Brush Mirrors feature to create a mirror image of whatever you draw.

- Spray painting.

- Drawing straight lines.

- Stretching and shrinking a selection.

- Drawing shapes with patterned lines and borders.

Many of these additional features are used in other projects later in this book. Those projects include a wine-shop circular, a display ad for a newspaper, a handbill for a nightclub, a map to a business, a yellow-pages display ad, a restaurant menu, a land-scaping diagram, a furniture-arrangement plan, a get-well card, a party announcement, a map to a home, a bulletin-board ad, and a 3 × 5 ad for a supermarket advertising board.

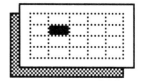

Figuring Your Net Worth With Multiplan

● *You'll learn about worksheets, rows, columns, cells, formulas, functions, cell references, cell formats, and more if you follow the detailed descriptions of this Multiplan project.*

Are you a prince or a pauper? Are you living beyond your means, or are you needlessly frugal? Could you handle a financial emergency right now? Are you accumulating enough to meet your long-term goals? How are you doing in the race with inflation? Figuring out your net worth can help you answer these questions.

Knowing your net worth tells you things a record of income and expenses never will. Lots of people mistakenly believe that income level is the sole measure of wealth. Very few people, though, take home a paycheck that could cover any expense that might arise. Instead, they must save, invest, and borrow to manage major expenditures such as a house, children's education, sudden unemployment, unexpected illness, vacations, and retirement.

Your net worth compares how much you have saved and invested, plus how much your savings and investments have appreciated, with how much you owe. The things you own— your assets—are balanced by your debts and obligations—your liabilities. Subtracting your liabilities from your assets tells you your net worth.

A simple worksheet computes your net-worth statement. As Figure 6 shows, it has two columns, one for descriptions, the other for dollar amounts. Assets are grouped together at the top of the worksheet, followed by liabilities. Net worth is computed at the bottom, along with an analysis based on the past year's performance and the inflation rate.

To prepare the net-worth statement, you could laboriously write down descriptions and amounts on ledger paper, and then calculate totals and percentages on a calculator. Multiplan makes the job easier and produces neater results, too. With Multiplan, you use the keyboard and mouse to enter and edit the descriptions and amounts. You also enter formulas that calculate totals and percentages. Multiplan performs the calculations and displays the results. Suppose you make a mistake, change your mind, or just want to see what happens to the totals if you alter one entry. Use standard editing methods to make the change; Multiplan recalculates the formulas and displays the new results.

Skills You Need

Before starting Multiplan, you should know some basic Macintosh skills, namely how to:

- Click, select, and drag with the mouse.
- Choose commands and features from menus.
- Open icons.
- Move, scroll, and resize windows.
- Perform cut-and-paste and copy-and-paste editing.
- Insert, eject, and handle disks.

These techniques are covered briefly in this chapter. If you need more detailed explanations, consult the first two chapters of this book or your Macintosh owner's manual.

You do not need a degree in mathematics or statistics to use Multiplan. A knowledge of arithmetic and a familiarity with algebra are all you need for the average Multiplan worksheet.

Starting Multiplan

When you switch on a Macintosh, it only knows how to do one thing: read instructions from a disk. It waits patiently until you insert a start-up disk from which it can get the instructions that tell it how to manage the electronic desktop and how to start applications. When you start an application, the Finder (the built-in program that locates and retrieves information on the disk) finds the application program and gives it control of the Macintosh. The application furnishes you with commands especially suited to working with one kind of information. Multiplan is an application that facilitates working with numbers.

Personal Net Worth Worksheet

	1	2	3	4
1	ASSETS			
2				
3	Cash	210.00		
4	Checking accounts	3,539.77		
5	Savings accounts	680.00		
6	Money market accounts	12,318.00		
7	Certificates of deposit			
8	Payroll savings plan	1,327.72		
9	Stocks--current value	2,675.00		
10	Company stock purchase plan	500.00		
11	Bonds--current value			
12	U.S. savings bonds	140.00		
13	IRA or Keogh	4,500.00		
14	Life insurance--cash value			
15	Deferred profit sharing	806.57		
16	Accrued pension benefits			
17	Home	86,500.00		
18	Other real estate			
19	Automobiles	21,100.00		
20	Rec. vehicle/boat/airplane	7,500.00		
21	Furniture	4,800.00		
22	Clothing	5,600.00		
23	Antiques and collections			
24	Hobby equipment	1,800.00		
25	Share in business or partnership	35,000.00		
26	Loans owed to us			
27				
28	Total Assets	$188,997.06		
29				
30	LIABILITIES			
31				
32	Credit cards	6,000.00		
33	Charge accounts	1,375.48		
34	Utilities	105.00		
35	Medical bills			
36	Tuition	1,200.00		
37	Automobile loan	10,830.12		
38	Appliance loan			
39	Furniture loan	1,629.32		
40	Home improvement loan			

● *Figure 6. The Multiplan worksheet
for figuring your net worth*

Personal Net Worth Worksheet

	1	2	3	4
41	Rec. veh./boat/plane loan			
42	Education loan			
43	Home mortgage	65,660.00		
44	Second mortgage			
45	Other real estate loan			
46	Income tax due			
47	Real estate tax due	927.81		
48	Personal property tax due	88.24		
49	Self employment tax due			
50	Homeowner's insurance	298.37		
51	Automobile insurance	1,307.44		
52	Life insurance	83.75		
53	Rec. veh./boat/plane insurance			
54	Medical insurance			
55				
56	Total Liabilities	$89,505.53		
57				
58	NET WORTH			
59				
60	Current	$99,491.53		
61	Last year at this date	$99,536.17		
62	Change	($44.64)		
63	Rate of change	-0.04%		
64				
65	Annual inflation rate	7.20%		
66	Adjusted net worth	$92,809.26		
67	Ahead of (behind) inflation	$6,682.27		
68				
69				
70				
71				
72				
73				
74				
75				
76				
77				
78				
79				
80				

 File Edit Select Format Options Calculate

R1C1		

Untitled

	1	2	3	4	5	6
1						
2						
3						
4						
5						
6						
7						
8						
9						
10						
11						
12						
13						
14						
15						

● *To start Multiplan, insert a disk that contains the Multiplan application program and open that disk's icon. Then find the Multiplan application icon and open it.*

Multiplan

If the Multiplan application icon is dimmed, it means the Multiplan program resides on a disk you inserted some time ago but ejected. When you open the dimmed icon to start the application, a dialog box appears telling you to switch disks. Insert the disk named in the dialog box so the Finder can locate the Multiplan program.

Multiplan Security Check

Multiplan may insist you temporarily insert the original Multiplan Master disk if you try to open the application from a copy of that disk. The original disk contains a security code that cannot be copied to another disk. Thus, without an original Multiplan disk, copies of it are useless. Generally, this security check occurs only the first time you open Multiplan after starting up the Macintosh.

● *To complete the Multiplan security check, insert the original Multiplan Master disk. Reinsert your Multiplan application disk when asked.*

> **Please insert the Multiplan Master disk**   [Cancel]

The Multiplan Desktop

Opening an application clears the desktop. The directory window vanishes along with the disk icon, the Trash icon, and any open windows. The menu bar is erased and replaced briefly by the name of the application, Multiplan. The pointer assumes a wristwatch shape, letting you know you must wait while the Finder transfers the Multiplan program from disk to memory. About 15 seconds after opening the Multiplan application icon (longer if a security check of the Multiplan Master disk is needed), the desktop assumes the standard look for Multiplan.

The Menu Bar

Across the top of the screen is a menu bar with seven menu titles. The Apple menu lists the desk accessories described in the first chapter. The File menu lists commands that act on an entire worksheet at once. The Edit menu lists cut-and-paste and copy-and-paste editing commands plus some features unique to Multiplan. Most of those new features, along with the commands in the Select, Format, Options, and Calculate menus, are described later in this chapter.

The Worksheet Window

A worksheet window occupies most of the screen. The new worksheet it displays is untitled and empty.

You can drag the worksheet window around on the desktop by its title bar. This title bar, unlike most, has no close box. The worksheet window cannot be put away, though the worksheet inside the window can be replaced by another worksheet. Only desk accessories and the Clipboard window can be put away in Multiplan.

The worksheet window has two scroll bars, which you can use to scroll the worksheet up and down, and from side to side. The worksheet window also has a size box, which you can use to shrink or enlarge the window.

Each of the two scroll bars incorporates a window-splitting control, a small black box called the *split bar.* One is located directly above the up arrow in the vertical scroll bar and the other is directly to the left of the left arrow in the horizontal scroll bar. By dragging the split bars along the scroll bars, you split the window into panes. The window can be split into two panes (right and left or top and bottom) using one split bar, or into four panes (top left, top right, bottom left, and bottom right) using both. Splitting the window also splits the scroll bar, so scrolling in one half does not affect the other half.

 Pointer Shapes

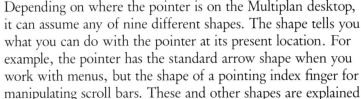 Depending on where the pointer is on the Multiplan desktop, it can assume any of nine different shapes. The shape tells you what you can do with the pointer at its present location. For example, the pointer has the standard arrow shape when you work with menus, but the shape of a pointing index finger for manipulating scroll bars. These and other shapes are explained thoroughly in the rest of this chapter.

The Worksheet

The dotted lines inside the worksheet window divide the worksheet into rows and columns. Rows are numbered from 1 to 255, columns from 1 to 63. You can only see some of the rows and columns at one time in the worksheet window. Use the scroll bars to see other rows and columns.

Selecting Cells

The space where a row and column cross is called a *cell*. A cell can contain a number, a description, or a formula that combines the values of other cells.

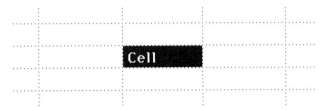

Before you can enter a number, description, or formula into a cell, you must select the cell. You can use the mouse to select any cell at random.

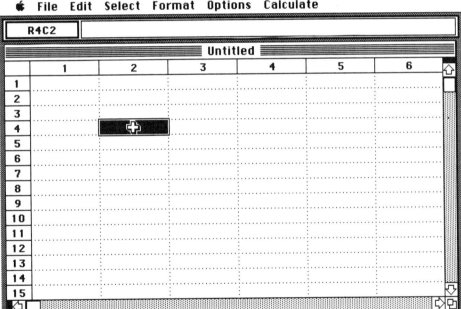

● *To select a cell, place the pointer on it and click the mouse button.*

The pointer assumes the shape of a large white cross when it is over the worksheet in a position to select a cell.

You can also change the selected cell from the keyboard. The Return key moves the cell selection down one cell, the Tab key moves the selection one cell to the right, Shift-Return moves the cell selection up one, and Shift-Tab moves it one cell to the left.

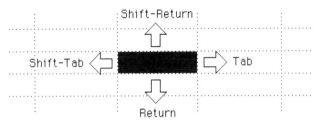

Multiplan highlights the currently selected cell by reversing the black and white colors in it and drawing a thin border around it. The selected cell is also called the *current cell* or the *active cell*.

Entering Cell Contents

You can enter a number, description, or formula by typing. Whatever you type appears in two places at once: in the selected cell on the worksheet and in the *formula bar,* which stretches across the screen below the menu bar. To see how this works, try typing the first description for the net-worth worksheet.

⌘ File Edit Select Format Options Calculate

```
┌─────────────┬───┬───────────────────────────────────────┐
│   R1C1      │ ⊗ │ ASSETS                                 │
└─────────────┴───┴───────────────────────────────────────┘
```

	1	2	3	4	5	6
1	ASSETS					
2						
3						
4						
5						
6						
7						
8						
9						
10						
11						
12						
13						
14						
15						

● *Select the first cell in column 1 and type the word* ASSETS.

The code at the left end of the formula bar identifies which row and column the selected cell is in. For example, R1C1 identifies the cell where row 1 crosses column 1.

When you start typing, a *Cancel button* appears in the formula bar next to the cell identification. Clicking the Cancel button tells Multiplan to disregard everything you've done in the formula bar since you selected the current cell.

⌘ File Edit Select Format Options Calculate

	R2C1						

═══ Untitled ═══

	1	2	3	4	5	6
1	ASSETS					
2	▮					
3						
4						
5						
6						
7						
8						
9						
10						
11						
12						
13						
14						
15						

● *Press the Return key to select the cell immediately below.*

Pressing the Return key enters the description you typed in the formula bar into the selected cell. (The description becomes the cell *contents*.) Pressing the Return key also switches cell selection to the next row in the same column.

Constructing a Prototype Worksheet

A complete net-worth worksheet consists of descriptions and amounts for individual assets and liabilities, and formulas for computing totals and analyzing the results. A prototype worksheet has everything but individual asset and liability amounts, which remain blank. You create the prototype once, save it on disk, and fill in the blanks on a new copy of it every time you want to prepare another complete net-worth statement.

Typing the Descriptions

Begin constructing the prototype worksheet by typing the descriptions in column 1. Use the descriptions that are shown in the sample worksheet or adapt them to your situation by changing the wording, omitting assets and liabilities that don't pertain to you, or adding new ones that do.

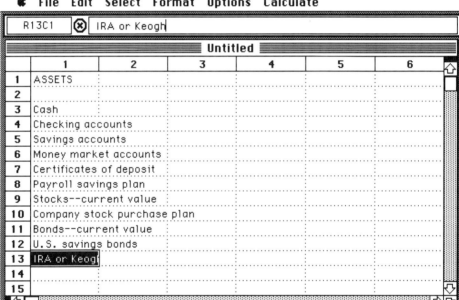

● *Enter the descriptions in column 1, typing the words that belong in the currently selected cell and pressing the Return key to advance from one row to the next.*

As you type a description, the formula bar shows the whole thing, letter for letter. The currently selected cell on your worksheet shows only as much as the column width allows. However, even the longest description appears in its entirety on your worksheet when you press the Return key.

Correcting or Changing Descriptions

If you see typing mistakes in the currently selected cell, correct them in the formula bar using the standard text editing methods summarized in Figure 7. Inside the formula bar, the pointer has an I-beam shape. Use the I-beam pointer to click an insertion point or to select and highlight text. Then type new text or choose commands from the Edit menu for cut-and-paste or copy-and-paste editing.

Objective	Method	Shortcut
Add text to the left of the insertion point	Type new text	None
Add text from the Clipboard to the left of the insertion point	Choose Paste from the Edit menu	Command-V
Remove the character to the left of the insertion point	Backspace	None
Remove highlighted text	Backspace	None
Remove highlighted text and put it on the Clipboard	Choose Cut from the Edit menu	Command-X
Remove the entire contents of the highlighted cell	Choose Clear from the Edit menu	Command-B
Copy highlighted text to the Clipboard	Choose Copy from the Edit menu	Command-C
Move highlighted text	Choose Cut from the Edit menu, click a new insertion point, and then choose Paste from the Edit Menu	Command-X plus Command-V
Replace highlighted text	Type new text	None
Replace highlighted text with the contents of the Clipboard	Choose Paste from the Edit menu	Command-X
Undo your last action	Choose Undo from the Edit menu	Command-Z

● *Figure 7. Standard text editing methods in Multiplan*

If you spot an error or wish to make a change in a cell that is not currently selected, click the cell to select it. The cell's contents appear in the formula bar, where you can edit them. If the cell's contents do not appear in the formula bar, you selected the wrong cell (the pointer was probably on a cell in column 2 or 3, instead of column 1).

To enter the revisions you made in the formula bar into the currently selected cell, press the Enter or Return key. To cancel changes you have just made in the formula bar and restore the previous the cell contents, click the Cancel button.

Saving Intermediate Work

Typing the complete list of asset and liability descriptions is tedious work. When you finish, save a copy of the list on disk. Then, in the event of a mistake or accident, you can reopen the worksheet with the descriptions intact. The more often you save a worksheet, the less you stand to lose in the event of a surprise power outage.

● *To save a new worksheet on disk, choose Save As... from the File menu. Type a name for the worksheet. Click the Save button.*

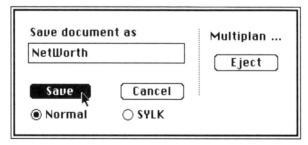

The Save As... command will be dimmed and you will be unable to choose it if you have not entered the contents of the formula bar into the currently selected cell. Press the Return or Enter key, or click the Cancel button in the formula bar to enable saving.

Naming the Worksheet

Whenever you choose Save As. . . from the File menu, a dialog box appears asking for the name you wish to give the worksheet. The Eject button in the dialog box lets you swap the current disk for another disk before saving the worksheet. If your Macintosh has both an internal and an external drive, the dialog box includes a Drive button, which lets you switch between the drives.

Before you click the Save button, double check the name you typed for the worksheet. You can use standard editing methods to edit the name, if necessary. Also, check the name of the disk, which is displayed directly above the Eject button, to make sure the worksheet will be saved on the correct disk. If not, swap disks or switch drives.

When you click the Save button, the Finder checks the name you typed against the names of worksheets and applications on the disk. If it finds a match, it displays a small dialog box asking whether you wish to replace the existing worksheet or application. You answer by clicking a displayed Yes or No button.

Multiplan Save Options

Multiplan includes the option to save the worksheet in Normal format or SYLK (Symbolic Link) format. For worksheets that will only be used on a Macintosh, Normal format is the most common choice. The SYLK format provides a standard for information interchange between Microsoft applications on different computers. So if you plan to transfer a worksheet to another kind of computer, choose SYLK format. Otherwise, choose Normal format.

Adjusting Column Width

Notice that all the descriptions line up against the left edge of column 1, and that the longer ones extend into columns 2 and 3. Later, when you enter asset and liability amounts in column 2,

Multiplan will no longer allow the lengthy descriptions to encroach on adjacent cells. Multiplan runs text into adjoining cells only if those cells are empty. Otherwise it shows as much as will fit in one cell and hides the rest. The hidden text is still part of the cell contents and can be seen by widening the column.

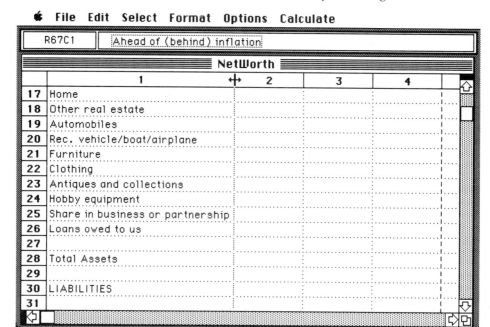

● *To change the column width, use the pointer to drag the column boundary right or left.*

Before widening column 1, scroll the worksheet up and down until you find the longest description, Share in business or partnership (row 25 in the sample worksheet). Then move the pointer along the line of column numbers until it points to the boundary line between columns 1 and 2. There the pointer changes shape to a two-headed arrow bisected by a vertical bar. Press the mouse button, drag the boundary line to the right until it clears the widest description, and release the mouse button. Multiplan then resizes column 1 and moves the other columns to the right, pushing column 6 and part of column 5 out of sight.

Centering the Headings

The process of arranging information so that the information is easier to understand or more pleasing to the eye is called *formatting.* Column width is one aspect of formatting; how cell values line up with the column margins is another. Multiplan normally aligns text at the left edge. With commands from the Format menu, you can align it at the right, or center it instead. Most of the descriptions in column 1 look best and are easiest to read aligned as they are at the left edge of the column, but the headings ASSETS, LIABILITIES, and NET WORTH (rows 1, 30, and 58 in the sample worksheet) will look better centered.

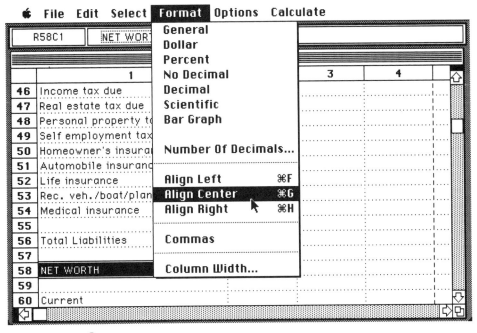

● *To center the three headings in column 1, first select the cells that contain them, then choose Align Center from the Format menu (or press Command-G).*

Choices you make in the Format menu, like most menu choices, affect only the cell or cells that are currently selected. You could select and format the three cells one at a time, but selecting all the cells and formatting them collectively is quicker.

To select nonadjacent cells as a group, you must use the Command key. First, select one of the cells in the ordinary way (point at it and click the mouse button). Then, for each additional cell, point at it, hold down the Command key, and click the mouse button. The Command key tells Multiplan not to deselect the existing selection, but to add to it. When you finish, all the selected cells will be highlighted and you can format them all at once.

Formatting for Numeric Values

The only choices you have for formatting text values, such as those in column 1, are adjusting the column width and aligning text in its cell. But for formatting numeric values, such as those you will enter in column 2, the Format menu provides seven more options: General, Dollar, Percent, No Decimal, Decimal, Scientific, and Bar Graph. The numeric formats table in Figure 8 summarizes their effects. None of the numeric formats affects the value in a cell, only the way Multiplan displays it. Multiplan uses General format unless you specify another.

You can choose to have commas punctuate all numbers on the worksheet that are 1,000 and larger. In addition, Multiplan will display values rounded to the number of decimal places you select—from 0 to 15—for Dollar, Percent, and Decimal formats.

Set the format for a cell or group of cells by selecting the cells to be formatted and then choosing the format options that apply from the Format menu. Do this now for the cells in column 2, before entering the amounts, so you never have to think about them again, no matter how often you reuse the prototype worksheet. None of this formatting causes any immediate visible change in the worksheet, but the effects will show up later when you enter numbers in column 2.

Format	Effect
General	Uses the best precision allowed by the column width; uses scientific format for a number longer than the column width. Samples:
Dollar	Prefixes a number with a dollar sign; puts a negative number in parentheses*. Samples:
Percent	Multiplies a number times 100 and suffixes it with a percent sign*. Samples:
No Decimal	Rounds to the nearest whole number*. Samples:
Decimal	Always shows the number of decimal places set by the Number of Decimals command*. Samples:
Scientific	Expresses a value as a number times 10 raised to some power. Samples:
Bar Graph	Draws a shaded bar (dark gray for positive values, light gray for negative) whose length represents the size of the value[†]. Samples:

General samples:

| 3 | 3000 | 0.03 |
| −3 | −3000 | −0.03 |

Dollar samples:

| $3.00 | $3000.00 | $0.03 |
| ($3.00) | ($3000.00) | ($0.03) |

Percent samples:

| 300.00% | 30000.00% | 3.00% |
| −300.00% | −30000.00% | −3.00% |

No Decimal samples:

| 3 | 3000 | 0 |
| −3 | −3000 | 0 |

Decimal samples:

| 3.00 | 3000.00 | 0.03 |
| −3.00 | −3000.00 | −0.03 |

Scientific samples:

| 3.00E + 00 | 3.00E + 03 | 3.00E − 02 |
| −3.00E + 00 | −3.00E + 03 | −3.00E − 02 |

Bar Graph samples:

*If the value is too long for the cell, Multiplan prints a string of # symbols.

[†]The shortest bar (a line) represents a value of 0.1 and each 0.1 increase in value lengthens the bar a line width.

● *Figure 8. Numeric formats*

● *Select all of column 2, then choose Commas and Decimal from the Format menu.*

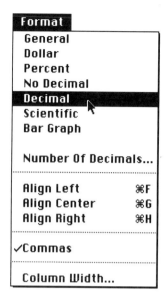

To select a whole column at once, place the pointer over the column number at the top of the worksheet window and click the mouse button. Multiplan highlights the whole column and outlines a single cell with a thin white border. The Decimal format affects only the highlighted cells, but the Commas option affects all cells on the worksheet.

● *Again in column 2, select the cells next to Total Assets and Total Liabilities and all the cells next to the descriptions under NET WORTH. Then choose Dollar from the Format menu.*

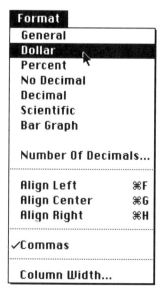

Use the Command key to select the nonadjacent cells that will show totals or net-worth amounts (rows 28, 56, 60, 61, 62, 66, and 67 in column 2 in the sample worksheet). Choosing Dollar from the Format menu overrides the Decimal format set earlier for the whole column and sets the Dollar format for all the selected cells.

● *Select the cells next to Rate of Change and Annual Inflation Rate and then choose Percent from the Format menu.*

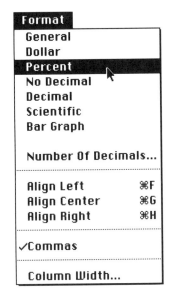

Choosing Percent for the two cells that show percentages (rows 63 and 65 in column 2 in the sample worksheet) overrides the Decimal format previously set for the whole column.

Setting a Precise Column Width

Multiplan's standard column width is 10 digits, which is not enough for dollar amounts in the hundreds of thousands. So you need to widen column 2 to show at least 13 digits.

● *Select column 2 and choose Column Width... from the Format menu. Then, in the dialog box that appears, type the new column width and click the displayed OK button.*

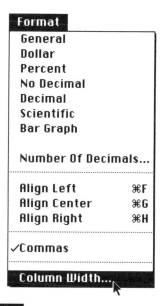

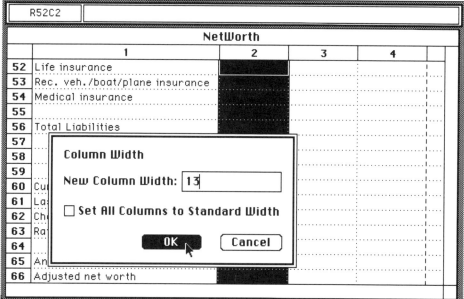

Instead of using the Column Width... command, you can set the size of column 2 by eye, as you did with column 1. Either way, widening column 2 pushes the rest of column 5 out of sight.

Entering Formulas

A cell can contain a formula just as it can contain words or numbers. If the first character in the cell is an equal sign, Multiplan knows the cell contains a formula. Instead of displaying the formula itself on the worksheet, it displays the formula's value.

Operators

Formulas can involve addition, subtraction, multiplication, division, and some other operations. The Multiplan operations table in Figure 9 lists the symbols, or *operators,* that designate the operations Multiplan allows.

Operator	Operation	Precedence*
( )	Grouping	1st
—	Negative number	2nd
%	Percent	3rd
^	Exponentiation	4th
*	Multiplication	5th
/	Division	5th
+	Addition	6th
—	Subtraction	6th
&	Text concatenation	6th
=	Equal	7th
<	Less than	8th
<=	Less than or equal	9th
>	Greater than	10th
>=	Greater than or equal	11th
<>	Not equal	12th

*Operations of equal precedence are performed as encountered, from left to right.

● *Figure 9. Multiplan operations*

If a formula involves more than one operation, Multiplan performs them in a standard order, also shown in the Multiplan operations table. Thus $6 + 4 / 2$ equals 8, not 5, since division takes precedence over addition. Parentheses can overrule the standard order. For example, $(6 + 4) / 2$ equals 5, not 8.

Functions

Formulas can also include *functions,* which are like powerful specialized operators. They perform mathematical and statistical calculations, extract pieces of text, test for true-or-false conditions, and more, thereby deriving new values from existing values. For example, the AVERAGE function computes the average (technically, the arithmetic mean) of two or more numbers; the value of AVERAGE(100,200,300) is 200.

Cell References

A formula must specify not only the operations to perform, but the values on which to perform them. If a value is always the same—a *constant*—you can simply write it in the formula. For example, $=3+4$ is a valid formula that adds two constants and always comes up with the same result, 7.

Formulas become useful when they include references to cells, because the values of cells can change. A formula that adds the values of two cells won't always yield the same result. If the cell values are 3 and 4, their sum will be 7, but if you change the second cell's value to 8, their sum becomes 11.

Multiplan offers a choice of three ways to refer to individual cells. All three rely on the fact that only one cell can occupy the space where a row and column cross. This means you can identify any cell by specifying a row number and a column number. For example, R2C3 refers to the cell where row 2 crosses column 3. This straightforward way of identifying cells is called *absolute reference.*

Any cell can also be specified by its location relative to the currently selected cell. The location is stated as a number of columns to the left ($-$) or right ($+$) and a number of rows up ($-$) or down ($+$) from the currently selected cell. For example, R[-2]C is the cell two rows up in the same column as the currently selected cell, and R[$+9$]C[-1] is the cell nine rows down and one column to the left. This way of referring to cells is called *relative reference.*

In addition, you can name a cell and refer to it by that name. You can also name a whole row, a whole column, or other group of cells. A name must be one word, have no blank spaces or hyphens, and contain no more than 31 characters. It must start with a letter and can include letters, digits, periods, and underscores. The same word with different capitalization is the same name, so ASSETS, Assets, and assets are just three ways to type one name.

If absolute, relative, and name references confuse you, it's probably the terminology, not the concepts. Think of Manhattan, where the Avenues run north-south and the Streets run east-west. Suppose you are standing at the intersection of 50th Street and 6th Avenue. Some tourist bleats, "Excuse me, where's the Oak Bar?" If you say, "59th Street and 5th Avenue," you are using absolute reference. Reply, "Nine blocks north, one block east," and you are using relative reference. Say, "Plaza Hotel" and you are using a name. You might also try to divert the wanderer to your brother-in-law's joint in Queens, a response for which Multiplan has no parallel.

Entering the Total Assets Formula

You enter the individual asset and liability amounts directly, but Multiplan computes seven amounts on the net-worth worksheet from the values of other cells. For each cell that requires a computation, you specify a formula in advance to tell Multiplan which cell values to use and what arithmetic operations to perform on them. The formula to compute Total Assets, for example, tells Multiplan to add up all the individual asset amounts no matter what they may be. It can use absolute, relative, or named cell references, as follows:

$$=SUM(R3C2:R26C2)$$

$$=SUM(R[-25]C:R[-2]C)$$

$$=SUM(Assets)$$

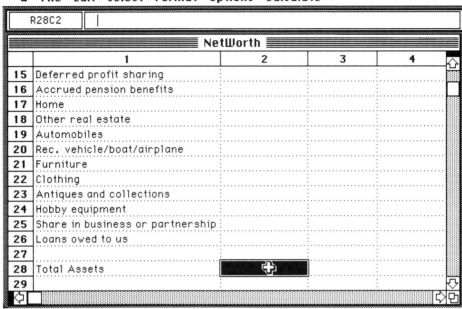

● *Select the cell in column 2 for*
the Total Assets formula.

Pasting Functions

The first part of the Total Assets formula is the word SUM, which names the function that adds up the values of the cells you specify in parentheses. You can type the function name or use the pointer and Edit menu to paste it from a list of available function names.

● *To display a list of function names available, choose Paste Function... from the Edit menu. Use the scroll bar to scan the list for the SUM function. Click it and then click the OK button.*

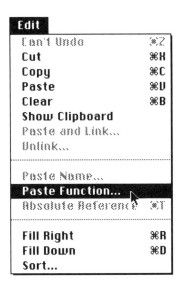

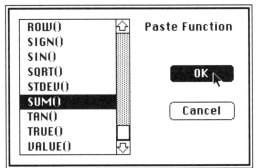

With no typing on your part, the Paste Function... command puts an equal sign, the function name you selected, and a pair of parentheses into the formula bar. The text insertion point moves between the parentheses to show where the next entry will go.

Specifying a Range of Cells

Between the parentheses that follow SUM you specify what you wish summed. You can list numbers and individual cell references (absolute, relative, or named) in any combination; separate the items you list with commas. Your list can also include references to whole rows or columns, partial rows or columns, rectangular cell blocks, and groups of nonadjacent cells. You can type cell references or point them out with the mouse.

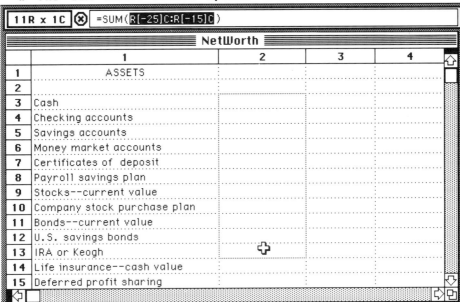

● *Scroll the worksheet so you can see the first asset description and place the pointer next to it in column 2. Press the mouse button and drag the pointer down column 2.*

When you press the mouse button, Multiplan determines the absolute location of the cell under the cross-shaped pointer. It also determines the location of that same cell relative to the currently selected cell (the cell in column 2 next to the Total Assets cell). It displays the absolute reference at the left edge of the formula bar and pastes the relative cell reference into the formula at the text insertion point (between the parentheses).

As you drag the pointer downward, Multiplan adds a colon to the formula, followed by the relative reference for the cell currently under the pointer. The pair of cell references separated by a colon defines either the first and last cells of a partial column or row, or two diagonally opposite corners of a rectangular block of cells that spans several rows and columns. Multiplan outlines the range of cells with a dotted line and, at the left of the formula bar, displays the dimensions of the range instead of a cell reference.

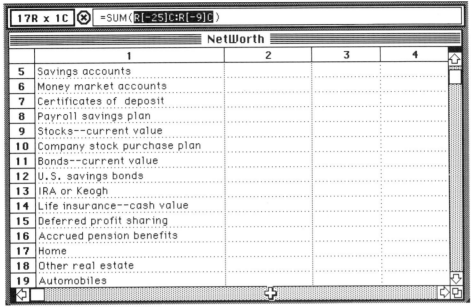

● *Continuing to hold the mouse*
button, extend the range further
down column 2 by dragging
the pointer to the bottom border
of the worksheet window.

Dragging the pointer into the scroll bar at the bottom edge of
the worksheet forces Multiplan to scroll the worksheet up. As
scrolling brings new cells into view, Multiplan incorporates them
into the range of cells to be summed.

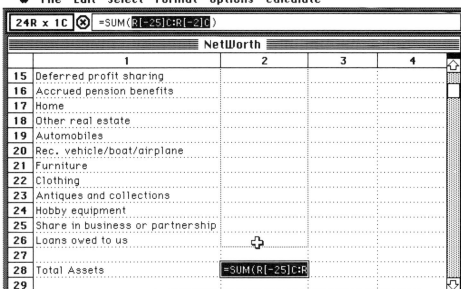

 When the last asset appears in the worksheet window, drag the pointer to the cell on that row in column 2, and release the mouse button.

Releasing the mouse button freezes the range of cells to be summed. Multiplan automatically scrolls the worksheet back to show the first cell in the range.

Pressing the Enter Key

You press the Enter key to enter the formula into the currently selected cell and to tell Multiplan to calculate its value.

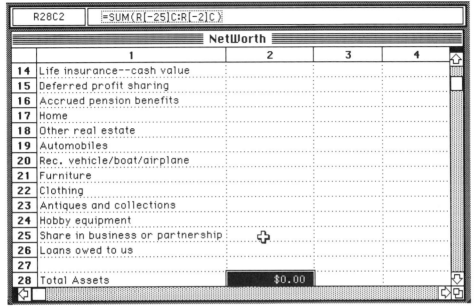

● *Press the Enter key to enter the formula into the cell you have selected for it.*

Multiplan scrolls the worksheet to the cell where the formula resides, and displays the calculated value there. The value appears in dollar format because that's the format you set for the cell earlier.

Entering the Total Liabilities Formula

The formula for Total Liabilities uses the SUM function to add up all the individual liability amounts. The following three versions of the formula use absolute, relative, or named cell references:

$$=SUM(R32C2:R54C2)$$

$$=SUM(R[-24]C:R[-2]C$$

$$=SUM(Liabilities)$$

Copying a Formula

You could use the procedure used for Total Assets to enter the
formula for Total Liabilities. The two formulas are identical
except for the range of cells to be summed. Instead, try copying
the Total Assets formula into the cell in column 2 next to Total
Liabilities and changing it to use absolute cell references.

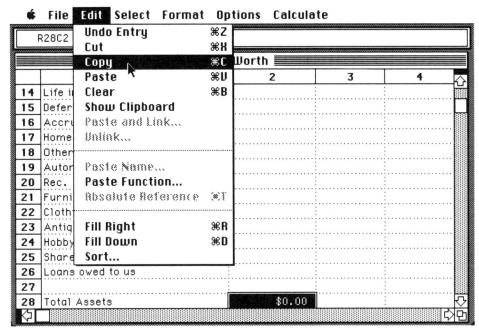

● *Start by selecting the cell that*
contains the Total Assets formula
you wish to copy. Then choose
Copy from the Edit menu.

The Copy command copies the contents of the selected cell
to the Clipboard. You can see the Clipboard by opening its window with the Show Clipboard command from the Edit menu.
In Multiplan, the Clipboard window shows the number of cells
on the Clipboard, but not cell references or cell contents.

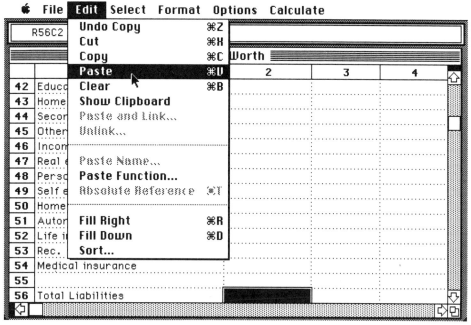

● *Next, select the cell that will contain the Total Liabilities formula and choose Paste from the Edit menu.*

The Paste command puts the contents of the Clipboard (the Total Assets formula) into the currently selected cell and the formula bar. After pasting, the active cell is no longer highlighted. Instead, Multiplan puts a lopsided heavy black cross at the cell's upper left corner. The cross marks the insertion point on the worksheet. If you have any doubt about which is the active cell, just check the cell reference at the left end of the formula bar.

Converting to Absolute Reference

Next you need to replace both relative references to asset cells with absolute references to liabilities.

| R56C2 | ⊗ | =SUM(R[-25]C:R[-2]C) |

● *Use the I-beam pointer to select the first cell reference inside the parentheses in the formula bar.*

To select the first cell reference in the formula bar, place the I-beam pointer on the leftmost letter R in the formula, press the mouse button, drag the pointer to the right as far as the first letter C, and release the mouse button. As a shortcut, you can select an entire cell reference by placing the pointer anywhere over it and double-clicking the mouse button.

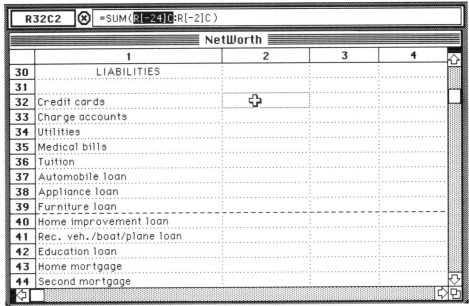

 File   Edit   Select   Format   Options   Calculate

● *Replace the selected cell reference by clicking the cell in column 2 next to the first liability description.*

The instant you click the mouse button, Multiplan replaces the highlighted cell reference with the relative reference for the cell under the pointer. The flashing insertion point has moved to the end of the new cell reference.

● *Choose Absolute Reference from the Edit menu (or press Command-T) to convert the new relative cell reference to an equivalent absolute cell reference.*

The Absolute Reference command converts the selected cell reference. If none is selected, the position of the insertion point designates which reference will be converted.

```
R54C2  ⊗  =SUM(R32C2:R[-2]C )
```

● *Replace the second cell reference with the absolute reference for the cell in column 2 next to the last liability description.*

Replacing the second cell reference in the formula is similar to replacing the first. Start by selecting the second cell reference in the formula. Next, use the scroll bar to bring the last liability description into view and click on the cell in column 2 next to it, replacing the selected cell reference. Then choose Absolute Reference from the Edit menu (or press Command-T).

Pressing the Enter key

When you press the Enter key, Multiplan uses the current values of the cells in the formula to calculate the formula's value.

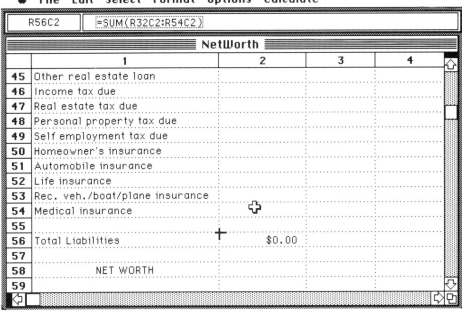

● *When all the changes are done, press the Enter key to put the Total Liabilities formula into its cell.*

Multiplan then displays the value in the currently selected cell according to the format already set for that cell.

Entering the Current Net Worth Formula

The Current Net Worth equals Total Assets minus Total Liabilities. The following three versions of that formula show how to write it using absolute, relative, and named cell references:

$$= R28C2 - R56C2$$

$$= R[-32]C - R[-4]C$$

$$= Total\_Assets - Total\_Liabilities$$

You've entered formulas using absolute and relative cell references. It's time to try a formula with named cell references. First you must name the cells that appear in the formula.

Naming Cells

Since you just finished entering the Total Liabilities formula, its cell should still be selected. If not, use the scroll bars to bring it into view and click on it to select it.

● *To name the currently selected cell, choose Define Name... from the Select menu (or press Command-N). Then enter a name for the selected cell; click the OK button to assign the name.*

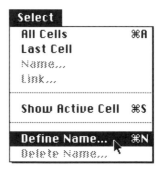

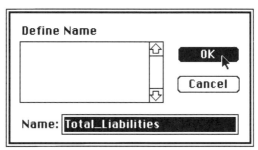

Choosing Define Name... makes a dialog box appear. It contains two windows and two buttons. The upper window lists the names that are already in use on this worksheet, but since there are none yet, the window is empty. In the lower window, you enter a name for the cell currently selected on the worksheet.

If the selected cell contains text, Multiplan proposes the text as the name for the cell. If the selected cell contains no text but the cell to its left or above it contains some, Multiplan proposes that text as the name. If none of those cells contain text or if you dislike the proposed name, you have to type one. Names Multiplan proposes are shortened to 31 characters if necessary, and blank spaces are converted to underscores. In this case, Multiplan has proposed the name Total_Liabilities.

Before clicking the OK button, check the name for accuracy. It must begin with a letter and can contain up to 31 letters, digits, periods, and underscores, but no blank spaces. Make any necessary changes with standard cut-and-paste editing methods.

A long name may not be completely visible in the dialog box. You can use the I-beam pointer to scroll the name left or right. Place the pointer anywhere over the name, press the mouse button, and drag the pointer to either end of the entry box. When the pointer reaches the end of the entry box, the name starts to scroll slowly in the opposite direction. The farther away you move the pointer from the edge of the entry box, the faster the name scrolls.

● *Select the Total Assets formula cell in column 2. Then choose Define Name... from the Select menu and click the OK button to approve the proposed name, Total_Assets.*

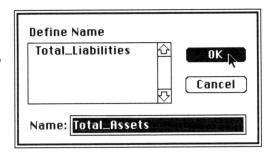

The upper window in the dialog box lists names you have already assigned. You can use any name in the upper window as the basis for the name you are going to give the currently selected cell. Click the name you want to use and it is highlighted and copied into the lower window, where you can edit it. Click the OK button and the edited name is assigned to the currently selected cell on the worksheet (not to the cell that has the unedited version of the name).

Pasting Cell Names

Having assigned names to the cells you are going to use in the Current Net Worth formula, it's time to enter the formula itself. You can either type the names in the formula bar or paste them from a list in a dialog box.

● *Select the cell in column 2 next to Current, choose Paste Name... from the Edit menu, then click Total_Assets and the OK button in the dialog box.*

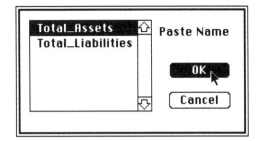

The Paste Name... command displays a dialog box that lists all the names that you have assigned. Clicking Total_Assets highlights the name and clicking the OK button pastes the highlighted name into the formula bar at the text insertion point.

Remember that every formula must begin with an equal sign. If you have not already typed one, Multiplan will furnish an equal sign when it pastes a name or function at the beginning of a formula.

● *Type a minus sign.*

The minus sign specifies subtraction. If you do not type a minus sign or some other arithmetic operator before pasting the second name, Multiplan prefixes the name with a plus sign.

● *Choose Paste Name... from the Edit menu again. In the dialog box, click Total_Liabilities, and then click the OK button.*

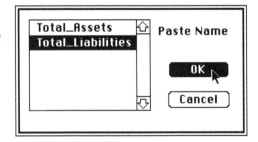

Pressing the Enter Key

When you press the Enter key, Multiplan calculates the Current Net Worth formula (in the formula bar) using the current value of the cells named Total_Assets and Total_Liabilities.

⚅ File Edit Select Format Options Calculate

R60C2	=Total_Assets-Total_Liabilities

NetWorth

	1	2	3	4
50	Homeowner's insurance			
51	Automobile insurance			
52	Life insurance			
53	Rec. veh./boat/plane insurance			
54	Medical insurance			
55				
56	Total Liabilities	$0.00		
57				
58	NET WORTH			
59				
60	Current	$0.00		
61	Last year at this date			
62	Change			
63	Rate of change			
64				

● *Press the Enter key to put the Current Net Worth formula in the selected cell.*

The result appears (in the Dollar format) in the currently selected cell on the worksheet.

Entering the Change Formula

Subtracting your net worth last year at this date from your current net worth tells you how your net worth has changed. Any of the following three versions of the formula will compute the change:

$$= R60C2 - R61C2$$

$$= R[-2]C - R[-1]C$$

$$= Current - Last\_Year$$

** File Edit Select Format Options Calculate**

R62C2	=R[-2]C-R[-1]C

NetWorth

	1	2	3	4
50	Homeowner's insurance			
51	Automobile insurance			
52	Life insurance			
53	Rec. veh./boat/plane insurance			
54	Medical insurance			
55				
56	Total Liabilities	$0.00		
57				
58	NET WORTH			
59				
60	Current	$0.00		
61	Last year at this date			
62	Change	$0.00		
63	Rate of change			
64				

● *In column 2, select the cell for the Change formula, type an equal sign, click the Current value, type a minus sign, click the cell next to Last year at this date, and press the Enter key.*

Typing an equal sign tells Multiplan you are entering a formula. After that, clicking on any cell pastes the relative reference for that cell into the formula at the spot marked by the text insertion point. You must type minus signs and other arithmetic operators as needed. If you forget to type the operator, Multiplan supplies a plus sign in front of the reference for the next cell you click.

Entering the Rate of Change Formula

The formula for Rate of Change calculates the percentage of increase or decrease from last year's net worth to this year's. The rate is equal to the amount of change divided by last year's net worth, as shown in the following three versions of the formula:

$$= R62C2/R61C2$$

$$= R[-1]C/R[-2]C$$

$$= Change / Last\_Year$$

🍎 File Edit Select Format Options Calculate

R63C2	=R[-1]C/R[-2]C

NetWorth

	1	2	3	4
50	Homeowner's insurance			
51	Automobile insurance			
52	Life insurance			
53	Rec. veh./boat/plane insurance			
54	Medical insurance			
55				
56	Total Liabilities	$0.00		
57				
58	NET WORTH			
59				
60	Current	$0.00		
61	Last year at this date	⊕		
62	Change	$0.00		
63	Rate of change	#DIV/0!		
64				

● *In column 2, select the cell for the Rate of change formula. Type an equal sign and click the Change value. Next, type a slash to designate division and click the cell next to Last year at this date. Finally, press the Enter key.*

Multiplan displays the message "#DIV/0!" as the value for the rate of change to advise you that the formula for that cell includes a division by zero. This occurs because the value for last year's net worth, which is the divisor in the Rate of change formula, is zero right now. Later, when you fill in a nonzero amount, the message will be replaced by a number.

Entering the Adjusted Net Worth Formula

Some of the increase in your net worth from one year to the next can be attributed to inflation. For instance, some of your assets are worth more this year than last year because of inflation. If you know the inflation rate for the last year, you can adjust your current net worth for inflation using the following formula:

adjusted net worth = current net worth
/(1 + annual inflation rate)

For example, suppose your current net worth is $110,000 with an annual inflation rate of 10 percent. Using the formula above, your adjusted net worth would be $110,000 / (1 + 0.10), or $110,000 / (1.10), which is $100,000.

Deriving Formulas Yourself

"Swell," you're thinking, "But where do I get the formulas for the worksheets I design myself?" The answer is simple: You find them in a book somewhere. Or, you derive them yourself using common sense and a little algebra. This section describes how you might derive the formula for adjusted net worth. (If you're not interested, skip ahead to the next section.)

Inflation artificially increases your net worth. It stands to reason, then, that your adjusted net worth will be less than your current net worth. In other words, your adjusted net worth equals your current net worth minus some amount attributable to inflation. The following formula says the same thing:

adjusted net worth = current net worth
− inflation amount

Or putting it another way:

current net worth = adjusted net worth
+ inflation amount

This formula contains two things you don't know: adjusted net worth and inflation amount. You have to reduce the number of unknowns from two to one. Then you can use rules of algebra to manipulate the equation so that it calculates the one remaining unknown term. The remaining unknown term must be adjusted net worth, since that's what you're seeking a formula for. So, is there any way to express the inflation amount in terms of the current net worth or adjusted net worth? Yes: The inflation amount equals the annual inflation rate times the adjusted net worth amount. Thus you can replace "inflation amount" in the formula with "annual inflation rate × adjusted net worth," as follows:

$$\text{current net worth} = \text{adjusted net worth} + \text{annual inflation rate} \times \text{adjusted net worth}$$

Now the formula contains just one unknown term, adjusted net worth. (If you don't know the annual inflation rate, you can look it up.) A simple algebraic maneuver changes the formula as follows:

$$\text{current net worth} = \text{adjusted net worth} \times (1 + \text{annual inflation rate})$$

Applying one more rule of algebra produces the final formula:

$$\text{adjusted net worth} = \text{current net worth} / (1 + \text{annual inflation rate})$$

The Multiplan Formula

Expressing the formula for adjusted net worth in terms of the three kinds of cell reference yields the following:

$$= R60C2/(1 + R65C2)$$

$$= R[-6]C/(1 + R[-1]C)$$

$$= \text{Current}/(1 + \text{Inflation\_rate})$$

File   Edit   Select   Format   Options   Calculate

R66C2	=R[-6]C/(1+R[-1]C)

NetWorth

	1	2	3	4
54	Medical insurance			
55				
56	Total Liabilities	$0.00		
57				
58	NET WORTH			
59				
60	Current	$0.00		
61	Last year at this date			
62	Change	$0.00		
63	Rate of change	#DIV/0!		
64				
65	Annual inflation rate			
66	Adjusted net worth	$0.00		
67	Ahead of (behind) inflation			
68				

● *Enter the formula for Adjusted net worth.*

Click the cell in column 2 next to Adjusted net worth to select it. For this formula, you have to type an equal sign, a division operator (slash), parentheses, and the number 1. You can put references to the Current net worth and Annual inflation rate into the formula by clicking the cells. Press the Enter key when you finish the formula.

Entering the Ahead of (Behind) Inflation Formula

By subtracting the Adjusted net worth from the Current net worth, you can determine how well you kept pace with inflation. If the result is zero, then you're even. A positive result means you're ahead and a negative result means you're behind. Use any of the following three versions of the formula:

$$= R60C2 - R66C2$$

$$= R[-7]C - R[-1]C$$

$$= Current - Adjusted$$

⚫ File   Edit   Select   Format   Options   Calculate

R67C2	=R[-7]C-R[-1]C

NetWorth

	1	2	3	4
54	Medical insurance			
55				
56	Total Liabilities	$0.00		
57				
58	NET WORTH			
59				
60	Current	$0.00		
61	Last year at this date			
62	Change	$0.00		
63	Rate of change	#DIV/0!		
64				
65	Annual inflation rate			
66	Adjusted net worth	0.00		
67	Ahead of (behind) inflation	$0.00		
68				

⚫ *Enter the formula for Ahead of (behind) inflation.*

Don't neglect to select the correct cell for the formula. Then type an equal sign, click on the Current net worth amount, type a minus sign, click on the Adjusted net worth amount, and press the Enter key.

Correcting and Changing Formulas

If you make a mistake setting up a formula or wish to change one, you can edit it using standard methods. First, select the erroneous cell to put its contents into the formula bar. Move the pointer into the formula bar, where you can select an insertion point or part of the formula. Then edit by typing, choosing commands from the Edit menu, or clicking and dragging on the worksheet itself to paste in relative cell references. While editing a cell, you can click the Cancel button to restore the cell's original contents. To move the edited version back into the active cell, press the Enter key.

Take a minute after finishing the formulas to save your work on disk again. If the power goes off, you'll be glad you did.

Setting Page Breaks

After you enter the asset and liability amounts, you will probably want to print the worksheet. The printed net-worth statement will look better if you check and adjust the page breaks now. Multiplan indicates a page break in the worksheet window with a line of dashes that is quite easy to distinguish from the dotted lines between rows and columns. You can spot these dashed lines by scrolling through the worksheet. This worksheet is narrow enough to fit across one page, but if it were wider, Multiplan would set page breaks vertically and horizontally.

With standard margins, the whole net-worth statement in the sample worksheet fits on two pages with room to spare. But left alone, Multiplan will put part of the liabilities on page 1 and the rest on page 2. You can force a page break earlier to get all of the liabilities together on page 2.

⌘	File	Edit	Select	Format	**Options**	Calculate

R29C1			

Freeze Titles
✓**Unfreeze Titles**

Set Page Break
~~Remove Page Break~~

Show Formulas
✓**Show Values**

Protect Document...
✓**Unprotect Document...**

Remove Cell Protection
Restore Cell Protection

	1		4
21	Furniture		
22	Clothing		
23	Antiques and collections		
24	Hobby equipment		
25	Share in business or partners		
26	Loans owed to us		
27			
28	Total Assets		
29			
30	LIABILITIES		
31			
32	Credit cards		
33	Charge accounts		
34	Utilities		
35	Medical bills		

● *Set a page break between assets and liabilities by selecting row 29 and then choosing Set Page Break from the Options menu.*

The Set Page Break command draws a page boundary above a selected row, to the left of a selected column, or above and to the left of a selected cell. If you change your mind about a page break you have already set, select the same row, column, or cell again, but this time choose Remove Page Break from the Options menu.

Protecting Your Worksheet Against Changes

Multiplan provides a scheme for protecting a worksheet against accidental changes. You can lock the protection with your secret password to prevent other people from making intentional changes. You might lock a worksheet that calculates sales commissions, for example, to prevent anyone from changing it in your absence.

The Protect Document... command in the Options menu institutes worksheet protection. When you choose it, a dialog box appears, asking you to type a password. Unless you have a specific reason to lock the worksheet with a password, do not type one. Instead, bypass the password lock by typing nothing and clicking the OK button.

Warning: If you must use a password, pick it carefully and make a note of it somewhere. You cannot remove worksheet protection unless you know the password.

Exempting Cells from Protection

Choosing Protect Document... protects every cell on the worksheet. However, you can expressly exempt particular cells in advance by selecting the cells you wish to remain unprotected and choosing Remove Cell Protection from the Options menu. When you protect the worksheet later, those cells you have exempted will not be protected, and you will be able to change their contents.

File   Edit   Select   Format   Options   Calculate

| R65C2 | | |

	NetWorth			
	1	2	3	4
52	Life insurance			
53	Rec. veh./boat/plane insurance			
54	Medical insurance			
55				
56	Total Liabilities	$0.00		
57				
58	NET WORTH			
59				
60	Current	$0.00		
61	Last year at this date			
62	Change	$0.00		
63	Rate of change	#DIV/0!		
64				
65	Annual inflation rate			
66	Adjusted net worth	$0.00		

● *In column 2, select all the cells that will hold individual assets, individual liabilities, last year's net worth, and the inflation rate.*

Start by placing the pointer over the first asset amount in column 2. Press the mouse button and drag the pointer down the column into the bottom scroll bar, forcing the worksheet to scroll up. When the last asset amount comes into view, drag the pointer to it and release the mouse button. Next, place the pointer over the first liability cell. Hold down the Command key to extend the selection, press the mouse button, drag the pointer down to the last liability amount, and release the mouse button. Move the pointer to the last year's net worth amount, hold down the Command key, and click the mouse button. Finally, move the pointer to the inflation rate, hold down the Command key, and click the mouse button.

● *Exempt the selected cells by choosing Remove Cell Protection from the Options menu.*

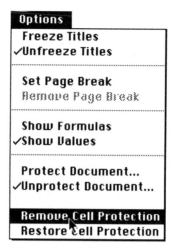

Removing cell protection has no visible effect on the worksheet. You can determine whether a particular cell is protected or not by selecting it and looking at the Options menu. If the Remove Cell Protection command is checked, the cell's protection has been removed. If the Restore Cell Protection command is checked, the cell's protection is intact.

Protecting the Prototype

After exempting the cells into which you will enter amounts, protect the prototype net-worth statement.

Protecting the worksheet removes the grid lines, the row numbers, and the column numbers. Unprotected cells are underlined. You can still select any cell on the worksheet and look at its contents in the formula bar, but you can only enter new contents or change existing contents of unprotected cells. On a protected worksheet, pressing the Enter key advances from one unprotected cell to the next one.

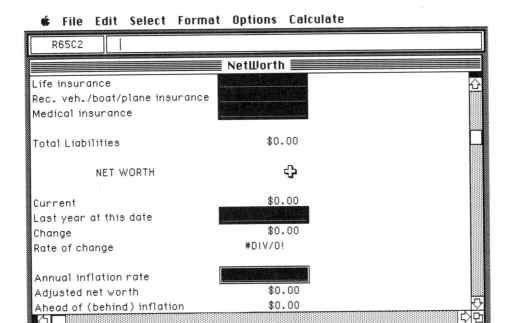

● *Choose Protect Document...*
from the Options menu. Unless
you really need password protec-
tion, bypass it.

Removing Protection

To remove worksheet protection, choose Unprotect Document... from the Options menu. If the worksheet is locked with a password, a dialog box appears asking you to type the password. Multiplan will not remove worksheet protection unless you supply the correct password.

Saving the Finished Prototype

Save the finished worksheet on disk. Whenever you want a complete net-worth statement, you will use a copy of the prototype worksheet as a basis.

● *To save an existing worksheet on disk, choose Save from the File menu.*

The Mac knows which disk a worksheet belongs on. If that disk is not inserted when you choose Save from the File menu, a dialog box tells you to insert the disk before the Mac saves the worksheet.

Since you have saved this worksheet before, the worksheet as it now exists replaces the previous version on the disk. That previous version is gone forever. Multiplan on the Macintosh does not automatically save the last version as a backup.

Multiplan will not let you choose the Save command if you have not yet entered the contents of the formula bar into the currently selected cell. If the Save command is dimmed in the File menu, press the Enter, Return, or Tab key, or click the Cancel button in the formula bar so that you can save your worksheet.

Quitting Multiplan

For best protection against accidentally changing or removing the prototype worksheet, return to the directory window and lock the worksheet icon. After locking, you can start Multiplan again or work with another application. You can even eject the disk, switch off the Macintosh, and take a break.

● *To return to the directory window, choose Quit from the File menu.*

If you changed the worksheet in any way since you last saved it, a dialog box appears, suggesting you save the worksheet again before quitting.

Upon return to the directory window, you will notice several changes. An icon for the new worksheet now appears in the directory window and there is less space available on the disk because of it. Any desk accessories that were open are now closed. Usually only one disk icon remains on the desktop, no matter how many were there prior to opening the application. The remaining disk icon is the one from which you opened Multiplan, and it is now considered the start-up disk.

Locking the Prototype

In the directory window, find and select the icon for the prototype worksheet. Next choose Get Info from the File menu (or press Command-I) and when the information window appears, click its Locked box. Close the information window.

Using the Prototype

When you are ready to calculate your net worth, gather your asset and liability figures. Your net-worth statement is a snapshot of your financial condition at one point in time, so try to gather numbers from about the same date. The end of a quarter or end of the year is usually convenient.

Opening an Existing Worksheet

When you are ready to prepare a complete net-worth statement, you must reopen Multiplan and the existing prototype worksheet. You can open an existing worksheet directly from a directory window by selecting the worksheet icon and choosing Open from the File menu, or by double-clicking the icon.

Opening a worksheet icon implicitly opens Multiplan. The Finder first tries to locate Multiplan on the current disk. Failing that, it looks on the other disks whose icons are on the desktop. If it finds Multiplan on a disk not currently inserted, it ejects the currently inserted disk and tells you to insert the disk it needs. You have to swap disks several times before the worksheet and Multiplan are both open.

If the Finder cannot find Multiplan on any of the disks it knows about, a dialog box tells you so. In that event, you must eject the current disk with the Eject command and insert a disk with Multiplan, thereby making it known to the Finder. Then you can try opening the worksheet again.

After the Finder opens Multiplan, it opens the worksheet you have selected.

The Mini-Finder

You can open existing worksheets from Multiplan instead of from the directory window. If you already have a worksheet on the screen, there cannot be changes pending in the formula bar (the Cancel icon cannot be present). If necessary, either press the Enter key to put the changes into the worksheet or click the Cancel icon to ignore them.

● *To get a list of worksheets you can open from Multiplan, choose Open... from the File menu.*

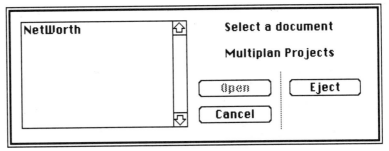

When you choose Open... from Multiplan's File menu, a large dialog box appears. This dialog box, called the *Mini-Finder,* has the Finder's ability to locate and retrieve a worksheet from disk. A window inside the dialog box lists the names of up to seven worksheets. If there are more than seven worksheets on the disk, a scroll bar lets you scroll more names into view.

The Mini-Finder lists the worksheets on only one disk at a
time. To see the names of worksheets on another disk, click the
displayed Eject button and insert the other disk. If your Mac
has an external drive, you can alternate between the internal
and external drives by clicking the displayed Drive button. The
disk name always appears in the Mini-Finder directly above
the Eject button.

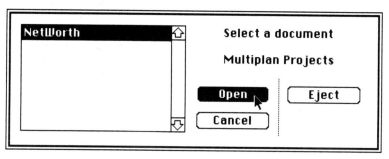

● *To open a worksheet listed in
the Mini-Finder, select it by
clicking its name, then click the
Open button. As a shortcut,
you can double-click the worksheet name.*

Creating a Copy of the Prototype

Before entering any amounts, save a copy of the prototype
worksheet under a new name with the Save As. . . command
from the File menu. Everything works just as if you were saving
the worksheet for the first time. A dialog box appears, in
which you must type the new worksheet name. Buttons displayed in the box allow you to eject the current disk and to
switch between internal and external drives.

After you save the worksheet under its new name, that name replaces the former name in the title bar of the worksheet window. If you subsequently save the worksheet with the Save command from the File menu, it will be saved under that new name. The old version of the worksheet still exists on disk under the old name, of course. You can go back to the old version at any time with the Open command.

It is especially important to create a copy of the prototype now if you did not lock the worksheet as recommended. If you wait until later, you could accidentally choose Save instead of Save As. . . , thereby replacing the prototype with an actual net-worth worksheet. The loss of the prototype would make it more difficult to do another net-worth statement in the future.

Adding and Removing Assets and Liabilities

There may be some assets and liabilities listed in the sample net-worth worksheet that don't pertain to you, and there may be others that do pertain but aren't listed. You can remove the categories you don't need by removing the rows they are on and you can insert new rows for the missing categories. But remember that before you can change the worksheet, you have to unprotect it with the Unprotect Document. . . command from the Options menu. After you make your changes, don't forget to reprotect the worksheet with the Protect Document. . . command.

Inserting Rows

First, identify the categories not included on this worksheet that you need to include in your own net-worth statement.

🍎 File Edit Select Format Options Calculate ▸

	1R		ASSETS			

	NetWorth 4/85				
	1	**2**	**3**	**4**	
31					
32	Credit cards				
33	Charge accounts				
34	Utilities				
35	Medical bills				
36	Tuition				
37	Automobile loan				
⊤	Appliance loan				
38	Furniture loan				
39	Home improvement loan				
40	Rec. veh./boat/plane loan				
41	Education loan				
42	Home mortgage				
43	Second mortgage				
44	Other real estate loan				

● *To insert a row, hold down the Shift key and place the pointer on the row number you want to insert above. Click the mouse button.*

While inserting a row, the pointer changes shape to resemble a miniature row. Multiplan pushes the row you pointed at, and all the rows below it, down. It automatically renumbers the rows and changes the cell references in all the formulas on the worksheet. For example, you might insert a row above Appliance loan (row 38 in the sample net-worth worksheet) so you could list a loan for a piano; the Total Liabilities formula would change as follows:

$$=SUM(R32C2:R55C2)$$

You can insert several rows at once. Place the pointer over the row number you want to insert above, hold down the Shift key, press the mouse button, and drag the pointer toward the bottom of the worksheet. As you drag, blank rows are inserted above the row number you started on. The number of rows that will be inserted when you release the mouse button appears at the left edge of the formula bar. Having created the blank rows, you can select the relevant cells to enter descriptions and amounts.

Don't forget to remove cell protection from column 2 for the new categories.

Removing Rows

Removing rows from the worksheet is just as simple an operation as adding them.

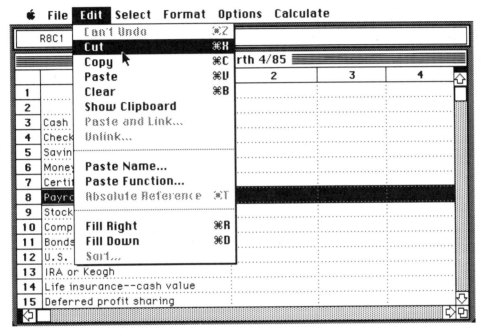

● *To remove a row, place the*
pointer over the row number,
click the mouse button, and
choose Cut from the Edit menu.

Removing a row moves up all the rows below it. Multiplan renumbers the remaining rows and adjusts cell references in formulas automatically. For example, after removing the Payroll savings plan asset (row 8 in the sample net-worth worksheet), the formula for Total Assets changes to this:

$$=SUM(R[-24]C:R[-2]C)$$

You can remove two or more adjacent rows by selecting them all and choosing Cut from the Edit menu. To select a group of rows, place the pointer on the lowest row number, press the mouse button, and drag the pointer down to the highest row number. All the rows are highlighted. Release the mouse button to confirm the selection.

Recalculating Formulas

Multiplan automatically recalculates every formula on the worksheet when you remove or insert a row. A message similar to "Calc: 7" appears at the left edge of the formula bar during calculation. The number in the message tells you how many formulas are being calculated.

Splitting the Worksheet Window

You can keep an eye on more than one part of the worksheet at a time by splitting the worksheet window. For example, you could watch the net-worth amount change in a bottom pane as you enter individual assets and liabilities in a top pane.

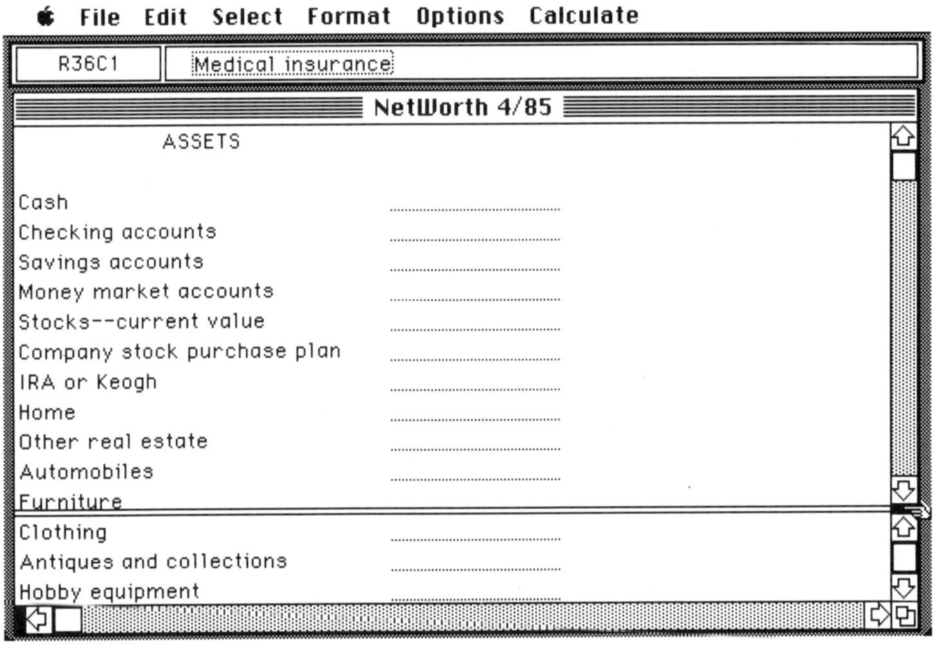

| **File** | **Edit** | **Select** | **Format** | **Options** | **Calculate** |

| R36C1 | | Medical insurance |

NetWorth 4/85

	ASSETS
Cash	
Checking accounts	
Savings accounts	
Money market accounts	
Stocks--current value	
Company stock purchase plan	
IRA or Keogh	
Home	
Other real estate	
Automobiles	
Furniture	
Clothing	
Antiques and collections	
Hobby equipment	

● *Split the worksheet window into a large top pane and small bottom pane by dragging the split bar about three-quarters of the way down the vertical scroll bar.*

To split the worksheet window horizontally, place the pointer on the split bar above the vertical scroll bar. The pointer will look like an index finger. Press the mouse button and drag the split bar down toward the bottom of the scroll bar. As you do, a dotted outline of a crossbar follows along. Drag it down until there are two or three rows below it and release the mouse button. If you change your mind and want to redo the split, drag the split bar, and with it the crossbar, to a new spot.

⊞ File Edit Select Format Options Calculate

R36C1	Medical insurance

NetWorth 4/85

ASSETS

Cash
Checking accounts
Savings accounts
Money market accounts
Stocks--current value
Company stock purchase plan
IRA or Keogh
Home
Other real estate
Automobiles
Furniture

NET WORTH

Current $0.00

● *Scroll NET WORTH into view in the bottom pane.*

A worksheet window split horizontally has two vertical scroll bars, enabling independent vertical scrolling of the two panes. The single horizontal scroll bar scrolls both panes synchronously from side to side.

Entering Amounts

Having a prototype worksheet set up in advance—with cell descriptions in place and all cells protected except those that you must enter—makes preparing a complete net-worth statement a matter of filling in the blanks.

⌘ File   Edit   Select   Format   Options   Calculate

R37C2		

NetWorth 4/85

Medical bills	1,200.00
Automobile loan	14,500.00
Piano loan	2,900.00
Appliance loan	467.33
Home improvement loan	938.28
Home mortgage	71,034.19
Second mortgage	30,100.15
Other real estate loan	12,955.41
Real estate tax due	1,355.00
Homeowner's insurance	535.75
Automobile insurance	880.63
Medical insurance	

NET WORTH	
Current	$95,473.45

● *Enter amounts for individual assets and liabilities, last year's net worth, and the inflation rate.*

Start by selecting the cell in column 2 for the first asset amount and typing its value. Press the Enter key to put the value in the cell. Since the worksheet is protected, the Enter key also advances the selection to the second asset amount. Type a value for it and press the Enter key to advance to the third asset amount. Continue in this vein to the end of the worksheet. You can skip past cells for which you have no entry by pressing the Enter key without typing anything.

In many cases, the amount for one asset or liability is the sum of several numbers. For example, you may have several checking accounts, the balances of which you have to add up so that you can enter the total as an asset. You can add up the amounts on a calculator or have Multiplan do the arithmetic for you. Simply express the amount as a formula, like this:

$$= 378.80 + 357.37 + 903.25 + 466.13$$

When you press the Enter key, Multiplan puts the formula in the cell, but it shows the formula's value on the worksheet.

Correcting or Changing Entries

Using standard editing methods, you can change any amount you have entered. First, select the offending cell to put its contents in the formula bar. There you may either completely retype the contents or edit them. Press the Enter key to put your revisions into the currently selected cell. Click the Cancel button in the formula bar to cancel your revisions and restore the former cell contents.

Suppressing Automatic Calculation

When you change the contents of a cell, Multiplan automatically recalculates all the formulas on the worksheet. You may notice a pause while it does that. The larger and more complex the worksheet, the longer the pause. You can, however, ask Multiplan to skip this step.

● *Choose Manual Calculation from the Calculate menu to suppress automatic formula calculation.*

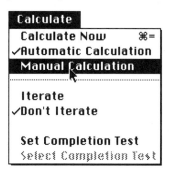

Once you suppress automatic calculation, you have to request formula recalculation as needed by choosing Calculate Now from the Calculate menu (or pressing Command − =). You can reinstate automatic calculation by choosing Automatic Calculation from the Calculate menu.

Analyzing Your Net Worth

After you have prepared net-worth statements for several years in a row, you should start to see a trend in your net worth. If your worth is positive and increasing, you are making progress toward your financial goals. If your worth is positive but static, you are spending too much; you had better look for ways to cut back if you want to get ahead. If your net worth is negative, you've either had a setback or are chronically spending beyond your means. Make austerity plans now so you can eliminate the red ink.

The last few lines of the net-worth worksheet help you see how you've done against inflation. You plug in your net worth from a year ago, and the worksheet computes the percent change between this year and last. Compare that rate to the annual inflation rate. The worksheet uses an inflation rate you enter to compute the amount you are ahead of inflation or behind, as well as to compute your current net worth adjusted for inflation.

Printing Your Net-Worth Statement

Multiplan gives you lots of control over the appearance and quality of printed worksheets. The Page Setup. . . and Print. . . commands in the File menu display dialog boxes full of options for tailoring printed worksheets to fit different situations. You can whip out a quick draft, produce a high-quality report, or print something between those two extremes, like the statement shown in Figure 10.

Whatever options you choose, check that your printer is connected to the Macintosh printer port and is switched on. Insert a fresh sheet of paper, or if you are using continuous paper, set the paper at the top of a new page. With an Imagewriter, make sure the Select lamp on the printer control panel is lit.

April 1, 1985 Personal Net Worth Statement Arlene Hitt

ASSETS

Cash	385.00
Checking accounts	2,105.55
Savings accounts	4,509.87
Money market accounts	27,331.95
Stocks--current value	3,750.00
Company stock purchase plan	1,349.25
IRA or Keogh	2,350.00
Home	142,500.00
Other real estate	21,350.00
Automobiles	16,250.00
Furniture	3,500.00
Clothing	3,000.00
Antiques and collections	4,500.00
Hobby equipment	400.00
Loans owed to us	250.00
Total Assets	$233,531.62

Page 1

Figure 10. Printout of net-worth statement

LIABILITIES

Credit cards	867.13
Charge accounts	289.30
Utilities	35.00
Medical bills	1,200.00
Automobile loan	14,500.00
Piano loan	2,900.00
Appliance loan	467.33
Home improvement loan	938.28
Home mortgage	71,034.19
Second mortgage	30,100.15
Other real estate loan	12,955.41
Real estate tax due	1,355.00
Homeowner's insurance	535.75
Automobile insurance	880.63
Medical insurance	457.38
Total Liabilities	$138,515.55

NET WORTH

Current	$95,016.07
Last year at this date	$80,553.27
Change	$14,462.80
Rate of change	17.95%
Annual inflation rate	8.50%
Adjusted net worth	$87,572.41
Ahead of (behind) inflation	$7,443.66

Reviewing Page Setup

The Page Setup. . . feature of the File menu displays a dialog box that shows the current state of ten page-layout options. You only need to set the options once; the settings are saved on disk with the worksheet the next time you save the worksheet.

Choose Page Setup. . . from the File menu. Select US Letter paper, Tall orientation, no row and column numbers, and no gridlines.

| Paper: | ◉ US Letter | ○ A4 Letter | OK |
| | ○ US Legal | ○ International Fanfold | Cancel |

Orientation: ◉ Tall   ○ Tall Adjusted   ○ Wide

☐ Print Row and Column Numbers

☐ Print Gridlines

Page Header: |

Page Footer:

Left Margin: 0.75   **Right Margin:** 0.75

Top Margin: 1   **Bottom Margin:** 1

Paper

Multiplan can adjust the printed worksheet to fit on any of the four different sizes of paper shown in the following table:

Paper Size	Wide	×	Tall
US Letter	8½	×	11
US Legal	8½	×	14
A4 Letter	8¼	×	11⅔
International Fanfold	8¼	×	12

Continuous paper with sprocket holes is wider than single sheets with the same usable width, usually by 1 inch. For example, continuous US Letter measures 9½ inches wide by 11 inches tall, but after subtracting an inch for the sprocket holes on either side, the usable width is 8½ inches.

Orientation

For normal upright printing, with the top line at the top of the page, choose Tall orientation. For sideways printing, with the top line printed down the right side of the page, choose Wide orientation. In Multiplan, Tall Adjusted orientation produces the same result as Tall.

Page Header and Page Footer

Multiplan can print a one-line *page header* at the top of every page and a one-line *page footer* at the bottom of every page. Headers and footers are also called *running heads.* The header is printed a half-inch from the top of the page; the footer a half-inch from the bottom edge. They have no effect on the size of the top or bottom margins.

Paper: ◉ US Letter ○ A4 Letter   **OK**
        ○ US Legal   ○ International Fanfold
Orientation: ◉ Tall   ○ Tall Adjusted   ○ Wide   [Cancel]
☐ Print Row and Column Numbers
☐ Print Gridlines

Page Header: `&LApril 1, 1985&CPersonal Net Worth Statement&RArle`

Page Footer: `&L&D &T&RPage &P`

Left Margin: `0.75`   Right Margin: `0.75`
Top Margin: `1`   Bottom Margin: `1`

● *As a page header, type "&LApril 1, 1985&CPersonal Net Worth Statement&RArlene Hitt." As a page footer, type "&L&D &T&RPage &P." Leave the margins unchanged. Then click the displayed OK button.*

A long header or footer will not be visible all at once in the Page Setup dialog box. You can use the I-beam pointer to scroll the text of the running head left or right within the entry box. To do that, place the pointer anywhere over the running-head text, press the mouse button, and drag the pointer to either end of the entry box. When the pointer reaches the end of the entry box, the running-head text starts to scroll slowly in the opposite direction. The farther away you move the pointer from the edge of the entry box, the faster the text scrolls.

In addition to regular text, you can include special commands to have Multiplan print the current date, time, or page number in the header or footer. You can also embed special commands to align parts of a running head at the left edge, right edge, or center of the page. The following commands are available:

Command	Effect
&L	Align the text that follows at the left margin
&C	Center the text that follows
&R	Align the text that follows at the right margin
&P	Print the page number
&D	Print the current date
&T	Print the current time

Margins

Standard top and bottom margins are 1 inch each; standard left and right margins are ¾ inch each. On an 8½- by 11-inch sheet of paper, the standard margins leave a 7- by 9-inch space for rows and columns of the worksheet. By enlarging the margins, you reduce the number of worksheet rows or columns that fit on a page. By shrinking the margins, you increase the number of rows or columns that fit on a page.

If the worksheet is narrower than the space allowed by the side margins, Multiplan centers it between them. In other words, it automatically widens both margins by the same amount. For example, the side margins on the net-worth statement end up about 1 inch each, not the ¾-inch set in the Page Setup dialog box. The right margin looks wider because Multiplan includes columns 3 and 4, which are blank, on the page with columns 1 and 2. In fact, you could center the net-worth statement by setting a page break between columns 2 and 3 (select column 3 and choose Set Page Break from the Options menu) before printing.

Side margins for the header and footer are always at least a quarter-inch less than the margins for the worksheet itself. Because Multiplan uses a proportionally spaced font, the number of characters that fits between the running head margins varies, but 90 characters is average. If you type more header or footer text than will fit on one line, Multiplan prints the center 8 inches, lopping off an equal amount of text from the beginning and the end.

Printing the Worksheet

The Print. . . feature of the File menu offers a choice of print quality and lets you specify which part of the worksheet to print, how many copies to make, and what style of paper you are going to use.

Choose Print. . . from the File menu. Select High quality, All pages, 1 copy, and Cut Sheet paper feed. Click the OK button to start printing.

Draft quality uses a high-speed font to quickly print a trial copy of a worksheet. Most special letters and symbols that you type with the aid of the Option key cannot be printed in draft quality, though the Imagewriter does make as many intelligent substitutions as possible.

Draft quality is not available if you choose Wide orientation (sideways printing) during page setup.

Standard- and high-quality printing both reproduce a displayed worksheet accurately and completely. Standard quality is about half as fast as draft quality and more than twice as fast as high quality. However, standard-quality characters are not nearly as dark and fully formed as high-quality characters.

Your choice of paper and the condition of your ribbon also affect print quality. A heavyweight, rag-content, rough-finish paper works best.

Interrupting Printing

Before Multiplan starts printing in standard or high quality, it takes a few seconds to copy the worksheet into a scratchpad area on disk. You cannot interrupt that process, but once printing begins you can cancel it by pressing the Command and Period keys simultaneously. When you do, Multiplan stops sending information to the Imagewriter, but printing does not cease immediately. First, the Imagewriter prints the residual information it has already received and stored in its own memory. This may take several seconds.

Printing from the Directory Window

You can print one or more Multiplan worksheets directly from a directory window. All you do is select them and choose Print from the File menu. The worksheets are printed one after the other in a sequence determined by the arrangement of the icons in the directory window. The Finder starts with the worksheet whose icon is located nearest the upper left corner of the directory window. After that one is printed, the Finder then proceeds across the window, then down to the next row of icons, across it from left to right, and so on.

For each worksheet you print from the directory window, page setup and print options are set individually. Most of the settings in effect the last time a worksheet was saved are used automatically. But regardless of previous settings, you always get one copy of all pages of each worksheet you selected.

In order to print a Multiplan worksheet, Multiplan must be present. If the Finder cannot locate it on the currently inserted disk, it checks the other disks whose icons are on the desktop. If Multiplan is on one of them, the Finder tells you to insert that disk. You may have to swap disks several times before printing is finished. If the Finder cannot locate Multiplan anywhere, it tells you so. In that event, you can eject the current disk, insert a disk with Multiplan, eject it, reinsert the worksheet disk, and try printing again.

You can cancel the printing of the current Multiplan worksheet by pressing the Command and Period keys at the same time. Multiplan advances the paper to the end of the page and begins printing the next worksheet you selected, if any.

Saving the Complete Net-Worth Statement

If you have not yet saved this particular net-worth worksheet, choose Save As... from the File menu; give the worksheet a unique name so it doesn't replace an existing worksheet. If you have already saved this worksheet, choose Save from the File menu to replace the previous version with the current version.

Beginning a New Worksheet

Once you're using Multiplan, you can start a new Multiplan worksheet without returning to the directory window. There cannot be changes pending in the formula bar (the Cancel icon should not be present). If necessary, either press the Enter key to put the changes into the worksheet currently on the screen or click the Cancel icon to ignore them.

● *To open a new worksheet from Multiplan, choose New from the File menu.*

If you changed the worksheet in any way since you last saved it, a dialog box appears, suggesting you save the worksheet again before starting a new one.

Summary

The net-worth worksheet presented in this chapter served as a vehicle for exploring some of Multiplan's features. You should now know how to:

- Start and quit Multiplan.

- Open and save new and existing worksheets on disk.

- Select cells singly, in blocks, and in odd-shaped groups.

- Adjust column width.

- Cut-and-paste cells.

- Align cell contents at the left, right, or center of the cell.

- Punctuate numbers with commas.

- Set numeric formats.

- Type and edit descriptions, numbers, and formulas.

- Paste function names into formulas from a list of names.

- Name cells.

- Paste cell names into formulas from a list of names.

- Enter formulas with relative, absolute, or named cell reference.

- Set artificial page breaks.

- Protect a worksheet.

- Exempt cells from protection.

- Remove and insert rows.

- Split the worksheet window.

■ Print the worksheet.

■ Suppress and reinstate automatic calculation.

Multiplan has many more features than the ones discussed in depth in this chapter. Some were mentioned in passing; others you have to discover yourself by perusing the menus and the Help pages incorporated in the About Multiplan. . . feature of the Apple menu. These additional features allow you to:

■ Remove and insert columns.

■ Cut-and-paste rows and columns.

■ Repeatedly recalculate the worksheet (called *iteration*).

■ Link values from one worksheet to another.

■ Freeze rows at the top and columns at the left of the worksheet.

■ Show formulas on the worksheet instead of values.

■ Set the number of digits displayed after the decimal point.

■ Select all cells.

■ Select the last cell on the worksheet.

■ Automatically scroll the currently selected (active) cell into view.

■ Duplicate a description, number, or formula down or across a selected range of cells.

■ Sort rows according to a selected column or part of a column.

Many of the features not covered in this chapter appear in worksheets elsewhere in this book. Those worksheets include a travel and entertainment account, a stock portfolio, a fee analysis, a sales commissions report, a budget, a wine-cellar inventory, an early loan payoff, and a profit study for the sale of your home.

More Projects for Work and Play

Part Three

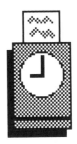

Nine
To Five

● *Get ideas from this collection of thirteen MacWrite, MacPaint, and Multiplan projects for your own job, profession, or business.*

The projects in this chapter show you how to design circulars, advertisements, announcements, analysis worksheets, and accounting worksheets. Be sure not to miss the written descriptions that accompany the projects. Most of them contain valuable tips for getting more out of MacWrite, MacPaint, and Multiplan. You'll probably find these project ideas more valuable if you're already familiar with the applications used to create them. In case you're not, Part Two of this book explains each application in detail.

Bob and Ray's Flier

My partner Bob and I have a small, independent painting service that we run out of his mother's basement. To drum up some business, Bob prepared a flier with MacPaint and I sent it out to all the names on a rented mailing list.

Bob started the flier by drawing the large paint brush. He used the hollow, rounded-corner rectangle with the widest line setting to outline the base of the brush. Drawing the handle required the hollow-rectangle and hollow-oval tools, plus the eraser to remove surplus lines. He used the straight-line tool, constrained by the Shift key to draw vertical lines, to draw a couple of the bristles. Then he lassoed those bristles and duplicated them repeatedly with the help of the Option key. He used the straight-line tool with two different line widths to draw the borders.

All the text is in the Athens font. The font size and style of the headline (Bob and Ray) is 36-point underlined bold shadow. The line under that is 18-point bold outline shadow. The seven bulleted items are 18-point bold. Bob did not type the bullets themselves. He drew one using the filled oval, then he selected it, and with the Shift and Option keys, he dragged a duplicate bullet straight down to each of the next six items on the list. The size and style for our slogan is also 18-point bold. The phone number for free estimates is 18-point bold outline shadow.

The swath of light gray "paint" over the headline type puzzled me at first. I figured Bob must have lassoed the type, cut it to the Clipboard, drawn the "paint," and pasted the text back in place. When I asked him if I was right, he laughed and said my method would leave the type solid white inside, not gray. His own method was much simpler. He selected the gray pattern, held down the Command key, and drew a borderless, filled rectangle right over the text. Instead of covering the letters, the pattern blended with them like a watercolor wash.

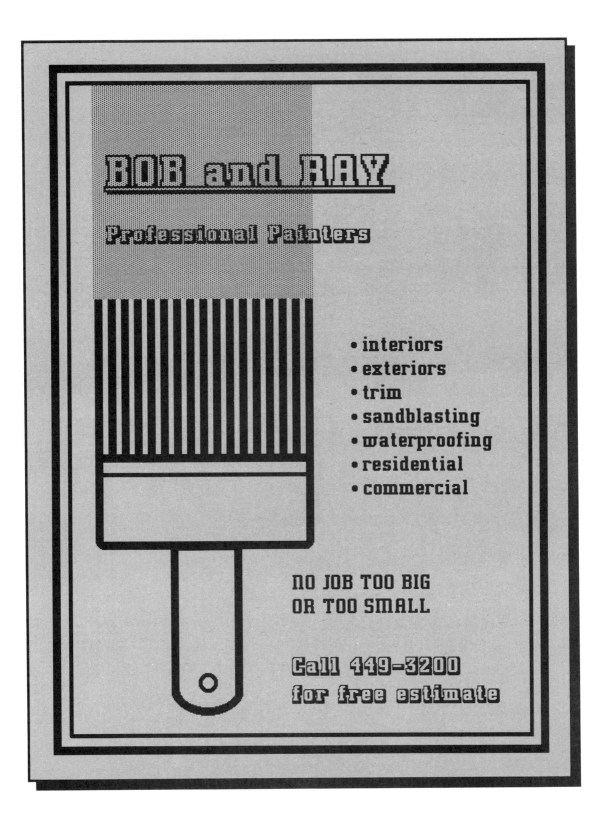

Fee Analysis

I am a hydraulics engineer considering going into business for myself. I developed a Multiplan worksheet that figures the daily and hourly billing rate I must charge in order to make a profit on the business, pay myself a salary, pay my overhead expenses, and cover the slack time when I'm between jobs. I also plan to use this same worksheet to re-evaluate my billing rate as my objectives and expenses change.

To use the worksheet, I enter the number of days I want to work each week, the number of holidays and vacation days I plan to take, the number of sick days I want to allow for, and a percentage that expresses the amount of time I expect to be out beating the bushes for work. From these factors, the worksheet computes the number of days I will work in a year. Next, I enter the amount I want to earn personally and the amount of profit, as a percent of gross income, that I want the business to make. After that, I enter an average monthly amount for each of several expenses.

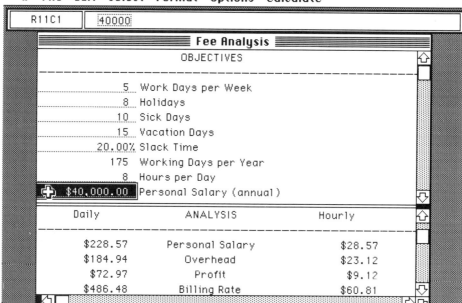

How It Works

The worksheet multiplies each monthly expense estimate by 12 to get the annual equivalents. The total of those amounts equals the total annual overhead. Dividing that amount by the number of working days calculated earlier computes a daily overhead amount. Similarly, dividing my desired salary by the number of working days computes a daily salary. From these two amounts and the profit rate I entered, the worksheet calculates the amount I need to charge for business profit. The total daily billing rate is simply the sum of the daily salary, daily overhead, and daily profit. The total hourly billing rate equals the daily rate divided by the number of hours I said I would work each day.

I used the ROUND or INT function where necessary to round the result of a calculation to match the number of decimal places with which the result is displayed. Otherwise, the sum of the actual values might not equal the sum you would get by adding up the displayed values.

The horizontal lines on rows 1, 3, 14, 15, 30, and 32 are generated by the formula $=REPT(" - ",55)$ in column 1 of each row. The character in quotes is not a regular hyphen, but a dash typed with the Shift-Option-Hyphen keystroke.

Formulas

Row 9, Column 1:

Working Days $= INT(Days\ per\ Week \times 52 \times (1 - Slack\ Time)$
$- Holidays - Sick\ Days - Vacation\ Days)$

R9C1	=INT(R[-5]C*52*(1-R[-1]C)-R[-4]C-R[-3]C-R[-2]C)

Rows 17 to 26, Column 3:

Yearly Overhead = Monthly Overhead $\times 12$

R17C3	=RC[-2]*12

Row 28, Columns 1 and 3:

Total Overhead $= SUM(Office\ Rent : Misc)$

R28C1	=SUM(R[-11]C:R[-2]C)

Row 33, Column 1:

Daily Salary = ROUND(*Annual Salary* ÷ *Working Days*, 2)

R33C1	=ROUND(R[-22]C/R[-24]C,2)

Row 34, Column 1:

Daily Ovhd = ROUND(*Yearly Total Ovhd* ÷ *Working Days*, 2)

R34C1	=ROUND(R[-6]C[+2]/R[-25]C,2)

Row 35, Column 1:

Daily Profit = ROUND((*Daily Salary* + *Daily Ovhd*) × *Profit Rate* ÷ (1 − *Profit Rate*), 2)

R35C1	=ROUND((R[-2]C+R[-1]C)*R[-23]C/(1-R[-23]C),2)

Row 36, Column 1:

Daily Billing = *Daily Salary* + *Daily Ovhd* + *Daily Profit*

R36C1	=R[-3]C+R[-2]C+R[-1]C

Row 33, Column 3:

Hourly Salary = ROUND(*Daily Salary* ÷ *Hours per Day*, 2)

R33C3	=ROUND(RC[-2]/R10C1,2)

Row 34, Column 3:

Hourly Ovhd = ROUND(*Daily Ovhd* ÷ *Hours per Day*, 2)

R34C3	=ROUND(RC[-2]/R10C1,2)

Row 35, Column 3:

Hourly Profit = ROUND(*Daily Profit* ÷ *Hours per Day*, 2)

R35C3	=ROUND(RC[-2]/R10C1,2)

Row 36, Column 3:

Hourly Billing = *Hourly Salary* + *Hourly Ovhd* + *Hourly Profit*

R36C3	=R[-3]C+R[-2]C+R[-1]C

FREE-LANCE FEE ANALYSIS

OBJECTIVES

5	Work Days per Week
8	Holidays
10	Sick Days
15	Vacation Days
20.00%	Slack Time
175	Working Days per Year
8	Hours per Day
$40,000.00	Personal Salary (annual)
15.00%	Business Profit

Monthly	OVERHEAD	Yearly
$800.00	Office Rent	$9,600.00
$80.00	Gas/Electricity	$960.00
$125.00	Phones	$1,500.00
$667.00	Payroll	$8,004.00
$125.00	Office Equipment	$1,500.00
$100.00	Office Supplies	$1,200.00
$100.00	Postage	$1,200.00
$150.00	Insurance	$1,800.00
$300.00	Promotion	$3,600.00
$250.00	Misc	$3,000.00
$2,697.00	Total	$32,364.00

Daily	ANALYSIS	Hourly
$228.57	Personal Salary	$28.57
$184.94	Overhead	$23.12
$72.97	Profit	$9.12
$486.48	Billing Rate	$60.81

Phyllis Tien Map

People contact the gallery from all over the country looking for unique art, and most express an interest in visiting the gallery personally. We're a little off the beaten track here in Gunsight, so I prepared a map to the gallery using MacPaint. I even found space in the lower right corner of the map for a short blurb about our next show.

All the roads were done with a small square brush. The county roads and side streets are one of the standard, medium gray patterns, but Route 66 is a custom-made pattern. This pattern automatically provided a center line for the highway, but it also put an extra broken line at the edge of the roadway. I got rid of it with the eraser.

I constructed the road signs at the side of the road and dragged them into place. For each sign, I outlined the sign first, with one of the hollow-shape tools. Then I typed the text in 9-point plain Geneva, lassoed it, and dragged it into the empty sign.

I drew most of the decorations freehand using the single-dot brush and pencil, with plenty of detail work in FatBits. The cacti are identical. I drew one, lassoed it, and duplicated it five times with the Option key. Lizard Lake was done with the kidney-shaped tool that draws filled free-form shapes (the wave pattern it's filled with is custom-made). Also, I used the rectangle-drawing tool to build the gas station, post office, church, and gallery buildings. The skull and flag were done freehand in FatBits, along with any necessary touching up.

Most of the text is 9-point plain Geneva. However, the letters for the Last Gas sign are my own FatBits creations. The gallery name is 12-point bold outline New York, and the address and phone number are 9-point bold, also New York.

I wanted to get a shadow behind the box in the lower right corner. First, I lassoed the box and chose Copy from the Edit menu, putting a copy of the box on the Clipboard. Then, I picked the solid black pattern in the pattern palette and chose Fill from the Edit menu; this made the box solid black. After that, I chose Paste from the Edit menu to get a copy of the original box from the Clipboard. Finally, I dragged that copy of the original box over the black box, leaving just the shadow showing on two sides.

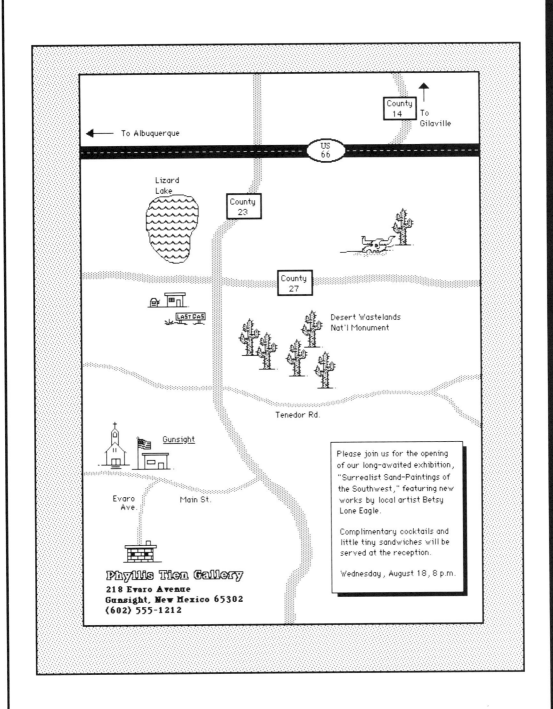

County 14
To Gilaville

To Albuquerque

US 66

Lizard Lake

County 23

County 27

Desert Wastelands Nat'l Monument

LAST GAS

Tenedor Rd.

Gunsight

Evaro Ave.

Main St.

Please join us for the opening of our long-awaited exhibition, "Surrealist Sand-Paintings of the Southwest," featuring new works by local artist Betsy Lone Eagle.

Complimentary cocktails and little tiny sandwiches will be served at the reception.

Wednesday, August 18, 8 p.m.

Phyllis Tien Gallery
218 Evaro Avenue
Gunsight, New Mexico 65302
(602) 555-1212

Sales-Commission Schedule

Our company has a fairly simple sales-commission schedule, so it was easy for me to set up a worksheet to compute the monthly commissions. We pay commission at higher rates for higher sales volumes. Salespeople get a 1 percent commission on the first $10,000, 1.5 percent on the next $10,000, 2.25 percent on the next $15,000, 3.5 percent on the next $15,000, and 6 percent on everything above that.

To set up this worksheet, I started by typing the headings across row 1. Next, I typed the names of the salespeople, last name first so that the Sort feature could later arrange them alphabetically. After that, I set up the commission table to the right of and well below the main report. I put the commission schedule below the list of salespeople so it would not be disrupted when I rearranged the list alphabetically. Putting the commission schedule to the right of the main report lets me collapse each of its four columns to a width of zero, making the whole schedule invisible. Then, protecting the worksheet with the Protect Document feature prevents others from seeing our commission rates.

The Commission Schedule

The commission schedule itself consists of a title, some column headings, and four columns by five rows of numbers. The first column of the table, which is labeled Breakpoint, lists the various breakpoints at which the commission rate changes. The second column, labeled Rate, lists the rate that takes effect when sales equal or exceed the matching breakpoint. The third column, labeled Minimum, shows the minimum commission amount that will be due at each breakpoint. The last column, labeled Hurdle, lists a hurdle for each breakpoint: The top rate at a breakpoint is paid only on the amount of sales that clears the hurdle. I enter the breakpoint values, rate values, first minimum amount, and first hurdle amount at the keyboard. Formulas compute the rest of the minimum and hurdle amounts.

I named three parts of the commission schedule for use with the LOOKUP function, which appears several times in the commission formula for each salesperson. By using the appropriate name, I have the LOOKUP function determine the proper commission rate, minimum commission amount, or sales hurdle for a particular sales amount. The name Rate refers to the two left-hand columns (columns 6 and 7 in rows 29 through 33 on the worksheet). Minimum covers the three leftmost columns (columns 6, 7, and 8 in rows 29 through 33 on the worksheet). Hurdle encompasses all four columns (columns 6 through 9 in rows 29 through 33 on the worksheet).

The Commission Formula

Having set up the table and named it, I entered the formula that computes the commission amount. Since the formula is the same for all salespeople, I only entered it for the first one, then used the Fill Down feature to copy it down column 3 for the other salespeople.

Using the Worksheet

To use the worksheet, I clear any old sales amounts from column 2, add new names to column 1, and enter the current sales amounts in column 2. Then I highlight the names in column 1, sort in ascending order, and print a copy of the resulting alphabetized report. Then I print a report without the grid or row and column numbers for the boss.

I have to be careful not to put any names on the rows occupied by the commission schedule. The one time I did, the schedule got rearranged when I sorted alphabetically, mixing up all the commission calculations. The Undo Sort feature saved the day.

Formulas

Rows 3 through 19, Column 3:

Commission = ROUND(LOOKUP(*Sales, Rate*)
$\qquad$ × (*Sales* − LOOKUP(*Sales, Hurdle*)), 2)
$\qquad$ + LOOKUP(*Sales, Minimum*)

R3C3	=ROUND(LOOKUP(RC[-1],Rate)*(RC[-1]-LOOKUP(RC[-1],Hurdle)) ,2)+LOOKUP(RC[-1],Minimum)

Drake Inc. Sales and Commissions

	1	2	3	4	5
1	Salesperson	Sales	Commission	Avg. Rate	Pct. Sales
2					
3	Baldwin, A	$47,587.06	$1,028.05	2.2%	7.8%
4	Beauty, R	$49,863.30	$1,107.72	2.2%	8.2%
5	Courtlands, V	$37,750.00	$683.75	1.8%	6.2%
6	Delicious, G	$24,110.00	$342.48	1.4%	4.0%
7	Golden, S	$84,680.58	$3,193.33	3.8%	13.9%
8	Gravenstein, P	$11,503.40	$122.55	1.1%	1.9%
9	Greening, D	$42,480.70	$849.32	2.0%	7.0%
10	Imperial, Y	$27,538.27	$419.61	1.5%	4.5%
11	Jonathan, T	$19,503.25	$242.55	1.2%	3.2%
12	MacIntosh, J	$19,207.31	$238.11	1.2%	3.2%
13	Pippin, M	$32,221.29	$524.98	1.6%	5.3%
14	Roman, N	$4,165.98	$41.66	1.0%	0.7%
15	Smith, G	$58,207.14	$1,604.93	2.8%	9.6%
16	Spys, N	$26,724.15	$401.29	1.5%	4.4%
17	Stayman, R	$56,291.19	$1,489.97	2.6%	9.3%
18	Wealthy, S	$22,671.39	$310.11	1.4%	3.7%
19	Winesap, B	$43,652.11	$890.32	2.0%	7.2%
20					
21					
22					
23					
24					
25					
26					
27	TOTALS	$608,157.12	$13,490.73	2.2%	100.0%
28					
29					
30					
31					
32					
33					
34					
35					
36					
37					
38					
39					
40					

Drake Inc. Sales and Commissions

	6	7	8	9	10
1					
2					
3					
4					
5					
6					
7					
8					
9					
10					
11					
12					
13					
14					
15					
16					
17					
18					
19					
20					
21					
22					
23					
24					
25		SALES COMMISSION SCHEDULE			
26					
27	Breakpoint	Rate	Minimum	Hurdle	
28					
29	0.00	1.00%	0.00	0.00	
30	10,000.01	1.50%	100.00	10,000.00	
31	20,000.01	2.25%	250.00	20,000.00	
32	35,000.01	3.50%	587.50	35,000.00	
33	50,000.01	6.00%	1,112.50	50,000.00	
34					
35					
36					
37					
38					
39					
40					

Rows 3 through 19 and 27, Column 4:

Avg. Rate = Commission ÷ Sales

R3C4	=RC[-1]/RC[-2]

Rows 3 through 19, Column 5:

Pct. Sales = Sales ÷ Total Sales

R3C5	=RC[-3]/R27C2

Row 27, Columns 2 and 3:

Total Sales = SUM(First Salesperson : Last Salesperson)

R27C2	=SUM(R[-25]C:R[-1]C)

Rows 30 through 33, Column 8:

Minimum = Previous Minimum + ROUND(Previous Rate
× (Hurdle − Previous Hurdle), 2)

R30C8	=R[-1]C+ROUND(R[-1]C[-1]*(RC[+1]-R[-1]C[+1]),2)

Rows 30 through 33, Column 9:

Hurdle = Breakpoint − 0.01

R30C9	=RC[-3]-0.01

Drake Inc. Sales and Commissions

Salesperson	Sales	Commission	Avg. Rate	Pct. Sales
Baldwin, A	$47,587.06	$1,028.05	2.2%	7.8%
Beauty, R	$49,863.30	$1,107.72	2.2%	8.2%
Courtlands, V	$37,750.00	$683.75	1.8%	6.2%
Delicious, G	$24,110.00	$342.48	1.4%	4.0%
Golden, S	$84,680.58	$3,193.33	3.8%	13.9%
Gravenstein, P	$11,503.40	$122.55	1.1%	1.9%
Greening, D	$42,480.70	$849.32	2.0%	7.0%
Imperial, Y	$27,538.27	$419.61	1.5%	4.5%
Jonathan, T	$19,503.25	$242.55	1.2%	3.2%
MacIntosh, J	$19,207.31	$238.11	1.2%	3.2%
Pippin, M	$32,221.29	$524.98	1.6%	5.3%
Roman, N	$4,165.98	$41.66	1.0%	0.7%
Smith, G	$58,207.14	$1,604.93	2.8%	9.6%
Spys, N	$26,724.15	$401.29	1.5%	4.4%
Stayman, R	$56,291.19	$1,489.97	2.6%	9.3%
Wealthy, S	$22,671.39	$310.11	1.4%	3.7%
Winesap, B	$43,652.11	$890.32	2.0%	7.2%
TOTALS	$608,157.12	$13,490.73	2.2%	100.0%

Bernini's Wine Shop Circular

We at Bernini's Wine Shop send out a circular every month to the 300 people on our mailing list. We print one copy of the circular on the Imagewriter, take it to our local printer, and have 750 copies duplicated every month. We put the extra copies next to the cash register for customers to carry away.

The drawings at the top and bottom of the circular we created once, using MacPaint. The top drawing consists of the bottle, the grapes, and the shop name and address; the bottom drawing consists of the goblet and the lines on either side of it. When we finished the drawings, we copied them to the Scrapbook. We reuse both of the drawings every month without change, copying them one at a time from the Scrapbook via the Clipboard to a new MacWrite document. Then, using MacWrite, we type a new list of featured wines between the two drawings.

The first time we tried to copy the drawings into a MacWrite document, we couldn't find them anywhere in the Scrapbook. Then we remembered that each disk has its own Scrapbook. So we renamed the Scrapbook File icon inside the System Folder on the MacWrite disk Old Scrapbook File, and copied the Scrapbook File icon from the MacPaint disk to the MacWrite disk.

The Drawings

We started the top part of the circular by drawing the grapes, but you could just as easily start with the bottle or the name and address. We used the filled-oval drawing tool with a medium gray fill pattern to draw one grape. Then we lassoed that grape, made duplicates of it with the help of the Option key, and dragged each duplicate into the bunch. We drew the leaves freehand using the single-dot brush, touched them up in FatBits, and filled them with a medium gray color. If you look closely, you'll see where we tried to show the veins in the leaves.

The bottle started out as two hollow rectangles, one for the neck and the other for the body. In FatBits, we added shoulders, rounded the corners at the bottom of the bottle, and drew a lip and a cork on top of the neck. We shaded the bottle with various widths of the round brush using black, white, and three shades of gray.

Bernini's
Wine Shop

**3447 Oak Street
Albany, California
(415) 555-1212**

May's featured wines:

◇ Simi Valley Ruby Cabernet, 1979...................$6.95
◇ Chateau St. Alphonso White Zinfandel, 1980..... $4.50
◇ Phillip Joseph Cabernet Sauvignon, 1979.......... $7.50
◇ Boar's Leap Chardonnay, 1982....................$14.95
◇ Ralph's Winery Tawny Port, 1977.................$9.95
◇ Mouton-Cochon Cellars Chenin Blanc, 1978....... $7.50
◇ Petaluma Cellars Zinfandel, 1982................. $4.00
◇ Gallows Hill Hearty Burgundy, 1984..............$3.95
◇ Chateau Apollinaire Rosé, 1976................... $8.95
◇ Poisson Vineyard Petite Sirah, 1974.............. $9.45
◇ Peter Cellars Pink Chablis, 1978................... $8.50

The store name is in 24-point plain Venice, which looks ragged unless you retouch it in FatBits. The address and phone number are in 14-point bold Venice.

The goblet in the bottom part of the circular was drawn entirely in FatBits.

The Wine List

The list of wines is 14-point Venice throughout. The heading (May's featured wines:) is bold, and the wine names and prices are all plain. We start each new list by typing the names and prices alone, no diamond-shaped bullets or periods leading to the prices. A decimal tab aligns the prices at the right edge of the page. We used to spell rosé without the accent over the "e," until we discovered that pressing Option-E before typing the "e" gives the vowel an accent.

After typing all the names and prices, we go back and insert the diamond-shaped bullets (◆). We sometimes have to use the Key Caps desk accessory to remind us which keys to press to get a diamond (Shift-Option-V). And because the Venice font doesn't have the diamond character, we use 12-point bold Chicago. Actually, we only type one diamond, copy it to the Clipboard, and then paste it at the start of every line.

To finish the list, we fill in the periods between the wine names and prices. On each line, we click an insertion point right after the year and type periods until they reach the dollar sign.

Easy Deal Dave Advertisement

I have a used-car lot full of reliable transportation and, every week, I advertise my best cars (you know, the ones on the front line with their hoods up) and some of the slow-moving dogs in the local paper. I hand in the ad as camera-ready copy and the newspaper uses it just as it is.

I do my ads entirely in MacPaint. All the type is in New York font, which looks the most like newspaper print to me. I put my name in large, 24-point boldface letters. Right below that, I put my motto in 14-point plain letters. The address and phone number of the lot are in 12-point plain letters.

I sketched my portrait with the single-dot brush, mostly in FatBits. The suit plaid is a custom pattern.

5 engine...

CLASSIFIED FLEA MARKET

Next comes my slogan in 12-point bold capital letters.

I type the list of cars in 9-point type. Since MacPaint has no tabs to help line up the column of prices, I type all the car descriptions in one pass, without prices. I click an insertion point, type a description, and press the Return key to go to the next line for the next description. After typing all the descriptions, I click another insertion point off to the side, change to boldface with right alignment, and type a separate list of prices. Then I select the column of prices with the selection rectangle and drag it into place next to the descriptions. Then I put in the periods.

The lot's hours, at the bottom of the ad, are in 9-point bold New York.

Mr. Earl's Club Announcement

Mr. Earl's Club features live entertainment three nights a week. Friday night is new-wave night, Saturday night is family night, and Monday night is blues night. The upcoming acts are posted every Tuesday in the showcase window in front of the club. Stacks of notices are left in laundromats, pizza parlors, liquor stores, and other consenting retail establishments. A reduced version of the notice appears in the newspaper on Wednesday and Friday.

Most of the lettering is 12-point Chicago, some plain, some bold, and some bold underlined. However, the headline is done in a custom-made display font. The parallel lines were all drawn with the straight-line tool, constrained by the Shift key to be horizontal or diagonal. The curves were done with the oval tool. Some letters were cannibalized from others. For example, the C was made from an A that was rotated once and flipped vertically. The U was based on an A that was flipped both vertically and horizontally.

The martini glass was done with the pencil in FatBits. The sides and stem are two dots thick and the rim is one dot thick. The olive was drawn with the filled oval tool, constrained by the Shift key to draw circles. The toothpick is a straight line. The black martini glass was drawn by duplicating a regular glass, filling it with the solid black pattern, and drawing a white olive inside it using the filled-oval tool with the solid white pattern.

MR EARL'S CLUB

PRESENTS . . .

Friday 7/1
<u>Bowl of Slugs</u>
8:30 PM $5.00

Saturday 7/2
<u>Polka Kings</u>
7:00 PM $4.00

Monday 7/4
<u>Muddy Waiters</u>
8:00 PM $2.50

Mr. Earl's Club ■ 219 LaRou St. ■ Gary, IN ■ (208) 443-1489

Stock-Performance Analysis

Over the last few years, I have purchased stock on 14 occasions. I developed a Multiplan worksheet to keep track of what I bought, when I bought it, how much I paid, and how much it is worth today. The worksheet calculates the dollar and percentage profit or loss I would realize if I sold at the current price. Based on the profit/loss rate, the worksheet also graphs the performance of each stock and of my whole portfolio.

Every stock purchase occupies its own row on the worksheet. On each row, I entered the information that identifies the stock, the date I bought it, the number of shares I bought, the price I paid per share, and the current price per share. All the rest of the cells in the row contain formulas. I had to enter all the formulas for the first stock on the list but, for subsequent stocks, the formulas can be duplicated from the row above with the Copy or Fill Down features.

The Bar Graph

The graph of stock performance occupies two columns. Losers (negative return) appear on the left, gainers (positive return) on the right. Aligning the loss column on its right and the gain column on its left makes the boundary between the two columns a zero-line, with losses extending to the left and gains to the right. Multiplan automatically graphs negative numbers in light gray and positive numbers in dark gray.

Since the rates of return have values generally between 0.1 and 1.0 (or -0.1 and -1.0 for losers), they must be multiplied by a scaling factor or the bar graph will be nearly invisible. A scaling factor of 10 works well with a column width of 17 or 18. For a portfolio with a wider or narrower range of return rates, the scaling factor may have to be changed.

Calculating the Commission

The worksheet calculates the round-trip commission for the number of shares and prices listed on each line. My broker has a sliding commission rate; the larger the dollar value of the purchase or sale, the lower the commission rate. For transactions of $3000 or less, the broker charges $18 plus 1.2 percent of the transaction amount. For transactions larger than $3000 but not more than $7000, the charge is $36 plus 0.6 percent of the transaction amount. Transactions between $7000.01 and $56,000 cost $57 plus 0.3 percent of the transaction amount. Above $56,000, the charge is $198 plus 0.15 percent. The formula that calculates the commission uses the LOOKUP function to get the various fees and rates out of a table on the worksheet.

I put the broker's commission table out of the way, in columns 16, 17, and 18 of rows 20 through 24. It consists of four rows and three columns. The first column lists the transaction amounts at which the fee and rate changes. The second column lists the fees and the third column lists the rates. Using the Define Name... feature, I named the eight value cells in columns 16 and 17 of the schedule Fee. I also named all 12 value cells Rate. The commission formula uses these names with the LOOKUP function to determine the appropriate fee and rate to use for a particular purchase or sale amount.

Totals versus Averages

The next-to-the-bottom line of the worksheet computes totals of the shares bought, original cost, current value, commission, and return on investment. Since totals of the prices paid and current prices would be meaningless, the bottom line shows averages for those columns instead.

The worksheet calculates both a total percent and an average percent gained or lost. It also creates a graph of these two rates. The total percent shows the overall performance of the portfolio; that is, how much the total dollars invested have gained or lost. The average percent is an average of all the issues' gain/loss percentages. If the total percent is higher than the average percent, I invested more money in the issues with the best performance. But if the average percent is higher than the total percent, I invested more heavily in the worst-performing issues.

Using the Sort Feature

The Sort feature really comes in handy on this worksheet. I can alphabetize the portfolio by stock name by selecting the list of stock names and choosing Sort from the Edit menu. I can just as easily arrange the list according to some other criteria by selecting a different column. For example, selecting the Percent Gain(Loss) column will arrange the stocks in order by performance.

Keeping the Worksheet Current

I always update the worksheet with the particulars of a stock sale or purchase. At other times, I update the current prices of all the stocks listed in my portfolio.

To make room for a purchase, I insert a new row anywhere in the existing list of stocks. Then I copy the formulas from another row, enter the information that describes the transaction, and re-sort the portfolio.

If I sell some shares, I reduce the number of shares listed for that particular company. If I sell all the shares, I remove the row from the worksheet with the Cut command.

Printing the Portfolio

The whole portfolio fits sideways on two sheets of paper. I finagled the first half to print near the bottom and the second half near the top of two consecutive sheets of continuous paper. Then, leaving the sheets connected, I turned them sideways and ended up with a wide, one-page report.

I got the first half of the portfolio to print near the bottom of a sheet of paper by using the Page Setup. . . feature to set the left margin to 1.75 inches and the right margin to 0. At the same time, I specified a header of &rStock and a footer of &l&d. I set up the paper in the Imagewriter so the top of the sheet was even with the top of the paper bail. Then, using the Print. . . command, I printed only the first "page" of the portfolio.

For the second half of the portfolio, I changed the left margin to 0, the right margin to 0.75 inch, and the header to &lPerformance. I cranked the paper backward about half an inch so the second half of the portfolio would print nearer the top edge of the second sheet of paper. Using the Print. . . command again, I printed only the second "page" of the portfolio.

Formulas

Rows 4 through 17, Column 9:

Original Cost = ROUND(*Shares Bought* × *Price Paid*, 2)

| R4C9 | =ROUND(RC[-3]*RC[-2],2) |

Rows 4 through 17, Column 10:

Current Value = ROUND(*Shares Bought* × *Current Price*, 2)

| R4C10 | =ROUND(RC[-4]*RC[-2],2) |

Rows 4 through 17, Column 11:

Commission = ROUND(LOOKUP(*Original Cost, Fee*)
                + LOOKUP(*Original Cost, Rate*) × *Original Cost*, 2)
                + ROUND(LOOKUP(*Current Value, Fee*)
                + LOOKUP(*Current Value, Rate*) × *Current Value*, 2)

| R4C11 | =ROUND(LOOKUP(RC[-2],Fee)+LOOKUP(RC[-2],Rate)*RC[-2],2)+ROUND(LOOKUP(RC[-1],Fee)+LOOKUP(RC[-1],Rate)*RC[-1],2) |

Rows 4 through 17, Column 12:

Return = *Current Value* − *Original Cost* − *Commission*

| R4C12 | =RC[-2]-RC[-3]-RC[-1] |

Rows 4 through 17 and 19, Column 13:

Percent = *Return* ÷ (*Original Cost* + *Commission*)

| R4C13 | =RC[-1]/(RC[-4]+RC[-2]) |

Rows 4 through 17, 19, and 20, Column 14:

Losing Issue = IF(*Percent* < 0, *Percent* × 10, 0)

| R4C14 | =IF(RC[-1]<0,RC[-1]*10,0) |

Rows 4 through 17, 19, and 20, Column 15:

Gaining Issue = IF(*Percent* > 0, *Percent* × 10, 0)

| R4C15 | =IF(RC[-2]>0,RC[-2]*10,0) |

COMPANY NAME	TICKER SYMBOL	WALL ST JRNL LISTING	EXCHANGE	DATE BOUGHT	SHARES BOUGHT	PRICE PAID	CURRENT PRICE
American Quasar Petroleum	AQAS	Am Quasr Pet	OTC	7/2/82	300	7.125	4.000
Apple Computer	AAPL	Apple Computr	OTC	11/9/83	200	18.000	29.125
Apple Computer	AAPL	Apple Computr	OTC	1/23/84	200	28.750	29.125
Church's Fried Chicken	CHU	Church	NYSE	8/3/79	500	17.250	25.500
Coca Cola Company	KO	CocaCl	NYSE	7/8/83	100	48.375	56.000
Eastman Kodak	EK	EsKod	NYSE	3/6/81	300	78.500	65.250
Mary Kay Cosmetics	MKY	MaryK	NYSE	2/17/82	200	10.750	12.000
Ozark Airlines	OZA	OzarkA	Amex	6/8/81	100	12.000	7.875
Pan American World Airways	PN	PanAm	NYSE	6/15/81	200	4.625	5.500
Pay 'n Save Corp.	PAYN	Pay'nSave	OTC	7/9/82	100	9.125	17.250
Rolm Corp.	RM	RolmCp	NYSE	2/16/82	100	33.625	34.625
Sunshine Mining	SSC	SunMn	NYSE	2/28/83	200	12.500	11.875
Texas Oil and Gas	TXO	TxOGs	NYSE	7/16/82	300	11.000	25.125
Yellow Freight Systems	YELL	YellFrtSys	OTC	7/23/82	200	15.250	24.750
Totals					3000		
Averages						21.920	24.857

308

Performance

ORIGINAL COST	CURRENT VALUE	COMMISSION (BUY+SELL)	RETURN ON INVESTMENT	PERCENT GAIN(LOSS)	--- RELATIVE PERFORMANCE ---	
					LOSING ISSUES	GAINING ISSUES
2137.50	1200.00	76.05	-1013.55	-45.79%		
3600.00	5825.00	128.55	2096.45	56.23%		
5750.00	5825.00	141.45	-66.45	-1.13%		
8625.00	12750.00	178.13	3946.87	44.83%		
4837.50	5600.00	134.63	627.87	12.63%		
23550.00	19575.00	243.38	-4218.38	-17.73%		
2150.00	2400.00	90.60	159.40	7.11%		
1200.00	787.50	59.85	-472.35	-37.49%		
925.00	1100.00	60.30	114.70	11.64%		
912.50	1725.00	67.65	744.85	75.99%		
3362.50	3462.50	112.96	-12.96	-0.37%		
2500.00	2375.00	94.50	-219.50	-8.46%		
3300.00	7537.50	135.41	4102.09	119.41%		
3050.00	4950.00	120.00	1780.00	56.15%		
===========	===========	==========	============			
65900.00	75112.50	1643.46	7569.04	11.21%		
				19.50%		

Row 19, Columns 6 and 9 through 12:

Column Total = SUM(*First Stock : Last Stock*)

R19C6	=SUM(R[-15]C:R[-2]C)

Row 20, Columns 7, 8, and 13:

Column Average = AVERAGE(*First Stock : Last Stock*)

R20C7	=AVERAGE(R[-16]C:R[-3]C)

	16	17	18
	Amount	Fee	Rate
20			
21	$0.00	$18.00	1.20%
22	$3000.01	$36.00	0.60%
23	$7000.01	$57.00	0.30%
24	$56000.01	$198.00	0.15%

Travel and Entertainment Account

I use a Multiplan worksheet to record my travel and entertainment expenses and to calculate the balance on my account. At the end of the month, I print a copy and turn it in to the bookkeeper at work. The first printed page, which occupies rows 1 through 20 and columns 1 through 7 on the worksheet, is a summary of the account balance. The second and third printed pages occupy rows 21 through 60 and columns 1 through 15. They detail my expenses day by day and show daily totals and totals by category.

Originally, I started the worksheet with the detailed expenses at the top, in row 1. I typed the column headings in the first two rows and adjusted the column widths so that everything would fit in two pages. Columns 1 and 14 have a width of 4; column 2 a width of 27; column 3 a width of 5; columns 4 through 12 a width of 8, and column 13 a width of 9. I also had to adjust the side margins to 0.5 inch using the Page Setup feature.

Next, I entered the dates in column 1. Rather than type the numbers 1 through 31 directly, I typed this formula:

$$= ROW() - 3$$

for the first day of the month and copied it into the next 30 cells with the Fill Down feature. Then I copied all of column 1 to column 14.

After entering the dates in columns 1 and 14, I entered the rest of the formulas and set the formats for each column. The Fill Down feature came in handy again in columns 4 and 13 for the auto expense and daily totals. The Fill Right feature saved retyping the same formula for the month totals at the bottom of the monthly detail in columns 3 through 13.

To finish the monthly detail section of the worksheet, I copied the column descriptions from the first two rows to the rows beneath the month totals. I also added descriptions at the bottom of columns 1 and 14 to point out the month totals.

Thinking I was done, I saved the worksheet on disk. Another glance at the company's standard form reminded me of the account-balance summary, so I decided to add it at the bottom of the worksheet.

Because of the peculiar column widths and formats needed for the expense-detail section of the worksheet, I chose not to use columns 1 and 2 in the summary section. The amounts fit nicely in columns 4 and 5, though. I put the matching descriptions in column 3 in spite of its narrow width, because the descriptions are aligned at the right and so spill into the empty column 2.

I ended up moving the account summary to the top of the worksheet with the Cut and Paste features. To get the right pagination, I had to add a page break between the summary and detailed-expenses sections (between rows 20 and 21). I also had to change the formulas that calculate the day numbers in columns 1 and 14 to the following:

$$= ROW() - 23$$

Formulas

Row 16, Column 5:

Month's Expenses = Month Total

R16C5	=R[+40]C[+8]

Row 18, Column 4:

Company Total = SUM(Last Company Balance : Company Expenses)

R18C4	=SUM(R[-10]C:R[-2]C)

Row 18, Column 5:

My Total = SUM(*My Last Balance : My Expenses*)

| R18C5 | =SUM(R[-10]C:R[-2]C) |

Row 20, Column 4:

Amount Due Company = IF(*Company Total* > *My Total, Company Total − My Total*, 0)

| R20C4 | =IF(R[-2]C>R[-2]C[+1],R[-2]C-R[-2]C[+1],0) |

Row 20, Column 5:

Amount Due Me = IF (*My Total* > *Company Total, My Total − Company Total*, 0)

| R20C5 | =IF(R[-2]C>R[-2]C[-1],R[-2]C-R[-2]C[-1],0) |

Row 24, Columns 1 and 14:

Date = ROW( ) − 23

| R24C1 | =ROW()-23 |

Rows 24 to 54, Column 4:

Auto Cost = *Auto Miles* × 0.25

| R24C4 | =RC[-1]*0.25 |

Rows 24 to 54, Column 13:

Daily Total = SUM(*Auto Cost : Misc*)

| R24C13 | =SUM(RC[-9]:RC[-1]) |

Row 56, Columns 3 to 13:

Month Total = SUM(*Day 1 : Day 31*)

| R56C3 | =SUM(R[-32]C:R[-2]C) |

TRAVEL AND ENTERTAINMENT ACCOUNT

	Due Company	Due Me
NAME: Blanche Noir		
ACCOUNT NUMBER: RD348		
EXPENSE MONTH: July		
Last Month's Balance	0.00	76.00
Reimbursement	76.00	0.00
Cash Advance	500.00	
Transportation Advance	677.98	
Month's Expenses		1616.35
	========	========
Totals	1253.98	1692.35
Amount Due	0.00	438.37

Blanche Noir

TRAVEL AND ENTERTAINMENT ACCOUNT

Date	Traveled To - From	Auto Miles	Auto Cost @.25/Mi.	Car Rental	Parking	Plane/ Train
1	San Francisco - Chicago	17	4.25			290.00
2						
3	Chicago - San Francisco	17	4.25		15.00	290.00
4						
5						
6	Fremont - San Francisco	110	27.50		4.50	
7						
8						
9						
10						
11	San Francisco - San Jose	106	26.50			
12						
13						
14						
15	Palo Alto					
16						
17						
18						
19	San Francisco - San Jose	114	28.50		5.00	
20						
21						
22						
23	San Francisco					
24						
25						
26	San Francisco - Los Angeles	34	8.50	140.37	9.50	97.98
27						
28						
29	Berkeley	26				
30						
31						
MONTH TOTALS =>		424	99.50	140.37	34.00	677.98
		Auto Miles	Auto Cost @.25/Mi.	Car Rental	Parking	Plane/ Train

Blanche Noir

Account RD348

314

TRAVEL AND ENTERTAINMENT ACCOUNT

Cabs/Bus	Hotels	Meals	Tips	Misc	Daily Totals	Date
12.00	89.50	57.00	8.00		460.75	1
9.50	89.50	85.00	14.00	3.50	201.50	2
6.00		8.00	4.00		327.25	3
					0.00	4
					0.00	5
		47.80	7.5		87.30	6
					0.00	7
					0.00	8
					0.00	9
					0.00	10
				8.56	35.06	11
					0.00	12
					0.00	13
					0.00	14
		33.78	5		38.78	15
					0.00	16
					0.00	17
					0.00	18
		72.90	11		117.40	19
					0.00	20
					0.00	21
					0.00	22
8.50					8.50	23
					0.00	24
					0.00	25
		58.25	12	3.50	330.10	26
					0.00	27
					0.00	28
					0.00	29
		8.46	1.25		9.71	30
					0.00	31
36.00	179.00	371.19	62.75	15.56	1616.35	<= MONTH TOTALS
Cabs/Bus	Hotels	Meals	Tips	Misc	Daily Totals	

Blanche Noir

Phone Directory

Who needs a Rolodex? I used to lose phone numbers all the time because I never could remember whether I filed them by last name, first name, or company name. I hit on this idea of listing them alphabetically in a MacWrite document. MacWrite's Find... feature helps me look up a number by first, last, or company name, or to zip to the first number listed under any letter of the alphabet. A few times I have even searched my MacWrite directory for a phone number that was scrawled on a scrap of paper to see whom the number belonged to. I print the directory too, because it isn't always convenient to open the phone-directory document on the Macintosh. There is a draw-back to the printed directory: It hasn't the bulk of my old card file and gets lost on my cluttered desk.

For the large alphabet headings, I used 24-point bold underlined Toronto for both the letters and underscores. The names and phone numbers are 9-point Geneva, with bold used for occa-sional emphasis—just like the phone book. A decimal tab at the 3¾-inch mark lines up the phone numbers. Two regular tab stops, at the 3⅞- and 6-inch marks, keep the addresses lined up. An occasional blank line makes it easier to scan the printed list.

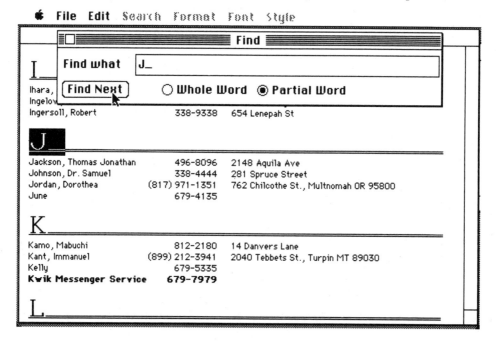

A

Peter Abelard	812-2877		
Al's Motor City	909-3458		
Susan B. Anthony	(658) 415-3755		

APPLE COMPUTER, INC.	(408) 996-1010	20525 Mariani Ave., Cupertino, CA 95014	
BARNUM P.T.	(408) 819-6570	Marketing	M/S 12Q
LAZARUS Emma	(408) 819-4822	Technical Support	M/S 99Z
RABELAIS Francois	(408) 819-3534	User Education	M/S 99Z
SCHOPENHAUER Arthur	(408) 819-4567	Public Relations	M/S 12Q

Jane Austen	(899) 212-2134	1071 Fifth Ave. New York NY

B

Honore de Balzac	496-2393	
Charles Baudelaire	679-4000	
Ludwig van Beethoven	338-1003	
Alexander Graham Bell	554-8737	
BERNINI'S Wine Shop	555-1212	3447 Oak St., Albany

Otto von Bismarck	(305) 812-3522	101 Strand, Miami Beach FL
William Blake	909-7874	
Simon Bolivar	679-5343	
John Wilkes Booth	554-1099	
James Boswell	906-8976	
Anne Bradstreet	496-8777	
Charlotte Bronte	338-6655	
Elizabeth Browning	554-3998	

Blanche	338-9703

C

William Camden	679-1551
Phoebe Cary	909-1824
Miguel de Cervantes	554-7676
Lydia Child	906-3298
Henry Clay	496-1777

Colonial Diaper Service	338-6900	
Dinah Craik	679-8338	
Dave Crockett	(606)-654-1951	350 Elm St., Winchester KY

D

Richard Dana	496-9080	
Charles Darwin	679-3818	
Daniel Defoe	338-6543	
Emily Dickinson	(203) 547-7557	985 Washington Ave., Goshen CT

Dinah's Diner	**906-5353**
Benjamin Disraeli	554-8122

Dr. Ruth Lessing Advertisement

I am a psychologist specializing in stress control. With stress running rampant in modern society, you'd think people would be beating down my door. They are, sometimes literally. Even so, the turnover in clients is high, so I advertise in the Yellow Pages. It's amazing how few people with stress problems know help is available.

The picture in my ad was drawn by a client using MacPaint. I've always encouraged my clients to draw, as the results can be quite revealing. This client used the small, square-shaped brush with the black pattern to sketch an angry face. To heighten the effect, he selected the whole sketch with the selection rectangle and, three times in succession, he chose Trace Edges from the Edit menu. To finish the drawing, he shaded the mouth black with the paint can.

To my client's drawing, I added some Geneva text. The first two lines are 12-point bold underlined. The three-line address and the telephone number are 12-point bold. The last three lines, which list my specialties, are 10-point bold. When I typed these three lines, I left a couple of extra blank spaces between specialties. Then I drew a small solid black dot and put a copy of it in each space.

Since the entire ad is taller than a single drawing window, I could not draw a border around it with the rectangle-drawing tool. So I used the straight-line drawing tool instead with the next to widest and the narrowest lines. I used the grabber to scroll and the shift key to make sure the lines were perfectly vertical or horizontal.

Psychologists–(Cont'd)

Criddle William D
PhD Clinical Psychologist
Fellow Institute For Rational-Emotive
Therapy
Certified Sex Therapist–AASECT
Individual–Group–Family & Marriage
Counseling
Stress Management
Evening Appointments
157 Yesler Wy ---------------------- 682-6959
Crow William R Maynard Bg -------------- 622-9931
DeCoster Don T ---------------------- 364-0233
DeNinno John A 9730 3d NE ------------ 522-3853
De Vore Anne I
Jungian Analysis & Problems Of Creativity
5608 15th NE ---------------------- 525-5836
Dineen Associates Learning &
Developmental Consultants
Susan K Dineen PhD–Certified School
Psychologist–Learning & Developmental
Disabilities
---------------------- 525-2381
Dortzbach Jan 1100 Olive Wy --------- 223-0050
Dream Psychology Northwest
1602 E Garfield ------------------ 325-6148
Dreiblatt Irwin S 1001 Broadway -------- 323-0905
Dunham Charles
5250 18th NE ---------------------- 525-7142
Dunham Jerome 5250 18th NE -------- 525-7142
Early Emmett 3826 Woodland Park N ------ 632-7331
East M Vicky 9730 3d NE ------------ 522-3853
Fallis & Associates
Industrial Psychology–See Management
Consultant
93 Pike Suite 312 ---------------- 625-0808
Family Crisis Service 1111 Harvard -------- 322-9095
Fehrenbach Peter
PhD Licensed–Adults Adolescents & Families
1507 Western Suite 403 ----------- 628-9580
Feldman Stephen R Maynard Bg --------- 621-7007
Feldman–Summers Shirley
3245 Fairview E ------------------ 328-1440
Fey Steven G
The Mason Clinic
PhD Clinical Psychologist
Pain Management
1200 9th ---------------------- 223-6954
Finkelstein Jay N 10909 NE 4th Bellevue ---- 451-1811
Fiore Joan
PhD Licensed–Individual–Marital–Adolescence
2200 24th E ---------------------- 328-0910
Forbes John L 4026 NE 55th --------- 525-3077
Freeman Charles M
The Pain Center Swedish Hospital
747 Summit ---------------------- 292-6582
Gawain Gary C V
PhD Clinical Psychology
Individual Psychotherapy–Marriage
Counseling
Psychosomatic Disorders–Clinical Hypnosis
Psychological Evaluations
Overlake Medical Center
1031 116th NE Bellevue ----------- 454-2809
Gerston Allan 1414 Alaskan Wy -------- 223-1729
Goldberg Irving A PhD Ltd PS
Medical Dental Bg ---------------- 622-6842
Goldenberg Samuel 2200 24th E -------- 328-0910
Goodrich Edward A
PhD Clinical Psychology
Office Located At 12221 NE 8th Bellevue
Bellevue ---------------------- 454-7321
Gordon Judith R 1415 Western Suite 406 ---- 447-9170
Gray Grady 3826 Woodland Park N ------- 545-8313
Gray Grady
PhD–Individual–Couple & Family Therapy
---------------------- 842-5348
Green G Dorsey 521 19th E ----------- 325-7435
Green Thomas K
Neuropsychology & Forensic Psychology
6850 35th NE ---------------------- 524-2668
Greff Nikolai N
PhD Licensed Clinical Psychologist
20061 19th NE ---------------------- 362-6222
Hammer Frank J
22506 66th W Mountlake Terrace ----- 778-7687
Hartsook Judy
PhD Licensed Clinical Psychologist
18631 Alderwood Mall Bv Lynnwood----771-3248
Hays Victor L
PhD Clinical Psychology
Stevens Health Center
21700 76th Av W Edmonds ---------- 771-5300
HEADACHE CLINIC THE
116 107th NE Bellevue ----------- 455-4545
Hedges Richard G
2661 Bellevue-Redmond Rd Rm 105
Bellevue ---------------------- 882-0700
Hervey Ellen P 1001 Broadway -------- 323-0905

Hill Byrde
PhD Clinical Psychologist
Psychotherapy
Individual & Group
Psychological Evaluation
Reconciliation–Marriage Or Divorce
Counseling
Bellevue ---------------------- 454-2400
Hill Emory PhD 220 106th Pl NE Bellevue ---453-8024
Hirschstein Ralph Dr 803 E Denny Wy ------ 324-0121
Hofman Kees C 9730 3d NE ------------ 522-9314
Hudgins Wren
Child–Adult–Family Therapy
401 S 43d Renton ---------------- 255-0920
Humphreys Lewis E
11225 Roosevelt Wy NE ----------- 363-9446
Hunsberger Peter
EdD Licensed–Individual–Couples–Family
2722 Eastlake E Suite 250 ----------- 324-4488
ILLIG DAVID P
PhD–Clinical Psychologist-Clinical
Hypnosis-Individuals & Couples
Counseling-Sex Therapy
1415 Western ---------------------- 625-9562
Inner Resource Associates 6328 22d NE----525-9119
INSTITUTE FOR RATIONAL LIVING
NW
Rational–Emotive Therapy
Certified Sex Therapist–AASECT
Individual–Group–Marriage & Family
Counseling
John Williams M A–Director
3216 NE 45th Pl ---------------- 527-4884
Johnson Patricia J ---------------------- 282-3533
Katz Arnold 4026 NE 55th Suite E 200 ---- 525-7444
King Nancy W ---------------------- 522-4505
Knowles Philip L
Individual Family & Group
Physicians Hospital Services Inc PS
509 Olive Wy ---------------- 583-0656
Koan Associates 219 1st S ------------ 621-7302
Kobler Arthur L 4709 16th NE -------- 525-1771
Krieger Margery H
PhD–Licensed Clinical & Consulting
Psychologist
14727 Bothell Wy NE -------------- 362-3924
Lamphere Arthur V 1001 Broadway ------ 323-0905
Lamson Frederick W 620 15th E -------- 322-3800
Lester Robert A
Marriage Sexual & Family Counseling–
Biofeedback Treatment Of Headaches
Hypertension & Stress–
Individual Psychotherapy–Diagnostic Testing–
Consultation
901 Boren ---------------------- 624-4512
Lindsay Franklin R 1100 Olive Wy -------- 223-0050
Livingston Goodhue
Psychotherapy–Marriage Counseling–
Diagnostic Testing–Cancer Counseling
1700 35th ---------------------- 322-2655
Lund Charles A 600 1st --------------- 624-1715
Manderscheid Lorraine
2513 152d Av NE Redmond ---------- 881-8314
Marlowe Wendy B
PhD Clinical Neurological Psychologist
Language Pathologys–Learning Disability
901 Boren ---------------------- 623-7444
Marshall Karol A 1715 114th SE Bellevue --- 455-2191
Martin Grant L
PhD Licensed Psychologist
CRISTA Counseling Service
19303 Fremont Av N -------------- 546-7215
Maurer Charles D 9730 3d NE ---------- 522-9314
McCarty Eileen R 901 Boren ---------- 624-4512
McCarty Gerald J Medical Dental Bg ---- 622-6675
McConville Bernard E
11671 SE 1st Bellevue ------------ 454-2002
Meeks Byrde Hill
PhD Clinical Psychologist
Psychotherapy–Individual & Group
Psychological Evaluation
Reconciliation–Marriage Or Divorce
Counseling
Bellevue ---------------------- 454-2400
Mendez Anita M 1004 E Galer -------- 325-2420
Miller Michael L 9730 3d NE ---------- 522-9314
Miller Richard
PhD Licensed Clinical Psychologist
Counseling & Psychotherapy
Diplomate In Clinical Psychology–American
Board Of Professional Psychology
1107 NE 45th ------------------ 329-4995
Morris Sharon K 1818 Westlake N -------- 285-7771
Mowatt Marian H
Psychotherapy & Psychological Evaluation
1107 NE 45th ------------------ 634-1706
Muscatel Kenneth 9730 3d NE ---------- 522-9314
Nelson Gary L
PhD Licensed Clinical Psychologist
The Parent Place
1608 NE 150th ------------------ 364-7274
Nelson Gayle Gulick ---------------------- 364-6981

Northwest Family Clinic
Nikolai N Greff PhD Clinical Psychologist
20061 19th NE ---------------------- 362-6222
Northwest Psychological Associates
9730 3d NE ---------------------- 522-9314
Nyman Barry A 3216 NE 45th Pl----------524-4639
Oakley Donald C
PhD Clinical Psychology
Marriage & Family Therapist AAMFT
Rational–Emotive Therapy
Individual–Group–Couples Counseling
Evening Appointments Available
157 Yesler Wy ------------------ 682-6959
Pacific Psychological Services
Pacific Center For Sexual & Marital
Counseling
1001 Broadway ------------------ 323-0905
Paige Albert B 9730 3d NE ------------ 522-9314

PATHFINDING INTERDIMENSIONS

William Stablein PhD
Leslie Schwartz MA

PSYCHOTHERAPY
RELATIONSHIPS
WHOLISTIC TRAINING
SPIRITUAL COUNSELING
NUTRITION

5253 15th NE ---------------------- 523-3147

Peterson Kevin
PhD–Licensed Psychologist–Evening
Appointments
1100 E 45th ---------------------- 324-4488
PETERSON MARIANNE
9806 S Carr Rd Renton -------------- 271-0986
Printz Dolph M 710 10th E -------------- 329-2331
Prosser Robert A
PhD Clinical Psychology
Stevens Health Center
21700 76th Av W Edmonds ---------- 771-5300
Psychological Advantage
Anita M Mendez PhD
1004 E Galer --------------------- 325-2420
Puget Counseling Center 1111 Harvard ----329-5050
RABKIN LESLIE Y
2200 24th E ---------------------- 328-0910

Rawlings Leslie H 550 16th -------------- 325-6812
Reilly James T
Licensed Clinical Psychologist
Medical Dental Bg---------------------- 622-6673
Rosen Gerald M Cabrini Medical Tower ------ 343-9474
Rosenbaum Edward
PhD–Clinical Psychology
1818 Westlake N ------------------ 284-0855
Rourke Philip G Cobb Medical Center ------ 623-2711
Sall Gary
PhD Licensed Clinical Psychologist
607 3d ---------------------- 682-3850
Shapiro Jay W
PhD Divorce Management–Family Evaluations
Bellevue ---------------------- 455-2759
Sion Alvin M 12333 35th NE ----------- 365-3464
Slosky Ron 401 S 43d Renton ----------- 255-0920
Smith David H 27 100th NE Bellevue ------ 454-3135
Snyder Arden
The Mason Clinic
PhD Clinical Psychologist
1100 9th ---------------------- 223-6748
Springer Harry C 844 N 161st Pl --------- 542-6606
Stein Eugene J 4026 NE 55th Suite E 200---525-7444
Taylor Evalyn W PhD Inc PS
Licensed Psychologist–Psychotherapy &
Couple Counseling–Psychological Assessment
1305 4th ---------------------- 622-9496
Thomson Solveig H PhD PS
Individuals–Group–Couples–Family Therapy
Transactional Analysis–Gestalt–Psychodrama
1107 NE 45th ------------------ 634-1706
Thorpe Sylvia A 3216 NE 45th Pl --------- 525-7081
Tracy James J
PhD Clinical Psychology
7614 195th SW Edmonds ------------ 775-4477
Troner Stephen P 1001 Broadway --------- 323-0660
Wall Tom W PhD PS 4026 NE 55th --------- 525-5700
Warren Judith L
PhD Clinical Psychology
2001 Western ---------------------- 583-0900
Washington State Psychological
Association
Referrals-Complaint Review
13500 Lake City Wy NE -------------- 362-4905
Wassmer Arthur C
10518 NE 68th Kirkland -------------- 827-5566

You get full value and continuous
circulation for every dollar spent in
Yellow Page Advertising.

Trade through the Yellow Pages

Dinah's Diner

The bill of fare changes daily at Dinah's Diner, so I use MacWrite to print a new menu every day. I selected 12-point Chicago for all the text. The margins are set at ½ inch on the left and 6½ inches on the right, and there is a decimal tab at the 6¼-inch mark. The whole menu is double-spaced.

When I first type a new menu, I type the names and prices of all the dishes but omit the periods that fill the empty space ahead of each price. Then I go back to each dish in turn, select an insertion point right after the name, and fill in the empty space by alternately typing a period and a blank space. That way, I can use the decimal tab to align the prices on the right.

My first menu was just a list of entrees and desserts, but a customer suggested adding a drawing of a coffee cup at the top. Everyone knows the diner for its free coffee refills. I played around in MacPaint until I got an illustration I liked, and then I copied it to the top of the menu in MacWrite with the Copy and Paste features. To get it centered above the menu, I used a separate ruler with the left margin set at 2⅝ inches.

Most of the basic shapes for the drawing were done with the hollow-oval tool, moved into place with the lasso, and trimmed with the eraser. Only the steam and cup handle were drawn freehand. I used the small round brush in white for the steam and the single-dot brush for the cup handle. The pencil did the three-dimensional shading. The tablecloth is a custom pattern created using the Edit Pattern feature. To get the phrase Fine Dinners in white, I typed it off to the side, selected it with the selection rectangle, and used the Invert feature of the Edit menu. Then I lassoed the words and dragged them into place.

The name of the diner is 18-point Chicago. I had to touch it up a little in FatBits. The address and phone number are 9-point, but 9-point Chicago looks terrible, so I used Geneva bold, which is very similar.

320

DINAH'S DINER

FINE DINNERS

1200 Yosemite Ave, Oakdale
454-3911

Wednesday's Entrees

Creamed chipped beef on toast $2.80

Chicken a la King $3.20

French dip sandwich with Au Jus sauce $3.50

Turki Surprise $3.75

Finn and Haddie $3.50

Beef on Wellington $4.35

(All dinners come with french fries, a dollop of cole slaw,
coffee or tea, and choice of dessert)

Wednesday's Desserts

Custard flambé $1.40

Gooseberry muffins $0.45

Maple flan $0.95

"Coffee refills are on us"

Shoe-Store Budget

Mr. Shoe is a chain shoe store that specializes in fashion shoes for the whole family. In September, the manager of each location prepares separate budgets for the next year's sales, purchases, personnel, overhead, operating income, cash flow, funds flow, and sometimes financing. The sample you see here is the 1983 operating-income budget for the Sunset Valley Mall location. It has had the actual 1983 revenue and expense totals entered to show how accurate the manager's predictions were. The manager will use a copy of the same worksheet for next year's budget, but will ignore the three right-hand columns until the actual amounts are available after the end of the year.

Setting up the worksheet was easy. We typed the column and row descriptions, set the column widths and formats, and entered the formulas. Sixty of the cells contain formulas, but there are only five different formulas on the worksheet. We typed each different formula once, then copied it to other cells using the Copy, Paste, Fill Right, and Fill Down features.

The budget is too wide for one page, so we printed it on two pages and taped them together. To fit the report on two pages, we had to specify side margins of 0.5 inch in the Page Setup dialog box. We did not type a header or footer there, since they would appear on both halves of the composite report. Instead, we put a title on the worksheet itself. The first half of the title is right-aligned at the top of column 9, and the second half is left-aligned at the top of column 10. The whole title ends up near the middle of the composite report.

Formulas

Row 22, Columns 2 through 14 and 16:

Total Expenses = SUM(Merchandise : Miscellaneous)

R22C2	=SUM(R[-10]C:R[-2]C)

Row 25, Columns 2 through 14 and 16:

Operating Income = Revenues – Total Operating Costs

R25C2	=R[-16]C-R[-3]C

322

Rows 9 and 12 through 20, Column 14:

Budget = SUM(*January* : *December*)

R9C14	=SUM(RC[-12]:RC[-1])

Rows 9, 12 through 20, 22, and 25, Columns 15 and 17:

Pct. Revenue = *Total* ÷ *Total Revenue*

R9C15	=RC[-1]/R9 C[-1]

Rows 9, 12 through 20, 22, and 25, Column 18:

DIFF = *Actual* − *Budget*

R9C18	=RC[-2]-RC[-4]

Rows 9, 12 through 20, 22, and 25, Column 19:

VARIANCE = IF(*Budget* > 0, *DIFF* ÷ *Budget*, − 1)

R9C19	=IF(RC[-5]>0,RC[-1]/RC[-5],-1)

Row 22, Column 19:

Average Variance = AVERAGE(*Merchandise* : *Miscellaneous*)

R22C19	=AVERAGE(R[-10]C:R[-2]C)

Row 25, Column 19:

Operating Income Variance = IF(ABS(*Budget*) > 0, *DIFF* ÷ *Budget*, − 1)

R25C19	=IF(ABS(RC[-5])>0,RC[-1]/RC[-5],-1)

Mr. Shoe Sunset Valley Mall

	January	February	March	April	May	June	July	August
Revenues	19896	20405	20104	20111	24815	27593	27881	30555
Expenses:								
Merchandise	22000	12000	6000	16000	14000	36000	12000	10000
Salaries	4500	4500	5000	5500	6000	6000	6000	6000
Rent	1200	1200	1200	1200	1200	1200	1425	1425
Utilities	185	175	170	150	135	125	125	125
Office Supplies	250	250	50	50	50	50	100	100
Equipment Rental	500	500	500	500	500	500	500	500
Company Travel	2000					3250		
Advertising & Promotion	750	750	1500	1500	2000		1500	1000
Miscellaneous	300	300	300	300	300	300	300	300
Total Expenses	31685	19675	14720	25200	24185	47425	21950	19450
Operating Income	-11789	730	5384	-5089	630	-19832	5931	11105

1983 Operating Income Budget

September	October	November	December	Budget Total	Pct. Revenue	Actual Total	Pct. Revenue	DIFF	VARIANCE
37144	39999	39129	42168	349800	100.0%	345645	100.0%	-4155	-1.2%
28000	9000	6000	4000	175000	50.0%	179114	51.8%	4114	2.4%
6500	7000	7000	7500	71500	20.4%	71000	20.5%	-500	-0.7%
1425	1425	1425	1425	15750	4.5%	15902	4.6%	152	1.0%
125	135	175	175	1800	0.5%	1500	0.4%	-300	-16.7%
100	150	150	100	1400	0.4%	1200	0.3%	-200	-14.3%
500	500	500	500	6000	1.7%	6000	1.7%	0	0.0%
1000				6250	1.8%	6524	1.9%	274	4.4%
500	500			10000	2.9%	9444	2.7%	-556	-5.6%
300	300	300	300	3600	1.0%	3850	1.1%	250	6.9%
38450	19010	15550	14000	291300	83.3%	294534	85.2%	3234	-2.5%
-1306	20989	23579	28168	58500	16.7%	51111	14.8%	-7389	-12.6%

After
Five

● *This collection of eleven MacWrite, MacPaint, and Multiplan projects offers ideas for your recreation and personal business.*

The projects in this chapter show you how to develop landscape designs, draw maps, prepare a wine-cellar inventory report, and create investment analysis worksheets, among other things. Be sure to read the written descriptions that accompany the projects. They describe some features of MacWrite, MacPaint, and Multiplan not mentioned elsewhere. To get the most out of a project, you should be familiar with the application used to create it. If you need more information, read Part Two of this book.

Landscaping a Garden

We recently moved to a new house and decided to completely redo the back yard. I wanted a deck with a hot tub and a small vegetable garden. My husband wanted a brick patio with a barbecue and a lawn. MacPaint helped us map out a plan that includes all those elements plus a couple of Japanese maple trees and several flowering bushes. We elected to retain the existing bamboo hedge at the back of the lot.

Drawing the house across the bottom of the document and the hedge across the top established the scale for the rest of the yard. The next step was blocking in the major areas—the deck, patio, walk, vegetable garden, lawns, and flower beds—using the hollow rectangle and rounded-corner rectangle. To draw rectangles with dotted lines, we selected the medium gray pattern and held down the Option key while drawing with the hollow-rectangle tool. It took lots of experimenting to fit in everything we wanted. The Show Page feature provided invaluable overviews of the whole yard during the design process.

Constructing and positioning the hot tub, bench, barbecue, and picnic table came next. First we outlined them with the hollow-rectangle and hollow-oval tools. Then we shaded them with different patterns using the paint can. We first filled the picnic table and benches with parallel lines and then used medium gray to fill between them. For the barbecue, we made a special pattern to replace one of the existing brick patterns.

Planting the yard was the next task. We outlined the trees with a small brush and filled them with a light gray pattern using the paint can. After that, the paint can also filled the lawns with a dark gray pattern and the hedge with a medium gray pattern. Rather than outline and fill every vegetable and bush in two steps, we drew them in various shades of gray directly. We used the filled, irregular-shape tool and the filled-oval tool, both with the no-border line thickness selected. To decorate the bushes, we drew a rose, a dahlia, and a camellia in the margin, mostly using the pencil in FatBits. Then we made copies of the flowers with the lasso and Option key, and dragged them into the bushes. For variety, we even turned a couple of the dahlias upside down with the selection rectangle and the Flip Vertical feature. We drew the row of pansies using the filled, rounded-corner rectangle with no border and a custom-made pattern.

328

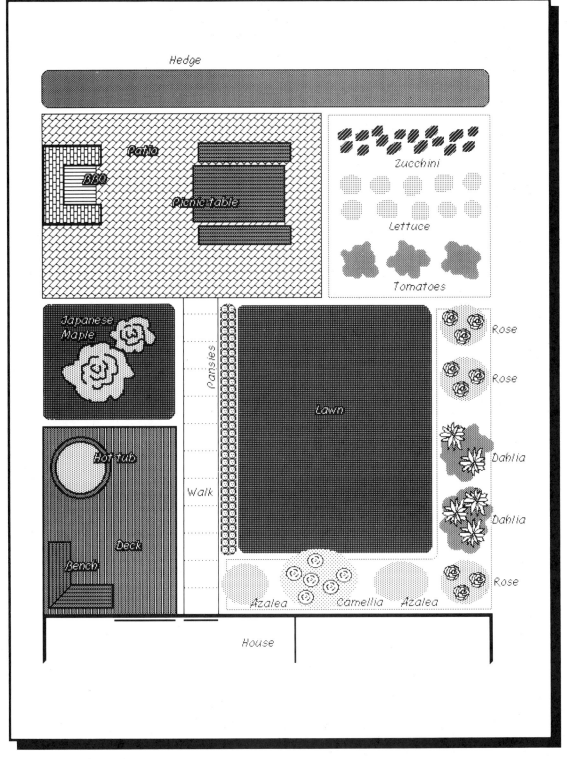

All that remained was to paint the patio and deck. For the patio, we used the standard diagonal brick pattern, but for the deck, we created a pattern to simulate redwood planks.

Naming the various parts of the landscape was the last step. We chose 12-point plain Los Angeles for all the text. (With the Font Mover program, we had already put the Cairo, Los Angeles, and Toronto fonts from the System Disk on our MacPaint disk.) One at a time, we typed each name in the margin, lassoed it, and dragged it into place. We turned the word Pansies sideways with the Rotate feature before moving it out of the margin. Words such as Lawn, Deck, and Patio we treated specially so they would show up against a dark background. First, we typed the word in the margin using plain Los Angeles. Next, we selected the word with the selection rectangle. Then, we pressed Command-E (the shortcut for choosing Trace Edges from the Edit menu) while also holding down the Shift key to add a shadow to the word as a whole. This method produces smaller words with more closely spaced letters than typing directly in shadow style.

Arranging Furniture

Whenever I get the urge to buy new furniture, I rearrange the furniture I already have instead. It gives me a fresh outlook on life. The only part I dislike is heaving the stuff to and fro to find the right new configuration, stirring up dust and scarring the floors in the process. MacPaint lets me experiment with different arrangements in a more civilized manner.

To get started, I had to draw the floor plan and each piece of furniture, but with that done, I can now drag furniture around with the aid of the lasso or selection rectangle. The Rotate feature of the Edit menu is handy for turning things around. However, Rotate only works on an object selected with the selection rectangle, not on something selected with the lasso, so sometimes I have to use the lasso to drag an object into the middle of the room where I can reselect it with the selection rectangle and rotate it. Then I select it again with the lasso and drag it to its new location.

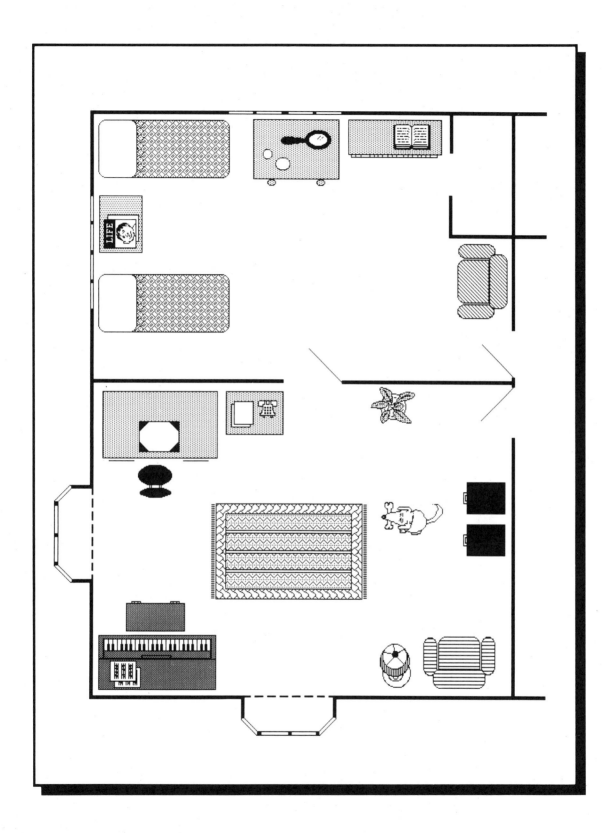

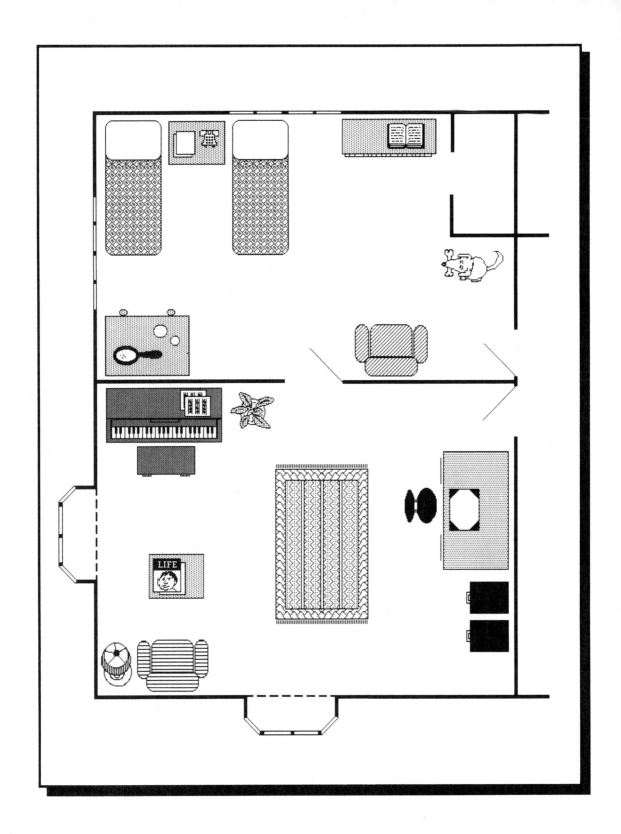

Moving furniture can be like solving the Puzzle from the Apple menu. I have to move one thing aside to make space to move another thing aside so I can move a third thing into place. In the process, objects tend to bump into each other and want to overlap. I have to be careful not to let one piece of furniture overlap another; it's very difficult to separate them unless I notice immediately and disentangle them with the Undo feature.

I use the Scrapbook as a giant closet. For example, MacPaint can't roll up the rug and stand it in a corner, so I cut it out of the room and paste it into the Scrapbook. Later, I reverse the cut-and-paste to put the rug back.

The floor plan and the basic furniture shapes required very little freehand drawing. The tools that draw straight lines, rectangles, rounded-corner rectangles, and ovals, together with the paint can, did most of the work. For example, the rug (excluding the fringe) consists of several rectangles filled with different patterns. The fringe was drawn by constraining the brush with the Shift key and drawing a straight line made of the pattern with closely spaced parallel lines. Embellishments such as the telephone, the open book, the hand mirror, the sheet music, and the magazine were drawn mostly with the single-dot brush and touched up in FatBits.

As you can see, the armchairs, beds, and file cabinets are identical or nearly so. I drew one of each, lassoed it, and dragged away a copy with the help of the Option key. The armchairs have different upholstery, because I drew one white armchair, duplicated it, and filled each chair with a different pattern.

One of the rooms has wall-to-wall carpeting and the other has hardwood flooring, which I once tried to show with custom-made patterns. But it was almost impossible to lasso the furniture without getting some of the floor pattern too. Even when I managed that, moving the furniture left big holes in the floor that I had to go back and fill. It just wasn't worth the effort.

Wine-Cellar Inventory

I moved to Northern California about a year ago and got heavily into wines. I'm not the kind of person who collects a few bottles here and there. When I discover a really fine wine,

I prefer to pick up a case or two. Using MacWrite and Multiplan, I developed a cellar-inventory report, which details rather completely my entire holdings.

My wine collection is housed along one wall of my basement in a wine rack that stores up to 500 bottles. The 25 columns of bins are labeled with letters of the alphabet from A to Y, and the 20 rows of bins are labeled with numbers from 1 to 20. Thus, any bin can be identified by a particular letter-number combination, which I call a bin number. For example, the bin in the upper left corner is A1.

I devised a cellar-plan worksheet to map which wine is in each bin. One cell on the worksheet corresponds to a bin in the wine rack. Since the cells are not wide enough for full descriptions of the wine in the corresponding bins, I use what I call a cellar code. The cellar-inventory report cross-references a description of each wine with the cellar code and bin numbers that appear on the cellar plan.

Knowing the cellar-inventory report would not fit on one page, I set out to do the whole report in Multiplan, reasoning that with Multiplan I could easily reorder and resize columns to control page breaks. I realized quickly, however, that two-thirds of the report would be text, and that I could do much more with text in MacWrite. The report's comments column, for example, was too long to do easily in Multiplan. Futhermore, Multiplan's 10-point Seattle font cannot produce as compact and classy a report as MacWrite's 9-point type with enhancements such as bold and italic.

The Macintosh can create diacritical marks above vowels. I pressed Option-U before typing the "u" in Gewürztraminer, Option-I before typing the "o" in Pinôt, and Option-E before typing each accented "e" in Fumé, Vigné, and Rosé.

The whole cellar-inventory report ended up spanning three pages. The left-hand page includes the Variety, Year, Vineyard, Vintner, and Origin columns. The middle page includes the Bottler, Bin Number, Cellar Code, Rating, and Comments columns. The right-hand page has the rest of the columns. I printed each page separately and pieced them together with scissors and tape. The left-hand and middle pages were done entirely in MacWrite. The right-hand page, with all the numbers, was done first in Multiplan and later copied to MacWrite using the Copy and Paste features. All three pages were printed by MacWrite using the High Quality option.

Spacing

The boldface column headings that run all the way across the report end seven lines from the top of the page. The blank space above the headings accommodates the report title, which I typed at the top of the middle page. I could not use the Header feature for the title because MacWrite would have repeated it at the top of all three pages.

The report groups the wines into reds, whites, and rosés. I put four blank lines between each group. In those spaces on the middle page, I centered italic subtitles that identify the groups.

Formatting Rulers

The margins for all three pages are set at the 1-inch mark on the left and the 7¼-inch mark on the right. In order to set the right margin, I widened the document window until the scroll bar was barely visible on the screen.

The whole report requires eleven formatting rulers. The first ruler takes care of the whole left-hand page. It sets single spacing and left alignment, and puts tabs at the 2⅝-, 3¹⁄₁₆-, 4½-, and 5¹³⁄₁₆-inch marks.

A pair of formatting rulers brackets the report title and an identical pair brackets each of the italic subtitles, for a total of eight rulers on the middle page. The first ruler of each pair sets single spacing and centering, while the second ruler of each pair sets single spacing, left alignment, and tabs at the 2⁵⁄₁₆-, 3⅛-, 3⁹⁄₁₆-, and 4⁵⁄₁₆-inch marks.

The right-hand page has two formatting rulers, one above the column headings and one below them. The ruler above sets single spacing, left alignment, and decimal tabs at the 1⅝-, 2⅝-, 3½-, 4½-, and 5½-inch marks. The ruler below moves the decimal tabs to the 1⅝-, 2⁷⁄₁₆-, 3⁵⁄₁₆-, 4⁵⁄₁₆-, and 5⁹⁄₁₆-inch marks.

None of the rulers sets double spacing. Each blank line you see on the report was made by pressing the Return key.

Cellar-Inventory Worksheet

The Multiplan worksheet I used to create the right-hand page of the cellar-inventory report has formulas in both totals columns.

Rows 5 through 18, Column 3:

Total Cost = Bottles × Bottle Cost

R5C3	=RC[-2]*RC[-1]

Rows 5 through 18, Column 5:

Total Value = Bottles × Bottle Value

R5C5	=RC[-4]*RC[-1]

I entered the formulas and amounts on the worksheet and made sure they were accurate. Next, I set the formats—Decimal, No Decimal, and so forth—that I wanted in the final report. After that, I selected the group of cells on rows 5 through 18 in columns 1 through 5 and chose Copy from the Edit menu, putting the selected group of cells on the Clipboard so that, from there, I could Paste it into MacWrite. Then, I quit Multiplan. In the dialog box that immediately appeared, I chose to save formatted (not unformatted) values on the Clipboard, so that the values would end up with the same format in MacWrite as they had in Multiplan.

With the cellar inventory numbers on the Clipboard, I opened the MacWrite document. I inserted a formatting ruler at the end of the document and set five decimal tabs on the ruler, one for each column that would come from the Multiplan worksheet. Finally, with the insertion point below the new formatting ruler, I chose Paste from the Edit menu. The invisible tab characters Multiplan inserted between values on the Clipboard made the values line up according to the tabs in the new formatting ruler.

Cellar-Plan Worksheet

The cellar-plan worksheet uses General format for all cells. It has no formulas. I entered everything directly from the keyboard. I did use the Fill Down feature to save some typing of repeated cellar codes such as R1 and W2.

Variety	Year	Vineyard	Vintner	Origin
Cabernet Sauvignon	1977	Whitehead Winery	Lewis Whitehead III	Sonoma County, CA
Zinfandel	1979	Luigi Brothers' Vineyard	Gregorio & Erni Luigi	Napa County, CA
Pinôt Noir (Casks 99-235)	1976	Cedarwood Cellars	Johann & Anna Lutz	Santa Clara County, CA
Gamay Beaujolais	1981	Charles M. Heliotrope	Charles M. Heliotrope	Napa County, CA
Burgundy	1981	New York Wine Co-op	Allied Vintners' Assoc	Hudson Valley, NY
Medoc	1976	Chateau Bizet	Jacques Bizet	Bordeaux
Fumé Blanc	1981	Charles M. Heliotrope	Charles M. Heliotrope	Napa County, CA
Chardonnay	1980	Whitehead Winery	Lewis Whitehead III	Sonoma County, CA
Gewürztraminer	1980	Cedarwood Cellars	Johann & Anna Lutz	Santa Clara County, CA
Sauternes	1978	Chateau Vigné	M. Proust	Bordeaux
Riesling	1982	Schloss Johann	Herr Schtumff	Rudesheim
Grenache Rosé	1982	Luigi Brothers' Vineyard	Gregorio & Erni Luigi	Napa County, CA

Bottler	Bin Number	Cellar Code	Rating	Comments . . .
--Red Wines--				
Whitehead Winery	A1–A12	R1	Excellent	Medium dark red; fruity aroma; very fruity taste, clean aftertaste; moderate body, tannin, and acid
Napa Bottlers	C1–C18	R2	Good	Medium red; soft fruity aroma; smooth taste; medium body; moderate acid and tannin
Cedarwood Cellars	E1–F4	R3	Very Good	Dark red; rich aroma; deep fruity taste; moderate body and acid; strong tannin
Charles M. Heliotrope	H1–H18	R4	Very Good	Light red; soft fruity aroma; light fruity taste; light body; low acid and tannin
NY Union Bottlers	J1–J18	R5	Good	Medium red; pleasing earthy aroma; fruity taste; light body; moderate tannin and acid
Chateau Bizet	L1–L12	R6	Very Good	Light red; fruity aroma; soft fruity taste; light body; moderate acid and tannin
--White Wines--				
Charles M. Heliotrope	M1–N4	W1	Excellent	Light yellow; fruity-woody aroma; very clean, dry taste; moderate body and acid
Whitehead Winery	P1–P18	W2	Very Good	Medium yellow; apple-like aroma; tart fruity taste; light body; moderate acid
Cedarwood Cellars	R1–R12	W3	Good	Pale gold; slightly spicy aroma; hint of sweetness; medium body; moderate acid
Chateau Vigné	T1–T12	W4	Very Good	Medium yellow; fruity-woody aroma; sweet not sugary taste; light body and acid
Schloss Johann	V1–V18	W5	Good	Medium yellow; fruity aroma; dry taste; medium body and acid
--Rosé Wines--				
Napa Bottlers	X1–X12	O1	Good	Pinky-orange; fruity aroma; fairly dry taste; medium body and acid

Bottles On Hand	Cost of Each Bottle	Total Cost	Value of Each Bottle	Total Value
12	8.75	105.00	21.50	258.00
18	4.25	76.50	6.75	121.50
24	5.50	132.00	14.25	342.00
18	5.00	90.00	9.75	175.50
18	2.45	44.10	6.00	108.00
12	6.50	78.00	24.25	291.00
24	6.40	153.60	18.50	444.00
18	12.25	220.50	25.50	459.00
12	5.75	69.00	10.40	124.80
12	6.00	72.00	15.50	186.00
18	4.85	87.30	6.75	121.50
12	2.85	34.20	5.95	71.40

Cellar Inventory Worksheet

	1	2	3	4	5	6
1	Bottles	Cost of	Total	Value of	Total	
2	On Hand	Each Bottle	Cost	Each Bottle	Value	
3						
4						
5	12	8.75	105.00	21.50	258.00	Reds
6	18	4.25	76.50	6.75	121.50	
7	24	5.50	132.00	14.25	342.00	
8	18	5.00	90.00	9.75	175.50	
9	18	2.45	44.10	6.00	108.00	
10	12	6.50	78.00	24.25	291.00	
11						
12	24	6.40	153.60	18.50	444.00	Whites
13	18	12.25	220.50	25.50	459.00	
14	12	5.75	69.00	10.40	124.80	
15	12	6.00	72.00	15.50	186.00	
16	18	4.85	87.30	6.75	121.50	
17						
18	12	2.85	34.20	5.95	71.40	Roses
19						
20						
21						
22						
23						
24						
25						
26						
27						
28						
29						
30						
31						
32						
33						
34						
35						
36						
37						
38						
39						
40						

Creighton R. A. Pembroke IV
Cellar Plan
1 April 1985

| | | | RED | | | | | | | ---> < --- | | | | | | | WHITE | | | | ---> < - ROSE -> | |
A	B	C	D	E	F	G	H	I	J	K	L	M	N	O	P	Q	R	S	T	U	V	W	X	Y
R1		R2		R3	R3		R4		R5	R6	W1	W1	W1		W2	W3		W4		W5		O1		
R1		R2		R3	R3		R4		R5	R6	W1	W1	W1		W2	W3		W4		W5		O1		
R1		R2		R3	R3		R4		R5	R6	W1	W1	W1		W2	W3		W4		W5		O1		
R1		R2		R3	R3		R4		R5	R6	W1	W1	W1		W2	W3		W4		W5		O1		
R1		R2		R3			R4		R5	R6	W1	W1	W1		W2	W3		W4		W5		O1		
R1		R2		R3			R4		R5	R6	W1				W2	W3		W4		W5		O1		
R1		R2		R3			R4		R5	R6	W1				W2	W3		W4		W5		O1		
R1		R2		R3			R4		R5	R6	W1				W2	W3		W4		W5		O1		
R1		R2		R3			R4		R5	R6	W1				W2	W3		W4		W5		O1		
R1		R2		R3			R4		R5	R6	W1				W2	W3				W5				
R1		R2		R3			R4		R5	R6	W1				W2					W5				
R1		R2		R3			R4		R5		W1				W2					W5				
		R2		R3			R4		R5		W1				W2					W5				
		R2		R3			R4		R5		W1				W2					W5				
		R2		R3					R5		W1									W5				
				R3							W1													
				R3							W1													

Get-Well Card

I made a get-well card for my friend Augie, who caught pneumonia when playing miniature golf in the rain. Making the card didn't take much longer than going to the card shop and buying a card, and this way Augie got a personalized message.

The front of the card is a MacPaint document. I started with a cloud, rain, and puddle. First, I drew the cloud using the spray can with a dark gray pattern and then I used a light gray pattern for final shading. With the grabber, I scrolled the cloud out of the way, leaving just the bottom of it showing at the top of the drawing window. Next came the rain. I modified one of the patterns, chose the no-border line thickness, and with the filled, irregular-shape tool, I outlined the shape of the rain. Releasing the mouse button filled the shape with the rain pattern and removed the border line. Some retouching around the edges using a medium-sized round brush with the white pattern was necessary. I used the same technique for the puddle as for the rain, but used a standard, medium gray pattern.

In an empty area of the document, which I got to using Show Page, I sketched the sad-faced man. I used the single-dot brush and some FatBits work. The paint-can tool filled his clothes with different gray patterns. I lassoed the finished man and put him on the Clipboard with the Cut command. Then, I went back to the rainy area on the document. There I pasted the man from the Clipboard and dragged him under the cloud, standing in the rain. I used the pencil in FatBits to trace a line around his shoes so they would stand out better.

Finally, I typed a message of regret below the puddle, in 14-point plain Geneva.

For the inside of the card, I opened another MacPaint document and typed the centered message in 14-point plain Geneva.

I printed the card on a 12-inch by 9-inch piece of green construction paper, folded in half widthwise. But before printing on the construction paper, I did a couple of trial runs on some plain paper, carefully noting the position of the top and right edges of the paper. That told me how far to the right to insert the folded construction paper, and how far to roll it through before starting the printing. I was just as careful about aligning the paper for the inside message.

Hey Augie, sorry to hear you're under the weather.

Too bad you caught double-pneumonia
by playing through the downpour
that drenched the last round of
the Dinah's Diner Invitational
Putt-Putt Golf Tournament
last weekend.

Congratulations anyway for
winning, you zany duffer!

Get well soon!

343

Shangri-La Open House

Having recently acquired new digs at the exclusive Shangri-La Bungalows, I determined to have my pals over for a look around the joint. I drew this combination map/invitation with Mac-Paint. The main map shows the general lay of the land, and an inset map shows how to get to my place from the nearest major intersection.

I did most of the lines in the main map with the brush. A wide, dark gray brush works well for freeways and a thin black brush does a good job for freeway on- and off-ramps and city streets. The Shift key forces the brush to draw horizontal or vertical lines for the straight stretches. I used the same type of brush for the shorelines as for the streets. The water is custom made using the Edit Pattern feature.

All the street names are 12-point plain New York. I typed the street names for Frontage Rd., Oak St., Della St., and Lois Ln. in place. But I typed the names for White Way, Broadway, and Knowe Way one at a time off to the side. I selected each name with the selection rectangle and rotated it 90 degrees, and then lassoed and dragged it into place. In fact, I dragged each letter of Knowe Way and of Lake Dr. into place separately.

To label Lake Lorenzo, I typed the name in the margin in 12-point bold New York. Then I added a shadow to the name as a whole by selecting the words with the selection rectangle, holding down the Shift key, and choosing Trace Edges from the Edit menu.

To construct the Interstate 80 sign, I typed a boldface 80, selected it with the selection rectangle, and reversed the selected area with the Invert feature, resulting in a white 80 inside a square of black. Then I used the pencil in FatBits to carve the shield out of the black square.

Except for the bushes in Peeble's Park, the inset map is a study in rectangles. Notice how the rooftop patterns suggest a slope by running in opposite directions from the peak lines. I got that effect by filling both halves of the roof with the same pattern, selecting one half with the selection rectangle, and flipping it with the Flip Vertical feature. I painted the center stripes on the roads with a small white brush, constrained by the Shift key to draw only straight lines.

344

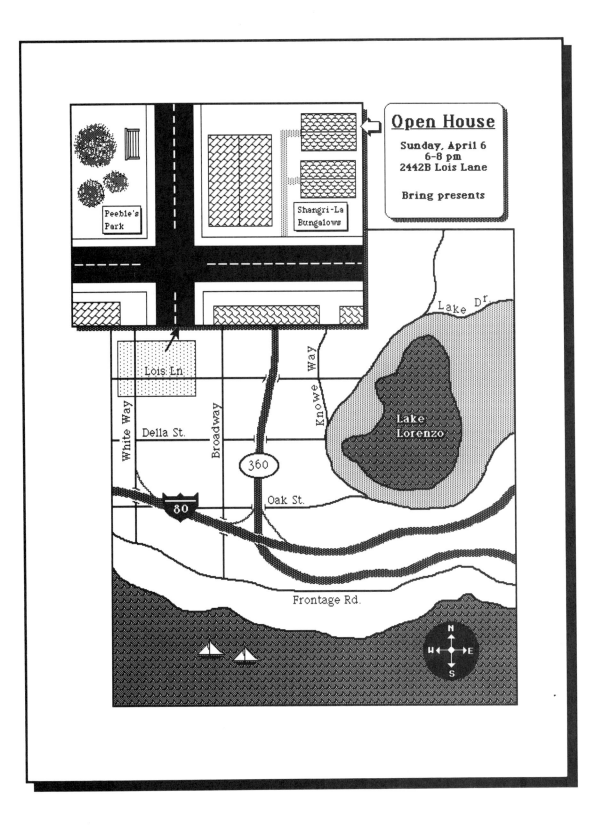

Open House

Sunday, April 6
6-8 pm
2442B Lois Lane

Bring presents

Peeble's Park

Shangri-La Bungalows

Lois Ln

White Way

Della St.

Broadway

Knowe Way

Lake Dr.

Lake Lorenzo

360

80

Oak St.

Frontage Rd.

N
W · E
S

The invitation itself, located in the upper right corner, is in 18-point and 12-point bold New York. The arrow that points to my place is one of the symbols from the Cairo font. Typing a lowercase "h" generates an arrow pointing to the right, which I selected, flipped horizontally, lassoed, and dragged into place.

Don Bosco Party Invitation

We posted a Macintosh notice on bulletin boards all over Don Bosco Technical High School to advertise the next '50s revival sock hop. An art student drew the shoes with MacPaint, and the general party committee drafted the rest of the notice in MacWrite. You can probably guess the shoes were done with the single-dot brush, with lots of detail work in FatBits. The words Dust Off Your Dancin' Shoes are part of the MacPaint drawing, too. They are 12-point bold Toronto (which someone on the committee copied to the MacPaint and MacWrite disks using the Font Mover program). The drawing was copied from MacPaint to MacWrite via the Clipboard with the help of the Copy and Paste features.

All the words typed in MacWrite are bold Toronto, either 12-point or 9-point. The formatting ruler at the top of the page has one tab, at the 4 5/16-inch mark, for lining up the decorations-committee sign-up list in the bottom half of the page.

The notices were printed one at a time on single sheets of colored paper by students who had to stay after school because they got caught in a food fight. They used MacWrite's High Quality option.

Dust Off Your Dancin' Shoes...

...and come to our party.

Don Bosco Technical High School is holding its fifth annual Sock Hop and Buddy Holly Look-Alike Contest.

When: Tuesday, October 29, at 7 p.m.
Where: In the gym, as usual.
Why: So we can all have an opportunity to make fools of ourselves in front of members of the opposite sex.

Sign up below if you want to be on a committee.

Refreshments

_____

_____

_____

_____

_____

_____

Decorations

_____

_____

_____

_____

_____

_____

Be there or be square!

Early-Payoff Analysis

The wind blew hot that morning, east across the basin from the desert. One of the air conditioners was out, naturally, along with half the office staff. I sat quietly sweating, feet up, staring out the window at the oil wells pumping steadily on Signal Hill across the street. Bill, my partner, had been working too hard for an hour now.

"I've got it," he said.

"What's that?"

"You know that second mortgage you just took out on your house so you could buy that property outside of Kalispell? I can show you how to save over $11,000 in interest by paying back just $50 a month more. Not only that, but you'll finish paying it off almost three years ahead of schedule."

"Okay, Bill, I'm thrilled. Why don't you show me what you've got there?"

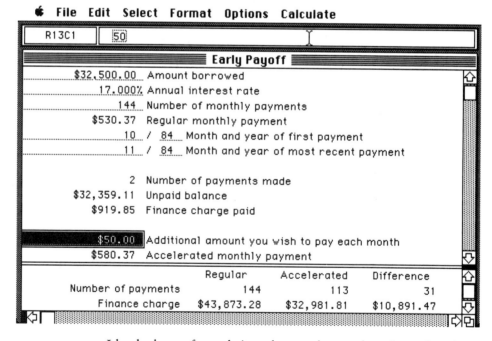

I lurched out of my chair and crossed around to sit on the edge of my desk where I could see what he had going. Jeez, it was another one of those Multiplan worksheets. The guy is nuts for them. This one was going to show me how much I would save by paying off my loan early. If I followed all of Bill's advice for saving money, I'd never have to work again. Kind of reminds me of the JC Whitney auto parts catalog, which lists about 500 additives and gizmos for saving gas. Each one saves you 2, 3, 7 percent—something like that. But if you go through and add up all those percentages, you end up saving more than 100 percent—you actually produce gas. I can just see myself driving down the street with gas pouring out of my tank. I told Bill about that once. He was not amused.

How It Works

Here's how Bill explained his worksheet.

The unpaid loan balance can only be computed by repeatedly recalculating some of the formulas on the worksheet, a process called *iteration*. For best results, you should choose Manual Calculation and Iterate from the Calculate menu before entering any formulas or amounts. In addition, select the cell at row 9, column 7 and choose Set Completion Test from the Calculate menu. That cell will contain what's called the *completion test* formula, which tells Multiplan when to stop iteration.

After entering the descriptions and formulas, use the Remove Cell Protection feature on these eight cells:

- Amount borrowed (R2C1).

- Interest rate (R3C1).

- Number of monthly payments (R4C1).

- Month and year of the first payment (R6C1 and R6C3).

- Month and year of the most recent payment (R7C1 and R7C3).

- Additional amount you want to pay from now on (R13C1).

Protect the rest of the worksheet with the Protect Document feature. This eliminates the clutter of grid lines and row and column numbers, making room for more of the worksheet in the window.

Multiplan underlines the eight unprotected cells; you enter amounts in them. The worksheet uses a standard formula to calculate the regular monthly payment. If your regular monthly payment is different, you should unprotect the worksheet, type the actual payment in place of the formula, and reprotect the worksheet.

When the amounts are ready, choose Calculate Now from the Calculate menu to start iteration. Multiplan recalculates the worksheet once for each of the payments you've already made on the loan. In the process, it tallies the number of payments, computes the unpaid loan balance after your most recent payment, and figures the total finance charge at that time.

Another formula, which doesn't require iteration, figures your new, accelerated monthly payment. Assuming you pay that amount every month, starting next month, the other formulas calculate how many payments you have yet to make and how much interest you have yet to pay before the loan is paid off. The last payment you make will probably be larger than the rest. This worksheet does not tell you how much larger the last payment will be, though you can be sure the extra amount will be smaller than one accelerated payment.

At the bottom of the worksheet, a small table compares the regular and accelerated payoffs. You can split the document window across and scroll this table into view in the bottom pane. The first column of the table lists the number of payments and the finance charge, assuming all your payments are the regular amount. The second column recaps the total number of payments and the finance charge, assuming you switch to an accelerated payment amount as indicated in the top part of the worksheet. The third column tells you how much less you will pay in finance charges by accelerating repayment. It also tells you how many fewer payments you will have to make.

The completion-test formula (R9C7) tells Multiplan when to stop recalculating the worksheet. The worksheet computes the number of payments you have already made from the two dates you entered. When the number of payments calculated equals (or exceeds) the number of payments you have already made, recalculation stops. The ITERCNT() function (in R9C1) tells the worksheet how many times it was recalculated.

Formulas

Row 5, Column 1:

$Regular\ Payment = ROUND((Amount\ Borrowed \times Interest \div 12) \div (1 - (1 + (Interest \div 12)) \char94 - Number\ of\ Payments), 2)$

| R5C1 | =ROUND((R[-3]C*R[-2]C/12)/(1-(1+R[-2]C/12)^-R[-1]C),2) |

Row 9, Column 1:

$Payments\ Made = IF(ISNA(ITERCNT(\ )), 0, ITERCNT(\ ))$

| R9C1 | =IF(ISNA(ITERCNT()),0,ITERCNT()) |

Row 10, Column 1:

$Unpaid\ Balance = IF(ISNA(ITERCNT(\ )), Amount\ Borrowed, Unpaid\ Balance - (Regular\ Payment - ROUND(Unpaid\ Balance \times Interest \div 12, 2)))$

| R10C1 | =IF(ISNA(ITERCNT()),R[-8]C,RC-(R[-5]C-ROUND(RC*R[-7]C/12, 2))) |

Row 11, Column 1:

$Finance\ Charge\ Paid = Regular\ Payment \times Payments\ Made - (Amount\ Borrowed - Unpaid\ Balance)$

| R11C1 | =R[-6]C*R[-2]C-(R[-9]C-R[-1]C) |

Row 14, Column 1:

$Accelerated\ Payment = Regular\ Payment + Additional\ Payment$

| R14C1 | =R[-9]C+R[-1]C |

Row 15, Column 1:

$Accelerated\ Payments\ Required = ROUND(-LN(1 - (Unpaid\ Balance \times Interest) \div (12 \times Accelerated\ Payment)) \div LN(1 + Interest \div 12), 0)$

| R15C1 | =ROUND(-LN(1-(R[-5]C*R[-12]C)/(12*R[-1]C))/LN(1+R[-12]C/ 12),0) |

Row 16, Column 1:

Finance Charge Payable = Accelerated Payments Required
× Accelerated Payment − Unpaid Balance

R16C1	=R[-1]C*R[-2]C-R[-6]C

Row 19, Column 4:

Number of Regular Payments = Number of Monthly Payments

R19C4	=R[-15]C[-3]

Row 19, Column 5:

Number of Accelerated Payments = Payments Made + Accelerated
Payments Required

R19C5	=R[-10]C[-4]+R[-4]C[-4]

Rows 19 and 20, Column 6:

Difference = Regular − Accelerated

R19C6	=RC[-2]-RC[-1]

Row 20, Column 4:

Regular Finance Charge = Number of Payments × Regular Payment
− Amount Borrowed

R20C4	=R[-16]C[-3]*R[-15]C[-3]-R[-18]C[-3]

Row 20, Column 5:

Accelerated Finance Charge = Finance Charge Paid + Finance
Charge Payable

R20C5	=R[-9]C[-4]+R[-4]C[-4]

Row 9, Column 7:

Completion Test = Payments Made > = 1 + Latest Payment Month
− First Payment Month + 12
× (Latest Payment Year − First Payment Year)

R9C7	=RC[-6]>=1+R[-2]C[-6]-R[-3]C[-6]+12*(R[-2]C[-4]-R[-3]C[-4])

EARLY LOAN PAYOFF

	1	2	3	4	5	6	7
1							
2	$32,500.00			Amount borrowed			
3	17.000%			Annual interest rate			
4	144			Number of monthly payments			
5	$530.37			Regular monthly payment			
6	10	/	84	Month and year of first payment			
7	11	/	84	Month and year of most recent payment			
8							
9	2			Number of payments made			TRUE
10	$32,359.11			Unpaid balance			
11	$919.85			Finance charge paid			
12							
13	$50.00			Additional amount you wish to pay each month			
14	$580.37			Accelerated monthly payment			
15	111			Number of accelerated payments required			
16	$32,061.96			Finance charge that will be paid			
17							
18				Regular	Accelerated	Difference	
19	Number of payments			144	113	31	
20	Finance charge			$43,873.28	$32,981.81	$10,891.47	
21							
22							
23							
24							
25							
26							
27							
28							
29							
30							
31							
32							
33							
34							
35							
36							
37							
38							
39							
40							

Free Kittens Advertisement

I thought my cat wanted to experience motherhood. I was wrong; she didn't seem to care for it. The kittens had to go, so I opened a new MacWrite document and typed up a notice using 14-point bold Geneva for the most part, but 24-point bold shadow Geneva for the headline.

I used three rulers altogether. The first ruler centered the headline, the second justified the body of the notice at both margins, and the third centered my name and phone number at the lower edge of the notice. All three rulers set the left margin at the 1-inch mark and the right margin at the 6-inch mark.

A friend of mine dropped by and lent a hand by drawing two kittens in a basket using MacPaint. She used the hollow-oval tool to draw the bottom of the basket and, an inch or so above that, the top of the basket. She drew the sides with the straight line tool, and erased the back part of the lower oval with the eraser. At this point, she used the paint can to fill the inside of the basket with a dark gray pattern.

Next, she drew a kitten. She used the small round brush with the medium gray pattern to sketch the general shape. Then she changed to a smaller brush and a darker gray pattern for shading. A small white brush allowed her to hollow out the eyes. She finished by drawing the whiskers, eyebrows, mouth, and other details with a small black brush.

She lassoed the kitten, held down the Option key, and dragged away a duplicate. She made a couple of quick passes at the second kitten with small gray brushes, making it look a little different from the first. Then she lassoed both kittens and dragged them into the basket. They overlapped the top of the basket, so she redrew the curve at the top of the basket with the single-dot brush and erased the part of the kittens that extended below it. Then she filled the front of the basket with the diagonal brick pattern.

I pasted her drawing into my notice, printed up two dozen copies on some 6- by 9-inch sheets of colored paper, and tacked them to telephone poles in the neighborhood. Got rid of those kittens in a week.

FREE KITTENS

Free to good home: two disgusting little hairballs that will most likely cost you a fortune in vet bills, insist on eating only the most expensive brand of catfood, exhibit little if any affection, and aggravate your allergies to boot. But what do you want for free?

Call Suzi at 345-8972 for further information.

Investment Analysis

Five years ago, before my wife Louise and I got married, she bought a shack in San Pedro. Her father had always told her buying a home, any home, was "the best investment you'll ever make." Well, my father, an old mutual-funds enthusiast, always told me real estate was a terrible investment and would lead to "your financial ruin." So I waited six months after getting married for the dust to settle before I started subtly campaigning to sell the albatross and invest the proceeds in some of the high-yield mutual funds available today. Louise demurred by preparing this Multiplan model that demonstrated what a sound investment her house had been.

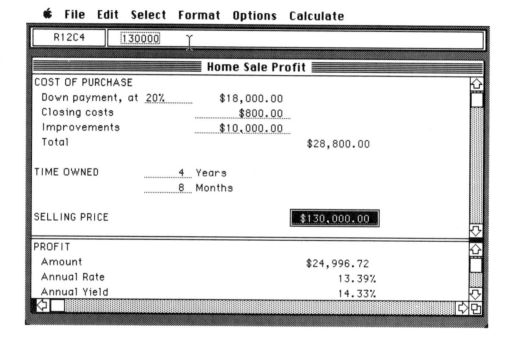

The Assumptions

Any investment can be made to look great, if you make the right assumptions. (My father told me that, too.) So I checked the assumptions and premises built into her worksheet:

▪ She got a pretty good deal on the terms: paid 20 percent down, assumed an existing loan with a balance of $46,000 at 9⅛ percent with 25 years left on a 30-year term; and got the previous owners to carry a $26,000 second at 15 percent for 12 years.

▪ Before she moved in, she had the plumbing completely redone and the bathroom remodeled, raising her investment cost by $10,000.

▪ She would have to pay standard broker's fee for selling: 6 percent.

▪ She deferred about $2,000 in pest control work when she bought the house, and expects that, plus other closing costs, would run $4,500.

▪ The analysis period, 1980 to 1985, was neither particularly good nor bad for home prices, so her figures were not skewed by unusual market conditions.

▪ She based the projected selling price on two independent appraisals.

▪ The carrying costs of owning equal the carrying costs of renting. The cost of utilities, insurance, and minor maintenance would be the same, renting or buying. The total rent paid would equal the total mortgage payment, plus major repairs (paint, roofing, etc., which the landlord would pay if renting), plus property taxes, minus the income-tax benefits from interest and property-tax deductions.

▪ All the proceeds from the sale of this property would be reinvested within 24 months in another home of equal or greater value, so no federal income tax would be due on the profit of this sale.

▪ In computing an interest rate, she used daily compounding of interest.

Based on these assumptions, the worksheet made her house look like a reasonable investment. But I am not completely convinced. It goes against my upbringing. I shall attack her assumptions and invest our money in a few "shares of America"—or bust.

The Main Worksheet

To compute the profit she would make from the sale of her house, Louise used three worksheets. The main worksheet determines the dollar profit, two interest rates, and some incidental totals. One of the interest rates, which Louise calls the Annual Rate, is the rate a savings account would have to have paid on the same investment to match the dollar profit. The other rate, which she calls the Annual Yield, is the average yearly appreciation rate on the investment.

Louise had to enter the purchase price, down-payment percentage, closing costs of buying, cost of capital improvements, years and months owned, broker's fee for selling, and closing costs of selling. The worksheet obtains the remaining balances on first and second mortgages from two auxiliary worksheets.

The main worksheet is protected, except for the cells that must be entered from the keyboard. Those cells remain unprotected by selecting them and choosing the Remove Cell Protection feature from the Options menu before protecting the whole worksheet.

Auxiliary Remaining-Balance Worksheets

Louise could not find a single formula that would calculate the balance remaining on a loan in any given month. It seems one must examine each payment in turn, determining how much of it goes to pay interest and how much to reduce the loan balance. So, for each loan, she set up an auxiliary worksheet with formulas that calculate the interest and principal reduction for any single payment. Then she used the Iteration feature to have Multiplan recalculate the auxiliary worksheet once for each month between the date the loan started and the date for which she wanted to know the remaining balance. For example, to calculate the remaining balance after two and a half years of monthly payments, Multiplan has to iterate (recalculate the worksheet) 30 times.

On each auxiliary worksheet, Louise had to enter the amount borrowed (the principal), the interest rate, the term of the loan as a number of years, the month and year the first payment was made, and the month and year the final payment was or will be made. The worksheet assumes payments are made on a monthly basis. It computes the amount of the regular payment, and the total number of payments. Then, using iteration, it calculates the interest paid with each payment, the amount paid toward reduction of principal, the total interest paid to date, the total principal reduction to date, and the remaining balance. The worksheet stops iterating when it has computed these amounts from the first payment to the last.

The first time the worksheet iterates, it does not process a loan payment. Instead it sets the interest and principal totals equal to zero and the remaining balance equal to the loan principal. At that time, the value of function ITERCNT( ) is #N/A (not available). The ISNA( ) function detects that fact and cues the interest total, principal total, and remaining balance cells to use their initial values.

Every iteration after the first, the worksheet calculates another loan payment. It uses the ITERCNT( ) function, which reports the number of iterations performed so far, to determine the current payment number. It figures out the interest due by multiplying the monthly interest rate by the current remaining loan balance. It subtracts that interest amount from the regular monthly payment and applies the difference to the loan balance, generating a new remaining balance. The new balance is used during the next iteration to figure the amount of interest due in the next month. The worksheet also keeps running totals of the total interest and total principal paid so far.

The worksheet cell that contains the so-called *completion test* formula determines when iteration stops. The formula has a value of False as long as the number of payments processed (the number of iterations) is less than the number of payments required. When the value of the completion test becomes True, iteration stops. The remaining balance displayed then is the one sought.

To set up the iteration, Louise chose Iterate and Manual Calculation from the Calculate menu. She also selected the cell containing the completion-test formula and chose Set Completion Test from the Calculate menu. After she entered all the values and was ready to calculate the remaining balance, she chose Calculate Now from the Calculate menu.

The auxiliary worksheets are identical except for the values entered. To create the first one, Louise entered the values for the first mortgage and used the Save As... feature to save the worksheet on disk under the name 1st Mortgage Balance. Then she linked the remaining balance from that worksheet to the main worksheet. She established the link by selecting the remaining-balance cell on the auxiliary worksheet and choosing Copy from the Edit menu. That put the selected cell on the Clipboard. Then she opened the main worksheet, selected the destination cell there, and chose Paste and Link from the Edit menu. That pasted a reference to the remaining-balance cell from the auxiliary worksheet into the main worksheet. Now, going back and changing the remaining balance in the auxiliary worksheet would automatically change the remaining balance in the main worksheet, too.

For the second mortgage, she used the first mortgage worksheet as a basis. First, she opened it and immediately saved it on disk (using the Save As... feature) under the name 2nd Mortgage Balance. Then, she changed the entries to reflect the second mortgage and saved it again, this time with the Save feature. After that, she linked the remaining balance of the second mortgage to the main worksheet.

Like the main worksheet, the auxiliary worksheets are protected, except for the cells that must be entered from the keyboard.

Formulas for Remaining-Balance Worksheets

Row 4, Column 2:

$$Payment\ Amount = \text{ROUND}((Principal \times Interest \div 12)$$
$$\div (1 - (1 + Interest \div 12)\,\hat{}\, -(12 \times Term)),\ 2)$$

```
R4C2    =ROUND((R[-3]C*R[-2]C/12)/(1-(1+R[-2]C/12)^-(12*R[-1]C)),
        2)
```

Rows 5 and 9, Column 1:

line of hyphens = REPT(" – ",45)

| R5C1 | =REPT("-",45) |

Row 11, Column 2:

This Payment Number = ITERCNT( )

| R11C2 | =ITERCNT() |

Row 12, Column 2:

This Payment Interest = ROUND(*Remaining Balance* × *Interest* ÷ 12, 2)

| R12C2 | =ROUND(R[+2]C[+1]*R[-10]C/12,2) |

Row 13, Column 2:

This Payment Amortized = *Payment Amount* – *This Payment Interest*

| R13C2 | =R[-9]C-R[-1]C |

Row 11, Column 3:

Total Number Payments = ROUND((*Last Payment Year* – *First Payment Year* + (*Last Payment Month* – *First Payment Month* + 1) ÷ 12) × 12, 0)

| R11C3 | =ROUND((R[-3]C-R[-4]C+(R[-3]C[-1]-R[-4]C[-1]+1)/12)*12,0) |

Row 12, Column 3:

Total Interest = IF(ISNA(*This Payment Number*), 0, *Total Interest* + *This Payment Interest*)

| R12C3 | =IF(ISNA(R[-1]C[-1]),0,RC+RC[-1]) |

Row 13, Column 3:

Total Amortized = IF(ISNA(*This Payment Number*), 0, *Total Amortized* + *This Payment Amortized*)

| R13C3 | =IF(ISNA(R[-2]C[-1]),0,RC+RC[-1]) |

Row 14, Column 3:

Remaining Balance = IF(ISNA(*This Payment Number*), *Principal*,
Remaining Balance – *This Payment Amortized*)

R14C3	=IF(ISNA(I+R[-3]C[-1]),R[-13]C[-1],RC-R[-1]C[-1])

Row 15, Column 2:

Completion Test = *This Payment Number* > = *Total Number Payments*

R15C2	=R[-4]C>=R[-4]C[+1]

Profit-Worksheet Formulas

Row 4, Column 3:

Down Payment = *Purchase Price* × *Down Payment Percentage*

R4C3	=R[-3]C[+1]*RC[-1]

Row 7, Column 4:

Total Cost of Purchase = SUM(*Down Payment* : *Improvements*)

R7C4	=SUM(R[-3]C[-1]:R[-1]C[-1])

Row 15, Column 3:

1st Mortgage Balance = [1st Mortgage Balance R14C3]

R15C3	[1st Mortgage Balance R14C3]

Row 16, Column 3:

2nd Mortgage Balance = [2nd Mortgage Balance R14C3]

R16C3	[2nd Mortgage Balance R14C3]

Row 17, Column 3:

Brokerage Fee = *Commission Rate* × *Selling Price*

R17C3	=RC[-1]*R[-5]C[+1]

Row 19, Column 4:

Total Cost of Sale = SUM(*1st Mortgage Balance : Other Selling Costs*)

R19C4	=SUM(R[-4]C[-1]:R[-1]C[-1])

Row 21, Column 4:

Net Proceeds = *Selling Price* − *Total Cost of Sale*

R21C4	=R[-9]C-R[-2]C

Row 24, Column 4:

Profit = *Total Cost of Purchase* − *Net Proceeds*

R24C4	=R[-3]C-R[-17]C

Row 25, Column 4:

Nominal Rate = $365 \times$ (*Net Proceeds* ÷ *Total Cost of Purchase*) ^ (1 ÷ ($365 \times$ (*Years Owned* + *Months Owned* ÷ 12))) − 365

R25C4	=365*(R[-4]C/R[-18]C)^(1/(365*(R[-16]C[-2]+R[-15]C[-2]/12)))-365

Row 26, Column 4:

Yield = (*Net Proceeds* ÷ *Total Cost of Purchase*) ^ (1 ÷ (*Years Owned* + *Months Owned* ÷ 12)) − 1

R26C4	=(R[-5]C/R[-19]C)^(1/(R[-17]C[-2]+R[-16]C[-2]/12))-1

	1	2	3	4
1	PURCHASE PRICE			$90,000.00
2				
3	COST OF PURCHASE			
4	Down payment, at	20%	$18,000.00	
5	Closing costs		$800.00	
6	Improvements		$10,000.00	
7	Total			$28,800.00
8				
9	TIME OWNED	4	Years	
10		8	Months	
11				
12	SELLING PRICE			$130,000.00
13				
14	COST OF SALE			
15	1st Mortgage balance		$43,147.97	
16	2nd Mortgage balance		$20,755.31	
17	Brokerage fee, at	6%	$7,800.00	
18	Other Selling Costs		$4,500.00	
19	Total			$76,203.28
20				
21	NET PROCEEDS			$53,796.72
22				
23	PROFIT			
24	Amount			$24,996.72
25	Annual Rate			13.39%
26	Annual Yield			14.33%

	1	2	3
1	Principal	$48,000.00	
2	Interest rate	9.125%	
3	Term in years	30	
4	Payment amount	$390.54	
5	-------------------	-------------------	-------
6		Month	Year
7	First payment made	6	75
8	Last payment made	3	85
9	-------------------	-------------------	-------
10		This payment	Total
11	Number	118	118
12	Interest	$328.58	$41,231.69
13	Principal reduction	$61.96	$4,852.03
14	Remaining balance		$43,147.97
15		TRUE	

	1	2	3
1	Principal	$26,000.00	
2	Interest rate	15.000%	
3	Term in years	12	
4	Payment amount	$390.23	
5	------------------	------------------	------------------
6		Month	Year
7	First payment made	8	80
8	Last payment made	3	85
9	------------------	------------------	------------------
10		This payment	Total
11	Number	56	56
12	Interest	$261.06	$16,608.19
13	Principal reduction	$129.17	$5,244.69
14	Remaining balance		$20,755.31
15		TRUE	

Fancy Lettering

While browsing at the bookstore, I ran across two books—*Art Deco Designs and Motifs* by Marcia Loeb (New York: Dover Press, 1972) and *Monograms and Decorations From the Art Nouveau Period* by Wilhelm Diebener (New York: Dover Press, 1982)—with complete display-type alphabets I just had to try in MacPaint. One was an ornate Art-Deco style; the other was a simple but elegant Art-Nouveau style. A friend of mine, whose hobby is calligraphy, happened to see me working on the decorative alphabets and insisted on drawing some foreign characters.

Art-Deco Alphabet

Thanks to MacPaint's ability to duplicate a selected piece of a picture, reproducing the Art-Deco alphabet was much easier than it might appear. I had to create only five letters completely from scratch: A, B, C, E, and O. Cannibalizing those five letters provided most of the parts for the other 21. For example, I made the D from a C flipped horizontally, joined with the left-hand part of a B, and touched up in FatBits. You will see parts of the B in the G, J, P, R, S, T, and U as well. The C also appears in the G, J, R, S, U, and Y. The F is nearly identical to the E, as is the L, but parts of the E also show up in the H, I, K, M, N, T, Y, and Z. The angled sides of the A, which took a lot of work in FatBits, came in handy for the K, M, N, V, W, and X. Another part of the A, the round circular crossbar, also appears in the E, F, and H. The last three choices on the Edit menu—Flip Vertical, Flip Horizontal, and Rotate—got lots of use creating this alphabet.

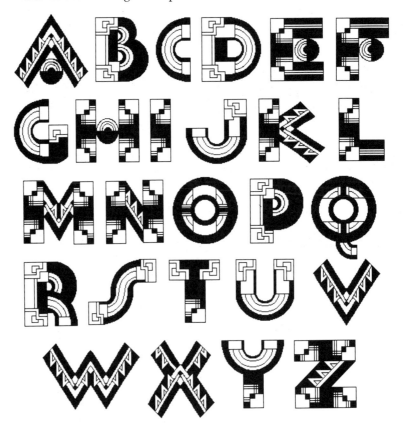

Art-Nouveau Alphabet

Compared to the Art-Deco alphabet, with its intricate geometric designs, the Art-Nouveau alphabet looks deceptively plain and simple. Almost every letter has a smooth curve in it somewhere, however. None of those curves can be drawn with the oval-drawing tool, either. I started by tracing and sketching letters from the book onto a piece of transparent acetate (available at artist supply stores). Then I taped the transparencies to the Macintosh screen and, with a single-dot brush, copied them into a MacPaint document.

With the letters outlined on the screen, I used the pencil in FatBits to smooth out the rough edges and personalize the design. I managed to fabricate the G from the C, the F from the E, the Q from the O, the W from the V, and the Y from the X. The thick vertical lines in other letters, such as B, H, M, and U, seemed at first glance to have the same width, but careful measuring revealed four different widths. The G, M, and U are one width. The B, D, E, F, J, P, R, and T are one dot wider. The H and K are another dot wider. The I and L are one dot wider still.

Shading the outlined alphabet black was the last step. I discovered I could shade several letters at once by lassoing them and choosing Fill from the Edit menu. The B, D, P, and R had to be filled individually with the paint can, since each completely encircles white space that must not be filled too.

ABCDEFGHIJK
LMNOPQRSTU
VWXYZ

Calligraphy

I thought the angled-line paint brushes would make a decent calligraphy pen, but my friend prefers the small square brush. It was the main tool he used to draw the Hebrew and Chinese characters. All the calligraphy required some touch-up with the pencil in FatBits.

Originally, he drew the Chinese characters in black. When they were finished, he selected them all with the selection rectangle and chose Trace Edges from the Edit menu, turning them into outlined white characters. He shaded the outlined characters medium gray with the paint can.

Hebrew

אבגדהוזחטיכל
מנסעפצקרשת

Chinese

賞 自 中 馬 冋 酒
詰 逳 人 間 女

Cadillac for Sale

My wife took one look at the beautiful pink '59 Cadillac I won at my Thursday-night Poker Club and said, "I wouldn't be caught dead in that thing. Either that car goes or I do." Women. Well, I had to sell her (the car). I decided to use MacPaint to make some 3 by 5 cards for posting on supermarket ad boards.

Being lousy at drawing but an ace at tracing, I looked through some back issues of *Detroit Classics* magazine for a picture I could copy. After finding the picture, I hopped into the Kitty and tooled on down to The Louvre Art Supply, where I bought some clear tracing plastic, which they called acetate.

Using a ballpoint pen, I traced the picture onto the acetate. Next, I opened a MacPaint document and taped the tracing over the blank drawing window. Using the single-dot brush, I traced the car from the acetate onto the Mac. I managed to copy most of the detail lines as well as the outline of the body, keeping the FatBits touch-up work to a minimum.

Below the picture, I typed a for-sale notice in 12-point Chicago.

In preparation for printing, I used the Show Page feature to move the ad to the top left corner of the drawing page. It was nearly impossible to crank the 3 by 5 cards into the Imagewriter and print them one at a time. So I used continuous 8½ by 11 pin-feed paper to carry the cards through. First I printed a sample of the ad on a sheet of the continuous paper. Then I taped each card in the upper left corner of a separate sheet of the continuous paper—in the exact position on the page where the ad printed on my sample. Thin strips of masking tape across the top and bottom edges of the cards worked best, since it holds fast yet can be removed fairly easily.

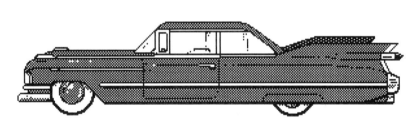

FOR SALE

'59 Cadillac De Ville Hardtop
124,000 miles, new tires, new transmission

$2000/bo   Call Chester at 232-4476

Reference

Part Four

Glossary

● *The distinctive terminology of MacWrite, MacPaint, Multiplan, and of the general Macintosh environment is defined in this chapter.*

Absolute reference: A method of identifying a cell in a Multiplan worksheet by specifying the row and column the cell is in. For example, R1C1 is the absolute reference for the cell where row 1 and column 1 cross.

Active cell: The Multiplan cell that is highlighted with a white border; its contents appear in the formula bar where they can be changed.

Active window: The currently selected window. If several windows have been opened, the active window is on top of the pile. The active window's title bar is striped, while the title bars of the other windows on the screen are white.

Alarm Clock: A desk accessory that reports the current date and time of day. The alarm can be set to go off at a specified time.

Alert box: A special window that warns you of a potentially dangerous situation, such as a disk becoming full. You must click a displayed button in order to proceed.

Apple menu: The menu at the far left of the menu bar, labeled with a picture of an apple rather than with a title. This menu contains the desk accessories and information about the current application.

Application program (also Application):   A program that performs a specific task, such as word processing, financial calculations, or graphics generation. MacWrite, MacPaint, and Multiplan are application programs.

Backup disk: A copy of a disk that can be used if the original is lost or damaged.

Button: A displayed circle or rounded rectangle that you click to select an option in a dialog box.

Byte: One unit of memory or disk space; enough space to store one letter.

Calculate: To compute the value of all the formulas in a Multiplan worksheet.

Calculator: A desk accessory that displays a four-function calculator. You enter numbers either by typing them at the keyboard or by clicking the pointer on the calculator's buttons.

Cell: A rectangle formed by the intersection of a row and a column in a Multiplan worksheet. You view and change a cell's contents—text, numbers, or formula—in the formula bar. You see the value of a cell's contents on the worksheet.

Character: A letter, number, or symbol typed at the keyboard. A space is also considered to be a character. The Return and Tab keys generate invisible characters in a MacWrite document.

Choose: To pick a command or feature from a displayed menu by dragging the pointer to the command or feature name and releasing the mouse button.

Clear: To completely remove selected text or graphics from a MacWrite or MacPaint document, rather than storing it in the Clipboard. To blank the selected cell (or cells) in a Multiplan worksheet.

Click: To place the pointer on an object (an icon, a displayed button, or a MacPaint tool, for example) and quickly press and release the mouse button. Clicking an object selects that object.

Clipboard: A temporary storage area that holds text, pictures, or numbers that have been cut or copied from a document. Unlike the Scrapbook, the Clipboard can hold only one item at a time.

Close: To remove a window and its contents from the screen by choosing Close from the File menu or clicking the window's close box.

Close box: The small square at the left end of some title bars. Clicking the close box removes the window from the screen.

Command key (⌘):   The key to the left of the space bar. This key, when pressed in conjunction with another key or key combination, causes a command or special feature to take effect. The design on this key is the international symbol for "extraordinary feature."

Comments box: An area in which you can type and store information about an application, document, or folder. You can view the information by selecting the appropriate icon and choosing Get Info from the File menu.

Completion test: The formula that controls iteration on a Multiplan worksheet. You may specify your own completion-test formula or use Multiplan's standard formula. As long as the condition specified by the completion-test formula is not satisfied (false), iteration proceeds. When, as a result of iteration, values change in such a way that they satisfy the condition (make it true), iteration stops.

Control Panel: A desk accessory that allows you to adjust nine system functions, including speaker volume, date and time, keyboard repeat rate, mouse tracking speed, and the desktop's background pattern.

Copy: To store a duplicate of a text, graphics, or cell selection in the Clipboard, leaving the original selection intact.

Current cell: The Multiplan cell that is highlighted with a white border; its contents appear in the formula bar where they can be changed.

Cut: To remove a text or graphics selection from a document and place it in the Clipboard.

Decimal tab marker: A movable triangle in the MacWrite formatting ruler that lets you line up columns of numbers on their decimal points or columns of text at their right edges.

Desk accessories: Features in the Apple menu, such as the Alarm Clock, Note Pad, Calculator, and Control Panel, that can be activated while an application is running.

Desktop: A screen layout that appears when you insert a disk. The desktop displays menu titles, icons, and windows.

Dialog box: A special window that asks you to enter information that an application needs in order to proceed.

Dimmed command: A menu command that is displayed in gray rather than black, indicating that it can't be chosen.

Directory window: The window that appears when you open a disk icon. It shows the contents of the disk.

Document: A collection of information that you create, modify, and save using an application program.

Double-click: To press and release the mouse button twice in rapid succession.

Drag: To move the pointer across the screen while pressing the mouse button.

Drawing: A MacPaint document.

Empty Folder: The icon in the directory window that you duplicate to create your own folders.

Enter key: The key on the right of the space bar. In Multiplan, pressing the Enter key puts the contents of the formula bar into the currently selected cell.

File: A collection of information stored on a disk.

Finder: A built-in program that keeps track of the applications and documents on a disk and retrieves them on command.

Folder: An icon representing a manila file folder into which you can drag application documents and other folders to help keep your desktop organized.

Font: A complete assortment of letters, numbers, and symbols with the same basic design. A variety of fonts can be selected from the Font menu in MacPaint and MacWrite.

Font Mover: An application that lets you transfer infrequently used fonts from one disk to another, thus freeing disk space for other uses.

Footer: The text and pictures that appear in the bottom margin of a MacWrite page. Icons optionally indicate where MacWrite will place the page number, date, and time.

Format: The arrangement of text and numbers on a MacWrite page or in Multiplan cells.

Formatting ruler: A ruler displayed in a MacWrite window that you use to set margins, indentation, tabs, line spacing, and alignment.

Formula: A rule or method for combining the values of specified worksheet cells, such as by arithmetic, that results in a new value. The first character in a Multiplan formula must be an equal sign.

Formula bar: The thin rectangle below Multiplan's menu bar. The location of the currently selected cell appears at the left end of the menu bar and the contents of that cell appear at the right end.

Function: A specialized Multiplan operator that uses the values of cells you specify to come up with a value according to a predefined method or rule.

Get Info: A command, selected from the desktop File menu, that provides information about a document, folder, or application.

Header: The text, pictures, and blank space that will appear in the top margin of a MacWrite page. Icons optionally indicate where MacWrite will place the page number, date, and time.

Highlight: To reverse the black and white elements of selected text or cells. An area is highlighted when you place the pointer on it and click the mouse button.

I-beam pointer: A pointer shape that indicates places where you can type and edit text. You move the I-beam pointer with the mouse, then click the mouse button to set an insertion point.

Icon: A small picture that represents an object or a concept. Common Macintosh icons include disks, file folders, and a trash can.

Indentation marker: A small arrow-shaped icon in a MacWrite formatting ruler that marks the position of the first word of a paragraph relative to the left margin.

Information window: A window that appears when you select Get Info from the File menu. The window displays information about a document, including its type, size, date of creation, and an optional description you write.

Initialize: The Mac's semi-automatic process of preparing a new disk by erasing it and writing reference marks on it.

Insertion point: The location where text will appear when you type at the keyboard or, in some cases, choose Paste from the Edit menu. The insertion point is indicated by a flashing vertical line.

Iteration: A Multiplan feature that enables automatic recalculation of a worksheet until the condition specified by a completion-test formula is satisfied.

Justified text: Text that is aligned at the left or right margin of a page, or at both the left and right margins.

K: A unit of measure that indicates how much disk space a document or application takes up. The symbol K stands for 1,024 bytes (characters' worth) of information.

Key Caps: A desk accessory that lets you see the characters that become available when you press a key in conjunction with the Shift, Option, or Caps Lock keys.

Line-thickness control panel: The box in the lower left corner of the MacPaint screen. Clicking on a line width in that box activates that width when the line and shape-drawing tools are used.

Link: A connection between cells on one Multiplan worksheet and cells on another Multiplan worksheet, so that changing the value of the first automatically changes the value of the second.

Lock box: A displayed button in an information window that allows you to prevent a document, application, or folder from being changed or removed.

MacPaint: A Macintosh application that facilitates drawing and manipulating graphics.

MacWrite: A word-processing application for the Macintosh.

Margin marker: A solid black triangle in a MacWrite formatting ruler marking the location of the right or left margin.

Menu: A list of commands available for a particular application. You can pull down a menu and view its contents by placing the pointer on the menu's title and holding down the mouse button.

Menu bar: The row of menu titles across the top of the screen. Menu titles vary from one application to the next.

Mini-Finder: A dialog box, activated by choosing Open from an application's file menu, that lists all the documents that are available for that application.

Mouse: A hand-held device that, when rolled across a flat surface, moves a pointer on the display screen. Pressing the button on the top of the mouse selects an object, chooses a command, or sets an insertion point.

Multiplan: An application by Microsoft that facilitates working with numbers and formulas.

Multiplan Master disk: Your original Multiplan disk (not a copy); it contains a code necessary to start Multiplan.

Note Pad: A desk accessory that allows you to view and change up to eight small pages of notes.

Open: To create a window for a disk, folder, or document in order to view its contents. To start up an application.

Operator: A symbol in a Multiplan formula that combines or compares the values of one or two cells according to a standard method or rule.

Option key: A key that, when pressed in conjunction with another key, produces an alternate symbol or character. It can also be used to make copies of a selected region in a MacPaint drawing.

Page break: The boundary between the bottom of one page and the top of the next. MacWrite and Multiplan mark these breaks with dotted lines.

Paste: To place text or pictures or cells stored in the Clipboard in a new location.

Pattern palette: The array of MacPaint patterns for filling and drawing that appears at the bottom of the MacPaint display screen. The currently selected pattern is shown at the extreme left end of the palette.

Pointer: A displayed graphic symbol that tracks the movement of the mouse. The shape and function of a pointer vary from one application to another.

Press: To place the pointer on an object (an icon or a menu title, for example) and press and hold the mouse button.

Protected cell: A Multiplan worksheet cell whose contents can't be changed. Protection can be canceled by selecting Remove Cell Protection from Multiplan's Options menu.

Puzzle: A desk accessory that displays a puzzle with 15 numbered tiles, which you rearrange into sequential order. Tougher than it sounds.

Relative reference: A method of identifying a cell in a Multiplan worksheet by indicating where it is in relation to the currently selected cell. For example, $R[-1]:C[+1]$ is one row up and one column to the right of the currently selected cell.

Return key: In MacWrite and MacPaint, pressing the Return key causes the text insertion point to jump to the beginning of the following line, ending the current paragraph. In Multiplan, pressing the Return key puts the contents of the formula bar into the currently selected cell and moves cell selection down one row.

Running head: A descriptive caption or heading repeated at the top or bottom of every page in a printed document.

Scrapbook: A desk accessory that stores text or pictures that you cut or copy from documents, drawings, or worksheets. The Scrapbook's contents are saved on disk.

Scroll: To move the contents of a document so that a different portion is visible in the area framed by a window.

Scroll arrow: A square containing an arrow, located at either end of a scroll bar. Clicking or pressing a scroll arrow moves the contents of a window in the opposite direction. For example, if you press the down arrow, the contents of the window move up.

Scroll bar: A thin rectangle along the right side or bottom of some windows. Clicking in a gray section of the scroll bar moves the window's contents in one-window increments.

Scroll box: The white square in a scroll bar. Dragging a scroll box up or down moves another part of the document into view in the window.

Select: To designate an object that will be affected by the next command. Generally accomplished by clicking or dragging across an object.

Selection: The object that will be affected by the next command you choose.

Shift key: A key that, when pressed in conjunction with another key, causes the uppercase version of a letter (or the upper symbol on two-character keys) to appear. The Shift key can also be used to constrain movement to a vertical or horizontal direction (no diagonals) in MacPaint, to select multiple icons in the directory window, or to extend a selection in MacWrite and Multiplan.

Size box: The small square in the lower right corner of some windows. Dragging the size box allows you to enlarge or shrink a window.

Split bar: A small black box above the vertical scroll bar and at the left end of the horizontal scroll bar that is used in Multiplan to divide a window into as many as four panes. This enables you to see more than one part of the worksheet at once.

Spreadsheet: Same as a worksheet.

Start-up disk: The first disk you insert after switching on the Macintosh. This disk must contain the Finder and System documents.

Style: A variation in the basic design of a font.

SYLK (symbolic link) format: A file format that standardizes the exchange of information between Microsoft applications on different computers.

System disk: A disk containing both the Finder and System document icons, which are necessary for starting up the Macintosh after switching on the power.

System Folder: A folder icon that contains system documents such as Finder, System, and Imagewriter.

Tab key: Pressing the Tab key moves the insertion point in MacWrite to the next tab. Tabs are set in the formatting rulers. In Multiplan, pressing the Tab key puts the contents of the formula bar into the currently selected cell and moves cell selection one column to the right.

Tab marker: A movable triangle in a MacWrite formatting ruler that lets you align columns of text at their left edges.

Tab wells: The two boxes at the lower left of a MacWrite formatting ruler. The plain triangle represents a regular tab, while the triangle with a dot in it represents a decimal tab.

Title bar: The thin rectangle along the top of some windows. The name of the currently selected document or application appears in the center of the title bar.

Tool rack: The box along the left side of the MacPaint screen that contains the program's various drawing tools, such as the pencil, paint brush, eraser, and paint can.

Trash: An icon that represents information to be removed from a disk. Select Empty Trash from the Special menu to dispose of the Trash contents.

Undo: An Edit-menu command that cancels your most recent action. Immediately selecting Undo a second time reverses the effect of the first undo.

Window: A rectangular area through which you view information contained in a disk, document, or folder. Windows can be opened (created), and closed (put away). You can often open several windows at once. Multiple windows can overlap but you can only work on the window that is on top of the pile.

Word processor: An application program you use for entering, editing, and formatting text.

Word wrap: A word-processing feature that causes a word that will not fit at the end of a line of text to automatically move to the beginning of the next line.

Worksheet: A Multiplan document. It contains cells of text, numbers, and formulas arranged in rows and columns. Cell values can be combined by arithmetic and other operations to generate the value of another cell. You can enter and edit the contents of a cell in the formula bar.

Wristwatch: A pointer shape that tells you to wait while the Finder locates a document or application.

Command
Shortcuts
And Modifiers

● *Save time and effort with the mouse and keyboard shortcuts available for the desktop, dialog and alert boxes, MacWrite, MacPaint, and Multiplan.*

On the Macintosh, the mouse is the basic tool for choosing commands and features from the pull-down menus. Several menu choices have keyboard shortcuts, however. Most of the shortcuts involve pressing the Command key while you press another key.

In addition, the Command, Shift, and Option keys allow you to modify the effect of clicking and dragging on the desktop and in MacWrite, MacPaint, and Multiplan.

In the tables below, the following symbols represent specific mouse actions:

    ↳   means click.

    ↳↳   means double-click.

    └⟋   means drag.

The Desktop

File

Action	Result
(icon)	Opens icon
(icon)	Closes window or desk accessory
Command-D	Duplicates selection
Command-I	Activates Get Info for selection
Command-E	Ejects selected disk(s)
Command-Shift-1	Ejects from internal drive
Command-Shift-2	Ejects from external drive
Command-Period	Stops printing MacWrite or Multiplan document
Command-Shift-3	Captures screen image as MacPaint document
Command-Shift-4	Prints current screen image
Caps Lock-Command-Shift-4	Prints active window

Edit

Action	Result
Backspace	Clears (removes) text selection
Command-X	Cuts text selection
Command-C	Copies text selection
Command-V	Pastes at text selection
Command-A	Selects all icons
Shift-↰	Adds to icon selection

Move

Action	Result
Command-⌐↗	Moves inactive window by its title bar without activating it

Dialog and Alert Boxes

Action	Result
Return	Confirms
Enter	Confirms
Tab	Moves to next entry (if any)

Edit

Action	Result
Backspace	Clears (removes) text selection
Command-Z	Undoes text edit
Command-X	Cuts text selection
Command-C	Copies text selection
Command-V	Pastes at text selection

MacWrite

File

Action	Result
document name	Opens named document from Mini-Finder
	Closes window or desk accessory
Command-Shift-1	Ejects from internal drive
Command-Shift-2	Ejects from external drive
Command-Period	Stops printing
Command-Shift-3	Captures screen image as MacPaint document
Command-Shift-4	Prints current screen image
Caps Lock-Command-Shift-4	Prints active window

Edit

Action	Result
Backspace	Clears (removes) selection
Command-Z	Undoes last command
Command-X	Cuts selection
Command-C	Copies selection
Command-V	Pastes at selection

Select

Action	Result
Shift- ↖	Extends current selection
Shift- ↗	Extends current selection
↖↗	Selects whole word

Style

Action	Result
Command-P	Plain
Command-B	Bold
Command-I	Italic
Command-U	Underline
Command-O	Outline
Command-S	Shadow
Command-H	Superscript
Command-L	Subscript

Move

Action	Result
Command- L↗	Moves inactive window without activating it

MacPaint

File

Action	Result
document name	Opens named document from Mini-Finder
	Closes drawing window or desk accessory
Command-Shift-1	Ejects from internal drive
Command-Shift-2	Ejects from external drive
Command-Shift-3	Captures screen image as MacPaint document
Command-Shift-4	Prints current screen image
Caps Lock-Command-Shift-4	Prints active window

Select

Action	Result
	Selects entire drawing window

Edit

Action	Result
Backspace	Clears selection
Accent/Tilde	Undoes last command
Command-Z	Undoes last command
Command-X	Cuts selection
Command-C	Copies selection
Command-V	Pastes at selection
Command-E	Activates Trace Edges inside selection
Command-Shift-E	Activates Trace Edges, with shadow, inside selection
	Erases entire drawing window
Shift-L	Moves selection up/down or left/right only
Command-L	Stretches or shrinks selection
Command-Shift-L	Proportionally stretches or shrinks selection
Option-L	Copies selection once
Command-Option-L	Copies selection repeatedly

Goodies

Action	Result
	Engages/disengages FatBits
	Shows page
	Can edit pattern
	Can change brush shape

Tool Modifiers

Action	Result
Option-	Scrolls with grabber in FatBits
Command-	Engages/disengages FatBits
Command-*filled shape*	Uses transparent fill pattern
Command-	Uses transparent fill pattern
Option-*any shape*	Uses patterned lines and borders
Shift-	Scrolls up/down or right/left only
Shift-	Sprays up/down or right/left only
Shift-	Brushes up/down or right/left only
Shift-	Draws line up/down or right/left only
Shift-	Draws line up/down, right/left, or at 45-degree diagonal only
Shift-	Erases up/down or right/left only
Shift-	Draws square only
Shift-	Draws rounded-corner square only
Shift-	Draws circle only
Shift-	Draws straight-sided shape with only vertical, horizontal, and 45-degree diagonal sides

Font

Action	Result
Command-Shift->	Lists next font in menu
Command-Shift-<	Lists previous font in menu

FontSize

Action	Result
Command->	Changes to next larger point size
Command-<	Changes to next smaller point size

Style

Action	Result
Command-P	Plain
Command-B	Bold
Command-I	Italic
Command-U	Underline
Command-O	Outline
Command-S	Shadow
Command-L	Aligns left
Command-M	Aligns center
Command-R	Aligns right

Multiplan

File

Action	Result
document name	Closes active document and opens named document from Mini-Finder
	Closes desk accessory
Command-Shift-1	Ejects from internal drive
Command-Shift-2	Ejects from external drive
Command-Period	Stops printing Multiplan worksheet
Command-Shift-3	Captures screen image as MacPaint document
Command-Shift-4	Prints current screen image
Caps Lock-Command-Shift-4	Prints active window

Edit

Action	Result
Backspace	Removes text selection or clears (blanks) active cell
Command-Z	Undoes last command
Command-X	Cuts selection
Command-C	Copies selection
Command-V	Pastes at selection
Command-B	Clears (blanks) cell selection
Command-T	Changes absolute/relative reference
Command-R	Fills cells right
Command-D	Fills cells down

Select

Action	Result
⬐⬐	Selects word or cell reference
Shift-⬐↗	Extends text or cell selection
Command-⬐	Adds to cell selection
Command-⬐↗	Adds to cell selection
Return	Moves down one row
Shift-Return	Moves up one row
Tab	Moves right one column
Shift-Tab	Moves left one column
Enter	Moves to next selected cell
Command-A	Selects all cells
Command-S	Shows active cell
Command-N	Defines name for cell selection

Format

Action	Result
Command-F	Aligns left
Command-G	Aligns center
Command-H	Aligns right

Calculate

Action	Result
Command-=	Calculates formulas now

Menus

● *A program's menus provide a snapshot of its commands and features. Here are the menus for the desktop, MacWrite, MacPaint, and Multiplan.*

Desktop Menus

About the Finder...

Scrapbook
Alarm Clock
Note Pad
Calculator
Key Caps
Control Panel
Puzzle

File

Open
Duplicate ⌘D
Get Info ⌘I
Put Back

Close
Close All
Print

Eject ⌘E

Edit

Undo ⌘Z

Cut ⌘X
Copy ⌘C
Paste ⌘V
Clear
Select All ⌘A

Show Clipboard

View

✓by Icon
 by Name
 by Date
 by Size
 by Kind

Special

Clean Up
Empty Trash
Erase Disk
Set Startup

MacPaint Menus

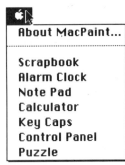

About MacPaint...

Scrapbook
Alarm Clock
Note Pad
Calculator
Key Caps
Control Panel
Puzzle

File

New
Open...
Close
Save
Save As...
Revert
Print Draft
Print Final
Print Catalog
Quit

Edit

Undo ⌘Z

Cut ⌘X
Copy ⌘C
Paste ⌘V
Clear

Invert
Fill
Trace Edges ⌘E
Flip Horizontal
Flip Vertical
Rotate

Goodies

Grid
FatBits
Show Page
Edit Pattern
Brush Shape
Brush Mirrors
Introduction
Short Cuts

Font

Chicago
✓Geneva
New York
Monaco
Venice
London
Athens

FontSize

9 point
✓12
14
18
24
36
48
72

Style

✓Plain ⌘P
Bold ⌘B
Italic ⌘I
Underline ⌘U
Outline ⌘O
Shadow ⌘S

✓Align Left ⌘L
Align Middle ⌘M
Align Right ⌘R

Multiplan Menus

É

About Multiplan...

Scrapbook
Alarm Clock
Note Pad
Calculator
Key Caps
Control Panel
Puzzle

File

New
Open...
Close
Save
Save As...

Page Setup...
Print...

Quit

Edit

Can't Undo	⌘Z
Cut	⌘H
Copy	⌘C
Paste	⌘U
Clear	⌘B
Show Clipboard	
Paste and Link...	
Unlink...	
Paste Name...	
Paste Function...	
Absolute Reference	⌘T
Fill Right	⌘R
Fill Down	⌘D
Sort...	

Select

All Cells	⌘A
Last Cell	
Name...	
Link...	
Show Active Cell	⌘S
Define Name...	⌘N
Delete Name...	

Format

✓General	
Dollar	
Percent	
No Decimal	
Decimal	
Scientific	
Bar Graph	
Number Of Decimals...	
Align Left	⌘F
Align Center	⌘G
Align Right	⌘H
Commas	
Column Width...	

Options

Freeze Titles
✓Unfreeze Titles

Set Page Break
Remove Page Break

Show Formulas
✓Show Values

Protect Document...
✓Unprotect Document...

Remove Cell Protection
✓Restore Cell Protection

Calculate

Calculate Now	⌘=
✓Automatic Calculation	
Manual Calculation	
Iterate	
✓Don't Iterate	
Set Completion Test	
Select Completion Test	

MacWrite Menus



About MacWrite...

Scrapbook
Alarm Clock
Note Pad
Calculator
Key Caps
Control Panel
Puzzle

File

New
Open...
Close
Save
Save As...
Page Setup
Print...
Quit

Edit

Undo Typing   ⌘Z

Cut   ⌘X
Copy   ⌘C
Paste   ⌘U

Show Clipboard

Search

Find...
Change...

Format

Insert Ruler
Hide Rulers
Open Header
Open Footer
Display Headers
Display Footers
Set Page #...
Insert Page Break
Title Page

Font

Chicago
✓Geneva
New York
Monaco
Venice
London
Athens

Style

✓Plain Text   ⌘P
Bold   ⌘B
Italic   ⌘I
Underline   ⌘U
Outline   ⌘O
Shadow   ⌘S
Superscript   ⌘H
Subscript   ⌘L

9 Point
10 Point
✓12 Point
14 Point
18 Point
24 Point

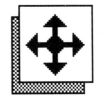

Pointers

● *Have you forgotten what some pointer shape signifies? Find out here.*

MacWrite Pointers

Pointer	Name	Purpose
	Arrow	General purpose
	I-beam	Text entry and editing
	Wristwatch	Mac is busy; wait

Multiplan Pointers

Pointer	Name	Purpose
	Arrow	Menus, desk accessories
	I-beam	Text entry and editing
	Cross	Cell selection
	(none)	Dragging the worksheet window by its title bar
	Index	Scrolling the worksheet and splitting the worksheet window
	(none)	Changing the worksheet window dimensions
	(none)	Inserting rows
	(none)	Inserting columns
	(none)	Changing column widths
	Wristwatch	Mac is busy; wait

MacPaint Pointers

Pointer	Name	Tools
▶	Arrow	Menus, tool rack, pattern palette, and line thickness
⬭	Lasso	Lasso
-¦-	Crosshairs	Selection rectangle
✋	Grabber	Grabber
I	I-beam	Text
🖌	Paint can	Paint can
⣿	Spray	Spray can
•	Brush*	Brush
✏	Pencil	Pencil
☐	Eraser	Eraser
+	Cross	Line- or shape-drawing
⌚	Wristwatch	Mac is busy; wait

*The Brush Shape command enables you to select from among the 32 pointer shapes shown below.

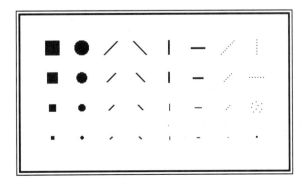

Chart
Of Fonts

● *These samples display twelve text fonts, indicate their best-looking sizes, and illustrate how style variations affect them.*

Athens

Athens
Athens Italic
Athens Bold
Athens Bold Italic
Athens Outline
Athens Bold Outline
Athens Shaded
Athens Bold Shaded
ABCDEFGHIJKLMNOPQRSTUVWXYZ
abcdefghijklmnopqrstuvwxyz
1234567890 !@#$%^&*() `~ -_+=[]\{}|;:'",.<>/?
Athens is available in an 18-point size

Cairo

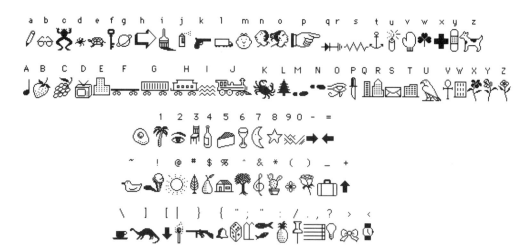

Chicago

Chicago
Chicago Italic
Chicago Bold
Chicago Bold Italic
Chicago Outline
Chicago Bold Outline
Chicago Shaded
Chicago Bold Shaded
ABCDEFGHIJKLMNOPQRSTUVWXYZabcdefghijklmnopqrstuvwxyz
1234567890 !@#$%^&*() `~ -_+=[]\{}|;:'",.<>/?
Chicago is available in a 12-point size

Geneva

Geneva
Geneva Italic
Geneva Bold
Geneva Bold Italic
Geneva Outline
Geneva Bold Outline
Geneva Shaded
Geneva Bold Shaded
ABCDEFGHIJKLMNOPQRSTUVWXYZabcdefghijklmnopqrstuvwxyz
1234567890 !@#$%^&*() `~ -_+=[]\{}|;:'",.<>/?
Geneva is available in a 9-point size
Geneva is available in a 10-point size
Geneva is available in a 12-point size
Geneva is available in a 14-point size
Geneva is available in an 18-point size
Geneva in a 24-point size

London

London
London Italic
London Bold
London Bold Italic
London Outline
London Bold Outline
London Shaded
London Bold Shaded
ABCDEFGHIJKLMNOPQRSTUVWXYZ
abcdefghijklmnopqrstuvwxyz   1234567890
!@#$%□&*() □□ -_+=[]\{}|;:'"",.□□/?
London is available in an 18-point size

Los Angeles

Los Angeles
Los Angeles Italic
Los Angeles Bold
Los Angeles Bold Italic
Los Angeles Outline
Los Angeles Bold Outline
Los Angeles Shaded
Los Angeles Bold Shaded
ABCDEFGHIJKLMNOPQRSTUVWXYZabcdefghijklmnopqrstuvwxyz
1234567890 !@#$%^&*() ~ -_+=()\{}|;:'"",.<>/?
Los Angeles is available in a 12-point size
Los Angeles in a 24-point

Monaco

Monaco

Monaco Italic

Monaco Bold

Monaco Bold Italic

Monaco Outline

Monaco Bold Outline

Monaco Shaded

Monaco Bold Shaded

ABCDEFGHIJKLMNOPQRSTUVWXYZabcdefghijklmnopqrstuvwxyz
1234567890 !@#$%^&*() `~ -_+=[]\{}|;:'",.<>/?
Monaco is available in a 9-point size
Monaco is available in a 12-point size

New York

New York

New York Italic

New York Bold

New York Bold Italic

New York Outline

New York Bold Outline

New York Shaded

New York Bold Shaded

ABCDEFGHIJKLMNOPQRSTUV WXYZabcdefghijklmnopqrstuvwxyz
1234567890 !@#$%^&*() `~ -_+=[]\{}|;:'",.<>/?
New York is available in a 9-point size
New York is available in a 10-point size
New York is available in a 12-point size
New York is available in a 14-point size
New York is available in an 18-point size
New York in a 24-point size
New York 36-point

San Francisco

San Francisco

San Francisco Italic

San Francisco Bold

San Francisco Bold Italic

San Francisco Outline

San Francisco Bold Outline

San Francisco Shaded

San Francisco Bold Shaded

ABCDEFGHIJKLMNOPQRSTUVWXYZ

abcdefghijklmnopqrstuvwxyz

1234567890 !@#$%□&*() □ -_+=[]\{}|;:'",.<>/?

San Francisco is available in an 18-point size

Seattle

Seattle

Seattle Italic

Seattle Bold

Seattle Bold Italic

Seattle Outline

Seattle Bold Outline

Seattle Shaded

Seattle Bold Shaded

ABCDEFGHIJKLMNOPQRSTUVWXYZabcdefghijklmnopqrstuvwxyz

1234567890 !@#$%^&*() `~ -_+=[]\{}|;:'",.<>/?

Seattle is available in a 10-point size

Toronto

Toronto

Toronto Italic

Toronto Bold

Toronto Bold Italic

Toronto Outline

Toronto Bold Outline

Toronto Shaded

Toronto Bold Shaded

ABCDEFGHIJKLMNOPQRSTUVWXYZabcdefghijklmnopqr
stuvwxyz   1234567890 !@#$%^&*() `~ -_+=[]\{}|;:'",.<>/?

Toronto is available in a 9-point size

Toronto is available in a 10-point size

Toronto is available in a 12-point size

Toronto is available in a 14-point size

Toronto available in an 18-point size

Toronto in a 24-point

Venice

Venice

Venice Italic

Venice Bold

Venice Bold Italic

Venice Outline

Venice Bold Outline

Venice Shaded

Venice Bold Shaded

ABCDEFGHIJKLMNOPQRSTUVWXYZ
abcdefghijklmnopqrstuvwxyz
1234567890 !□#$%^&*() `~ -_+=[]\{}|;:'",.<>/?

Venice is available in a 14-point size

Multiplan
Functions

● *Check this list of built-in Multiplan functions for the values you must supply when you use a function in a formula.*

A function is a built-in mathematical or statistical operation that Multiplan can perform using one or more values you specify. There are functions for mathematic and trigonometric calculation, logical evaluation, text extraction and creation, and for creating values in other ways. Some functions perform calculations that can't be done with arithmetic operators alone, and some convert one type of value into another.

Each function starts with its name. After the name are the values the function operates on, called arguments, enclosed in parentheses and separated by commas. Some functions have one argument, some have more. Even if a function doesn't use arguments, the parentheses must be included. A function can use another function as an argument, that argument can use another function as an argument, and so on. This nesting of functions can go to as many as seven levels in one formula.

There are several different types of arguments. This directory uses words in parentheses to represent arguments as follows:

Number: A number, a formula that yields a number, or a reference to a cell containing a number or a formula that yields a number.

List: A list of numbers, formulas, or references separated by commas.

Text: Text, a formula that yields text, or a reference to a cell containing text or a formula that yields text.

Value: Any type of value: a number, text string, error value, logical value, or a reference to a cell containing any of these.

Mathematic Functions

ABS(number)	Absolute value of a number
AVERAGE(list)	Average of the values in the list
COUNT(list)	Counts the number of items in the list
EXP(number)	Exponentiation
INT(number)	Integer portion of a number
LN(number)	Logarithm, natural
LOG10(number)	Logarithm, base 10
MAX(list)	Maximum value in list
MIN(list)	Minimum value in list
MOD(number to divide, number to divide by)	Remainder after division
NPV(rate,list)	Net present value of list at rate
ROUND(number, number of digits)	Rounds a number to number of digits
SIGN(number)	Sign of a number (1 positive, -1 negative)
SQRT(number)	Square root
STDEV(list)	Standard deviation
SUM(list)	Sum of numbers in list

Trigonometric Functions

ATAN(number)	Arctangent
COS(number)	Cosine
SIN(number)	Sine
TAN(number)	Tangent

Logical Functions

IF(logical expression, value if true, value if false)	Chooses which value to give depending on the logical value of an expression
AND(list)	True if all values in list are true
NOT(logical expression)	True if false, False if true
OR(list)	True if any value in list is true
ISERROR(value)	True if value is any error value
ISNA(value)	True if value is #N/A
FALSE()	False (logical value)
TRUE()	True (logical value)

Text Functions

DOLLAR(number)	Dollar representation of a number
FIXED(number, decimals)	Fixed format of a number
LEN(text)	Length of text
MID(text, start-position, number of characters)	Extracts characters from a text value
REPT(text, number of times)	Repeats text number of times
VALUE(text)	Changes text value to number

Other Functions

COLUMN()	Column number
ROW()	Row number
INDEX(area, subscripts)	Gets a value from area located by subscripts
LOOKUP(number, table)	Looks up a value in a table
DELTA()	Maximum change between iterations
ITERCNT()	Iteration count
NA()	#N/A (error value)
PI()	The constant 3.141592653589

Optimal Use of Disks

● *Use the Font Mover program to adjust the amount of space available on a disk by adding or removing fonts and font sizes.*

Every disk starts out with 409,600 bytes of space available, or 400K for short. Disk space is measured in individual bytes or in K, where one K equals 1,024 bytes. One byte will store a single character, a few dots on a drawing, or some similarly small piece of information.

How Many K Does It Need?

The System Folder and the five or six documents it contains—System, Finder, Imagewriter (Multiplan and MacWrite only), Note Pad File, Clipboard File, and Scrapbook File—occupy at least 140K. They can take up 250K or more, depending on the number of clippings in the Scrapbook and the number of fonts and font sizes in the System document.

The MacWrite application program accounts for 55K, the Mac-Paint application program for 61K, and the Multiplan application program for 92K. Using MacPaint requires between 40K and 100K for a scratchpad area, and MacWrite and Multiplan may need more than 30K in order to print a document.

The size of a document varies greatly depending on what it contains. A typical letter done with MacWrite takes about 5K, an average MacPaint drawing occupies about 20K, and a one-page Multiplan worksheet uses about 5K.

A single disk would need 600K for the System Folder, all three application programs, and the workspace to use them; adding an assortment of documents would require even more.

What Should You Put Where?

Clearly, separate disks for each application are in order. To minimize disk swapping, every disk that has an application on it should also have the System and Finder documents from the System Folder. Applications rely on the Finder to open and save documents, so it must be present. The System document is just as important, since it has all the information on how to display characters. In addition, the Imagewriter document must be present in order to print MacWrite and Multiplan documents.

Ideally, the application disk should contain the document you are working on, though this is not always possible. Eventually, you will create so many documents for an application that they simply will not all fit on the application disk. You will have to save the overflow documents on some other disk. Overflow disks will hold many more documents if they do not contain the application, Finder document, or System document.

MacWrite, MacPaint, Multiplan, and most other applications will let you work with a document from any disk, whether it is another application disk or a documents-only disk. If the document is on a disk not currently inserted, you are prompted to swap disks to open the document and swap again to save your changes to it.

One way to free up space on an application disk for your documents is to remove some of the fonts that you rarely use and store them on a different disk.

Fonts and Font Mover

The System document, which is usually located in the System Folder, contains the specifications for the various text fonts available to an application program. There may be different versions of a font present for different font sizes. The tables in Figures 11, 12, and 13 list the optional fonts in the Fonts document on the System disk, and all the fonts and font sizes available on standard Write/Paint, System, and Multiplan disks.

Size	Font	Bytes
18-pt.	Cairo	5840
12-pt.	Los Angeles	2440
24-pt.	Los Angeles	6444
36-pt.	New York	13780
18-pt.	San Francisco	2984
9-pt.	Toronto	2200
12-pt.	Toronto	3034
14-pt.	Toronto	3658
18-pt.	Toronto	5688
24-pt.	Toronto	8854
	Total	54922

*Not removable

Figure 11. Disk space requirements for Fonts document on the System disk

Size	Font	Bytes
18-pt.	Athens	4468
12-pt.	Chicago*	2940
9-pt.	Geneva*	2152
10-pt.	Geneva	2200
12-pt.	Geneva*	2734
14-pt.	Geneva	3568
18-pt.	Geneva	4864
20-pt.	Geneva	5848
24-pt.	Geneva	7568
18-pt.	London	3268
9-pt.	Monaco*	2026
12-pt.	Monaco	2464
9-pt.	New York	2032
10-pt.	New York	2200
12-pt.	New York	2734
14-pt.	New York	3352
18-pt.	New York	4516
20-pt.	New York	5260
24-pt.	New York	6832
14-pt.	Venice	3604
	Total	74630

*Not removable

Figure 12. Disk space requirements for System-document
fonts on Write/Paint and
System disks

Size	Font	Bytes
12-pt.	Chicago*	2940
9-pt.	Geneva*	2152
9-pt.	Monaco*	2004
12-pt.	New York*	2734
10-pt.	Seattle	2410
20-pt.	Seattle	6302
	Total	18542

*Not removable

Figure 13. Disk space requirements for System-document fonts
on Multiplan disk

The Font Mover application lets you selectively remove fonts and font sizes from the System document and store them in a document named Fonts. You can also use Font Mover to add fonts to the System document from the Fonts document.

Larger font sizes take more disk space than smaller ones, but don't rush off and delete the larger sizes to gain disk space. Even if you don't use the larger sizes directly, you need them for best results with high-quality printing of MacWrite and Multiplan documents. The best-looking high-quality print is obtained by condensing a font size that is double the size to be printed. For example, the best-quality 12-point New York is obtained if 24-point New York is available for use in the System document.

MacWrite, MacPaint, and Multiplan all adjust automatically for changes in font and font-size availability. The Font menu in MacWrite and MacPaint lists each available font. The MacWrite Style and MacPaint FontSize menus use outlined text to identify which font sizes are present. Multiplan uses a fixed set of fonts and font sizes. It ignores any you add and substitutes for any you remove.

You can even remove a font size that you have already used in a document. When you reopen the document and the Macintosh finds out it needs to use a font size that's no longer in the System document, it shrinks or enlarges the closest available size. Some coarseness results. If you use a font in a document and later remove that font altogether from the System document, the Macintosh substitutes another font when you reopen the document.

Starting Font Mover

Font Mover must be on the same disk as the System document in which you want to change fonts or font sizes. If you plan to add fonts or font sizes, the Fonts document that contains them must also be on the same disk. To achieve this, you may have to copy the Font Mover application and Fonts document by dragging their icons from the System Disk or another disk.

Warning: Never use Font Mover on the original System or application disk, only on copies. It is possible to accidentally and permanently remove a font from a disk. If that happens, you may have to copy the entire System document from another disk.

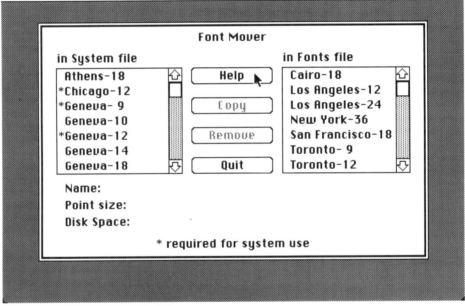

● *To start Font Mover, open the Font Mover application icon or the Fonts document icon.*

If the Font Mover application icon is dimmed, it means the Font Mover program resides on a disk you inserted some time ago but ejected. When you open the dimmed icon to start the application, a dialog box appears telling you to switch disks. Insert the disk it names so that the Finder can locate the Font Mover program.

The Font Mover Desktop

Starting Font Mover clears the desktop. The directory window vanishes along with the disk icon, the Trash icon, and any open windows. The menu bar is erased and replaced briefly by the name of the application, Font Mover. The pointer assumes a wristwatch shape, letting you know you must wait while the Finder transfers the Font Mover program from disk to memory. About 25 seconds after opening the Font Mover application icon, the desktop assumes the standard look for Font Mover.

The Font Mover desktop has no menu bar or conventional windows. Instead, it has a single, large dialog box, which contains two windows, four buttons, and a font-description area.

The window on the left lists the fonts and font sizes in the System document, and the window on the right lists the fonts and font sizes in the Fonts document. If there is no Fonts document on the disk, the right window is empty. Each window lists up to seven font sizes at a time. If there are more than seven font sizes, a scroll bar lets you scroll more font sizes into view.

Removing Fonts from the System Document

Before removing fonts from the System document (left window), you should copy them to the Fonts document (right window). That way you can change your mind later and move fonts back from the Fonts document to the System document.

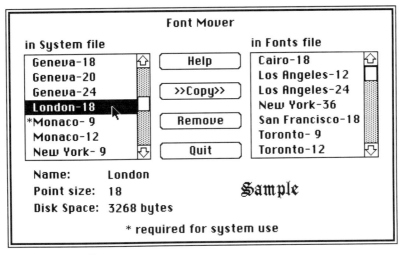

● *Scroll the font size you wish to*
remove into view and select it
by clicking it.

Select a group of fonts by pointing at the first one, pressing the mouse button, and dragging the pointer down the list. Add to a selection by holding down the Shift key while you click the name of another font size.

As you select font sizes to be copied, their names are high-lighted in the window. If you select a single font, some sample text appears along with the amount of disk space the font occupies. A multiple-font selection shows only the total disk space that all the selected fonts use.

If the Fonts window is empty, a new Fonts document is created to store the fonts that you copy from the System document.

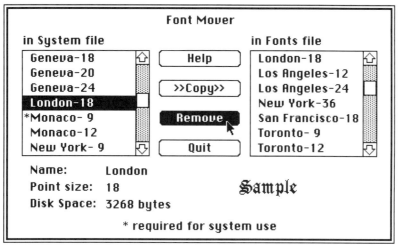

●*After selecting the font or fonts to copy, first click the Copy button and then click the Remove button.*

Clicking the Copy button copies the fonts you have selected from the System document to the Fonts document. Be absolutely sure the fonts that are highlighted in the System-document window also appear in the Fonts-document window before you click the Remove button. Font Mover has no Undo command to cancel a mistake.

Adding Fonts to the System Document

You add font sizes to the System document by selecting them in the Fonts window and clicking the copy button. There is generally no need to remove them from the Fonts document.

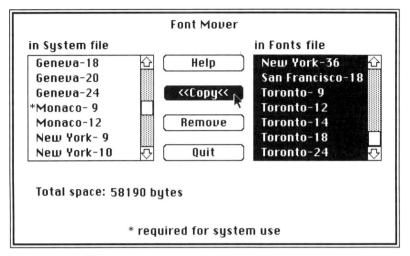

● *In the Fonts window, select the font sizes to be added to the System document. Then click the Copy button.*

After copying, the font-size names appear in both windows.

Quitting Font Mover

To quit and return to the directory window, click the Quit button. A message appears advising you that it may take a minute or so to rearrange the System and Fonts documents. When you are returned to the directory window, drag the Fonts document to another disk for safekeeping.

Index

Lon Poole

Lon Poole has been writing about personal computers and their practical applications since 1976, when micros were first introduced. Upon graduation from the University of California at Berkeley in 1972, with a B.A. in Computer Science, Lon joined Osborne and Associates, where he wrote custom computer programs for small businesses. He co-authored his first book, *Some Common BASIC Programs*, in 1977, followed by several more books on using BASIC for specific business applications. In 1981, Lon wrote the now classic *Apple II User's Guide*, and has continued to be one of the leading authorities on emerging Apple technologies.

A Californian most of his life, Lon Poole now lives in Oakland, sharing the sentiments expressed by Jack London: "You take Paradise, I'm going back to Oakland." He enjoys flying, house remodeling, and an occasional trip to Mexico.

The manuscript for this book was prepared and submitted to Microsoft Press in electronic form. Text files were processed and formatted using Microsoft Word.

Cover and text design by Ted Mader and Associates. Printed on the Mergenthaler 202 by ImageSet Corporation, Sunnyvale, California, the high-resolution screen displays and figures were created on the Apple Macintosh using MacWrite, MacPaint, and Microsoft Multiplan.

Text composition in Stempel Garamond with display in Helvetica Heavy, using CCI Book and the Mergenthaler Linotron 202 digital phototypesetter.

Cover art separated by Color Masters, Phoenix, Arizona. Printed on 12 pt. Carolina by Strine Printing Company, York, Pennsylvania. Text stock, 60 lb. Glatfelter Offset, supplied by Carpenter/Offutt. Book printed and bound by Fairfield Graphics, Fairfield, Pennsylvania.